The Judean Desert
Monasteries
in the
Byzantine Period

YIZHAR HIRSCHFELD

The Judean Desert
Monasteries
in the
Byzantine Period

Yale University Press

New Haven and London

Designed by Nancy Ovedovitz. Set in Fournier type by Tseng
Information Systems Inc., Durham, North Carolina. Printed in the
United States of America by Hamilton Printing Company, Castleton,
New York.

Library of Congress Cataloging-in-Publication Data
Hirschfeld, Yizhar.
The Judean desert monasteries in the Byzantine period /
Yizhar Hirschfeld.
p.   cm.
Includes bibliographical references and index.
ISBN 0-300-04977-3
1. Monasticism and religious orders—Judaea, Wilderness of.
2. Monasteries—Judaea, Wilderness of.   3. Judaea, Wilderness of—
Antiquities, Byzantine.   4. Judaea, Wilderness of—Church history.
I. Title.   II. Title: Desert monasteries in the Byzantine period.
BX2465.H49   1992
271'.0095694'09021—dc20   91-19249
CIP

The paper in this book meets the guidelines for permanence and
durability of the Committee on Production Guidelines for Book
Longevity of the Council on Library Resources.

1   3   5   7   9   10   8   6   4   2

To Hannah, my wife

Contents

Illustrations

FIGURES

TABLES

Preface

The Byzantine period was the golden age of the Judean desert monasteries. These monasteries were settled by monks who arrived from all over the Byzantine Empire, but mainly from Asia Minor and Greece. For them, this was "the desert of the Holy City," an expanse of land in which wondrous figures had lived and worked: the Prophets, John the Baptist, and Jesus Christ. Here, amid the wild, desolate landscape, the monks could retreat from the settled world and create their own way of life.

Because of the large number of monasteries in the area and their proximity to Jerusalem and the Christian holy places, as well as the involvement of various of the monks in the affairs of the church, Judean desert monasticism became a major movement. From the fifth century onward, the Judean desert was one of the most important centers of monasticism in the empire.

Recent years have seen a revolution in the study of the Judean desert monasteries. Since 1967, when the Judean desert fell into Israeli hands, Israeli scholars have been able to investigate directly the monastic sites in the region. These scholars, most of whom are natives of Jerusalem of the younger generation of archaeologists, have also had access to equipment and means of transportation that were unavailable to scholars of preceding generations. The short distance between Jerusalem and the interior of the desert and the development of new roads have also contributed to the progress of the research.

The major breakthrough in the study of Judean desert monasteries has been in the field of archaeological surveying. In recent years, five survey teams have worked simultaneously all over the desert. Teams headed by Haim Goldfus, Nitzan Hanin, and Uri Dinur have worked in the northern part, while teams headed by Joseph Patrich and by me have worked in the central and southern parts. In the course of this work, many previously unknown monasteries have been discovered, more than doubling the number of known monasteries in the Judean desert. The map in Derwas Chitty's *The Desert a City*, published in 1966, includes about twenty-five monasteries, but we are now familiar with more than sixty monastic sites scattered throughout the desert area, from Phasaelis in the north to Masada in the south (see map 1). The Israeli teams have made measurements of the remains of many of these monasteries, as very little measuring had been done earlier.

In addition to making surveys of monasteries in the Judean desert, archaeologists have carried out a number of new excavations. Two monasteries—that of Martyrius east of Jerusalem and Khirbet el-Kilya in the north of the region—have been excavated by Yitzhak Magen. The monastery of Martyrius proved to be one of the largest and grandest of the Judean desert monasteries of the Byzantine period. Another monastery that has been excavated almost completely is Khirbet ed-Deir, in the south of the region. In addition, excavations have been carried out at the monastery of Chariton and have been resumed at the monastery of Euthymius, east of Jerusalem; I headed the three latter projects. Exploratory excavations were carried out by Joseph Patrich at the various monasteries founded by Sabas in the Kidron valley, as well as at a newly discovered site near the Dead Sea.

While the fieldwork was going on, Yad Yitzhak Ben-Zvi's Institute for the Research of Eretz Yisrael, Its People and Cultures, based in Jerusalem, initiated and financed the translation of all the Byzantine sources on Judean desert monasticism from Greek into Hebrew. The translations, by Leah Di Segni, gave the historical background for the discoveries being made in the field and supplemented the archaeological evidence with a wealth of details regarding daily life in the monasteries.

The new information, which has accumulated in astonishing amounts, has been summarized in two unpublished dissertations recently submitted to the Hebrew University in Jerusalem. The first, my own, includes an overall discussion of the phenomenon of monasticism in the Judean desert, as well as a detailed typological classification of the monasteries and their components, based on archaeological finds. The second, by Joseph Patrich, focuses on Sabas and the monasteries he founded in the Kidron valley. These two dissertations complement one another and provide a comprehensive picture of monasticism in the Judean desert at its peak, from the fourth to the seventh centuries.

I first became acquainted with the subject of monasticism in the course of a survey of the Judean desert. I found monasticism very interesting as a sociohistorical phenomenon, and this, along with the allure of the desert landscape, prompted me to choose the Judean desert as the object of a systematic archaeological survey. I began the survey in 1981, under the auspices of the Israel

Antiquities Authority. After 1986, I extended the survey beyond the limits of the Judean desert, and the results of both phases of the survey form the basis for the archaeological discussion in this book.

Fieldwork, by its very nature, requires the assistance of many people. Rivka Birger-Calderon was co-director of the excavations at Khirbet ed-Deir and the monastery of Euthymius. Zeev Radovan took the photographs of the sites. Erez Cohen, David Huli, Israel Vatkin, and Leen Ritmeyer were involved in taking the measurements; and Erez Cohen and Leen Ritmeyer were also responsible for the reconstruction drawings. Tanya Gornstein gave the other drawings—maps and plans—their final form. My deepest thanks go to all of them, especially Leen Ritmeyer, whose contribution to the book has been major.

While preparing the doctoral dissertation on which the comparative study is based, I enjoyed the encouragement of professors Yoram Tsafrir and Amnon Linder, who contributed greatly to the formulation of the research methodology. Shortly after submitting the dissertation, I was invited for a post-doctoral year (1987–8) in the Department of Religious Studies at Yale University. There, under the guidance of Bentley Layton, I was able to expand and develop my research. My discussions with Professor Layton and his students at Yale and with other leading American scholars—Peter Brown of Princeton University, Robert Wilken of the University of Virginia, and Sidney Griffith of the Catholic University of America in Washington, D.C.—had a major influence on the form that the book eventually took.

I wish to extend my sincere thanks to the Rothschild Foundation, which sponsored my trip to the United States, and to the Dorot Foundation for helping to finance the publication of this book. I also thank Joy and Philip Mayerson for their consistent interest throughout the research. The completion of the writing was made possible by a Lady Davis Foundation Fellowship from the Hebrew University of Jerusalem for 1989–90.

I enjoyed the full cooperation and stimulation of my colleagues, the above-mentioned researchers of monasticism in the Judean desert, in the course of conversations and joint field trips. Special thanks go to Joseph Patrich, whose dissertation shed new light on the monastic movement in the Judean desert, and to John Binns, who read and commented on the manuscript. But I owe the most to Leah Di Segni, who generously shared her considerable scholarship and skills with me. Her translations of hagiographic literature gave me access to the fascinating world of Judean desert monasticism during the Byzantine period.

I was fortunate in being able to complete the final stages of writing at the monastery of St. John the Baptist, near 'Ein Kerem in the Judean hills. The peace and quiet that reign there, the still largely "Byzantine" way of life of the monks, and their warm hospitality were a constant inspiration.

I should also like to thank Judy Davidson for her skilled help in editing the manuscript.

Finally, I should like to express my deepest gratitude to my wife, Hannah, for her unwavering support.

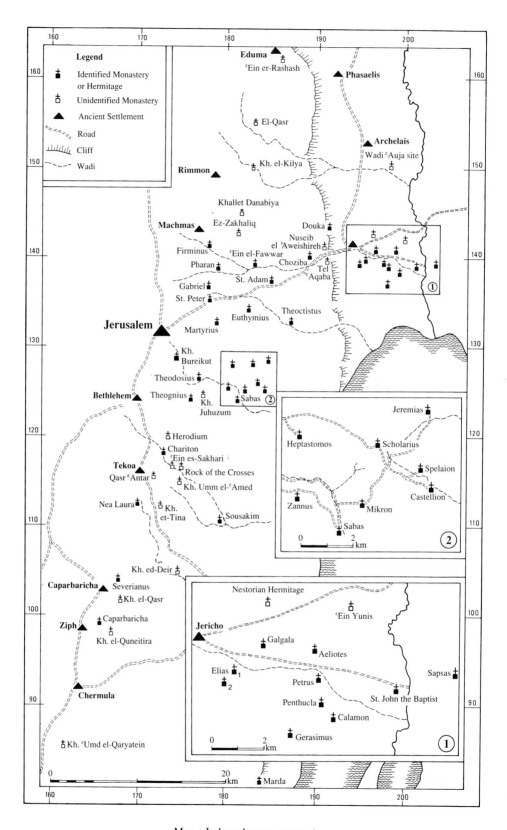

Legend

- ■ Identified Monastery or Hermitage
- ⌂ Unidentified Monastery
- ▲ Ancient Settlement
- ⊥⊥⊥⊥ Cliff
- ─── Road
- --- Wadi

Eduma
'Ein er-Rashash
Phasaelis

El-Qasr

Archelais
Wadi 'Auja site

Rimmon

Kh. el-Kilya

Khallet Danabiya

Machmas   Ez-Zakhaliq   Douka

Nuseib
el 'Aweishireh

Firminus   'Ein el-Fawwar   Choziba

Pharan   Tel
                              Aqaba
Gabriel   St. Adam
St. Peter

Jerusalem   Martyrius   Euthymius   Theoctistus

Kh.
Bureikut

Theodosius

Heptastomos   Jeremias
Scholarius
Spelaion
Castellion
Zannus   Mikron
Sabas

Bethlehem   Theognius   Kh.   Sabas ②
                          Juhuzum

Herodium

Chariton
'Ein es-Sakhari
Tekoa   Rock of the Crosses
Qasr 'Antar   Kh. Umm el-'Amed

Nea Laura   Kh.   Sousakim
             et-Tina

Kh. ed-Deir

Caparbaricha   Severianus
             Kh. el-Qasr

Ziph   Caparbaricha
        Kh. el-Quneitira

Chermula

Kh. 'Umd el-Qaryatein

Nestorian Hermitage

'Ein Yunis

Jericho   Galgala

                    Aeliotes

Elias 1   Sapsas
       2   Petrus
                    St. John the Baptist
    Penthucla
              Calamon

        Gerasimus

0   2
           km   ①

0   20
                     km   Marda

0   2
           km   ②

Map 1 Judean desert monasteries

Alphabetical List of Monasteries

Aeliotes 190/140

Calamon ('Ein Hajla) 190/130

Caparbaricha (Khirbet Umm-Rukba) 160/90

Castellion (El-Mird) 180/120

Chariton (Souka; Old Laura; Khirbet Khureitun) 170/110

Choziba (St. George's Monastery; Deir Mar Jariys) 180/140

Douka (Doq, Dagon, Deir el-Quruntul) 190/140

'Ein el-Fawwar 180/140

'Ein er-Rashash 180/160

'Ein es-Sakhari 170/110

'Ein Yunis 190/140

Elias (Eunuchs; Rujum Mugheifir; Khirbet Mugheifir) 190/130

El-Qasr 180/150

Euthymius (Khan el-Ahmar) 180/130

Ez-Zakhaliq 180/140

Firminus (El-Maqtara; Aleiliyat) 170/140

Gabriel (Qasr er-Rawabi) 170/130

Galgala (Ghalghala) 190/140

Gerasimus (Deir Hajla) 190/130

Heptastomos (Khirbet Jinjas) 170/120

Herodium (Khirbet Firdaus) 170/110

Jeremias (Khirbet ez-Zaraniq) 180/120

Khallet Danabiya 180/140

Khirbet Bureikut 170/120

Khirbet ed-Deir 170/100

Khirbet el-Kilya 180/150

Khirbet el-Qasr 160/100

Khirbet el-Quneitira 160/90

Khirbet et-Tina 170/110

Khirbet Juhuzum 170/120

Khirbet 'Umd el-Qaryatein 160/80

Khirbet Umm el-'Amed 170/110

Marda (Masada) 180/80

Martyrius (Khirbet el-Murassas) 170/130

Mikron (Small Coenobium) 180/120

Nea Laura (New Laura; Bir el-Wa'ar) 160/110

Nuseib el-ʾAweishireh 190/140

Penthucla 190/130

Pharan ('Ein Fara) 170/130

Qasr 'Antar 170/110

Rock of the Crosses 170/110

Sabas (Great Laura; Deir Mar Saba) 180/120

Scholarius (Khirbet el-Muntar) 180/120

Severianus (El-Qasrein) 160/100

Sousakim (Khirbet el-Quseir) 170/110

Spelaion (Cave; Bir el-Qattar) 180/120

St. Adam (Khan Saliba) 180/130

St. John the Baptist (Prodromos; Qasr el-Yahud) 190/130

St. Peter (Qasr 'Ali) 170/130

Tel 'Aqaba (Cypros) 190/130

Theoctistus (Deir Mukallik) 180/130

Theodosius (Deir Dosi) 170/120

Theognius (Khirbet el-Makhrum) 170/120

Wadi 'Auja site 190/150

Zannus (El-Bourj) 170/120

Introduction

In the fourth century, the Byzantine world was just beginning to emerge from late classical culture, and Constantine's imperial Church was slowly coming to assume a major role in Mediterranean life. Yet early Christianity remained a patchwork of different groups, heretical sects, diverse schools of theological thought, and alternative religious movements. Out of this rich variety of forms, only one was destined to become a central stream in Christian life, surviving into modern times: that of Christian monasticism.

The concept of monasticism is older than Christianity. Its roots are to be sought in Jewish asceticism, either in the solitary life in the desert of Nazirites like John the Baptist, or in the communal life of such sects as the Essenes in the Judean desert and the Therapeutae in Egypt.[1] It has also been suggested that, at least in the East, Christian monasticism was originally inspired by Manichean asceticism.[2] As far as the cradle of the monastic movement—Egypt—is concerned, however, there is no evidence of continuity between Jewish practice and the beginnings of Christian monasticism. In Palestine, too, a clear time gap separates the flourishing of the Essene communities and the rise of the first Christian monasteries.

But throughout the Roman and late Roman periods, both in Egypt and in Palestine, there is abundant evidence of a steady trickle of people into the desert, a process known as *anachoresis*. People went there for a variety of practical reasons, but basically they all sought security of one kind or another. They included deserters, citizens who could not cope with the heavy taxation, debtors, rebels, criminals, and victims of political and religious persecution. Some of these fugitivies left archaeological traces of their presence in the very places later frequented by the monks.[3]

As for the Judean desert, tradition has it that the first anchorites in the region were Christians fleeing from religious persecution.[4] After the Edict of Constantine in 313, there was no longer any need to seek refuge in the desert. But many of the desert-dwellers refused to go back to "normal" life after the persecution had ceased. They could not renounce the ideal of martyrdom and proceeded to transfer it from the public arena to the area of private life. This motivation was quite openly acknowledged and is often mentioned in monastic literature.[5]

With the growing strength of the monastic movement and its increasing economic resources, a new sociological factor came into play: the monastery became a means of social elevation and a source of economic security. It provided assistance to the poor and attracted people of the lower classes as a place providing a better, easier, and more satisfying way of life.

Religious fervor can also be counted as a sociological factor. Judean desert monasticism was largely dependent on the stream of pilgrims to the holy places, not only for the income they brought with them, but also—and primarily—for their manpower. Many pilgrims, euphoric from some kind of religious experience, decided to promote their further spiritual elevation by adopting a monastic form of life—a decision that was reinforced by the sight of many of their countrymen already living in the desert. Religious zeal was an equally strong factor among locals who joined monasteries, although the Christianization of Palestine came relatively late.

THE STUDY OF MONASTICISM: SOURCES

Monasticism has always been a major topic of ecclesiastical history; yet its origins were obscure until the past few decades. The nature and evolution of organized monasticism in Coptic Egypt (possibly the earliest monastic movement) are only now being unraveled through intensive study of the Pachomian system. In the past twenty years, hundreds of monasteries and hermitages have come to light in the Nile Delta.[6] Archaeological surveys and explorations of monastic sites in the Syrian desert have been conducted since the beginning of this century.[7]

Far less work has been done on the origins of the monastic movement in Palestine. Researches devoted to Palestinian monasticism include Simeon Vailhé's "Répertoire" and other articles.[8] Derwas Chitty, in his well-known book *The Desert a City*, gives a summary and analysis of the history of monasticism in Egypt and Palestine (mainly in the Judean desert and the Gaza region), on the basis of the written sources.[9] But, for lack of evidence, he is unable to paint a coherent picture on the basis of data from the field. This book, therefore, may be used as a companion to Chitty's book. The recent exploration of numerous monastic sites, relatively untouched for a millennium and a half except for the action of natural elements, has yielded a better understanding of the nature of Palestinian monasticism.

The monastic movement spread throughout Palestine. Remains of monasteries have been found in a variety of places, within areas that were settled, as well as outside them. Many monasteries were established in or around large cities or near villages. But monasteries established in desert areas were the most numerous and enjoyed the greatest enhanced status, at least in the eyes of believers. As already noted, the great number of monks in the Judean desert, their proximity to Jerusalem and the holy places, and their involvement in Church and state matters made the Judean desert the most important monastic center in the country. From the fifth century on, it became one of the foci of world monasticism.[10]

The main sources of information regarding the history of monasticism in the Judean desert are the hagiographies and collections of anecdotes written by monks who lived in the area during the Byzantine period. Although hagiographic writing follows a fixed literary form, the writers' close acquaintance with those whom they venerated and with the daily life of the monks increases their historical credibility. This is especially true of descriptions of life in the monasteries, their geographical location, and other practical aspects (see table 1).

Most useful are the writings of Cyril of Scythopolis (Beit She'an), which tell the stories of seven monks: Euthymius, Sabas, John Hesychast, Cyriac, Theodosius, Theognius, and Abramius. Cyril completed his work in about 560, but his narration begins with the arrival of Euthymius in the Judean desert about 150 years earlier.[11]

The second most valuable source is the collection of stories and anecdotes by John Moschus, a monk in the Judean desert in the late sixth century. Moschus traveled frequently between the monastic centers of Egypt, Syria, Palestine, and Asia Minor. He collected his stories during his travels and compiled them in a Greek work known as *Pratum spirituale* (*Leimonarion*, or "Spiritual Meadow").[12]

Further light is thrown on Judean desert monasticism by the biography of Chariton, written by an anonymous monk living in the laura of Chariton in the second half of the sixth century.[13] This is the only source dealing with the beginnings of Judean desert monasticism in the first half of the fourth century.

The main source relating to monastic life in the Judean desert during the period between the events described in the biography of Chariton and the beginning of Cyril's biography of Euthymius is Palladius's work *Historia Lausiaca*, named after Lausus, a chamberlain in the court of Theodosius II (408–50), to whom the book was dedicated.[14]

T A B L E 1

Main literary sources for the history of Judean desert monasticism

Source	Date of Composition	Period Covered	Main Monasteries Described	Person(s) Discussed	Best Modern Edition
Cyril of Scythopolis, *Vitae*	ca. 560	405–557	The Great Laura and its dependents Nea Laura Euthymius Theoctistus Theodosius Theognius	Euthymius Sabas John Hesychast Cyriac Theodosius Theognius Abramius	Schwartz (1939)
John Moschus, *Pratum spirituale*	ca. 620	ca. 500–600	Monasteries in the Jordan valley	Numerous	Migne, *PG* 87.3
Anon., *Vita Charitonis*	Second half of sixth century	ca. 330–350	Pharan Douka Souka	Chariton	Garitte (1941)
Palladius, *Historia Lausiaca*	ca. 420	ca. 400	Douka	Elpidius	Butler (1898–1904)
Anon. (pseudo-Cyril of Scyth.), *Vita Gerasimii*	Second half of sixth century	ca. 450–520	Gerasimus	Gerasimus	Koikylides (1902)
Anthony of Choziba, *Vita Georgii, Miracula*	ca. 630	ca. 420–630	Choziba Calamon	George of Choziba	House (1888)
Theodore of Petra, *Vita Theodosii*	ca. 556	ca. 460–530	Theodosius	Theodosius	Usener (1890)
Paul of Elusa, *Vita Theognii*	ca. 526	ca. 470–552	Theognius	Theognius	van den Gheyn (1891)

Our primary reference regarding Gerasimus is a biography, formerly ascribed to Cyril of Scythopolis, but now thought to be the work of an anonymous monk who made use of sections from Cyril's work.[15] This work is the main source for information on the character of monasticism along the Jordan River, particularly in the laura of Gerasimus. Another important work, which describes monasteries in the Jordan valley and the monastery of Choziba, is the biography of George of Choziba, written by George's disciple Anthony of Choziba, ca. 630.[16] It depicts life in Judean desert monasteries from the early fifth century to the first years after the Persian conquest of 614.

The lives and monasteries of Theodosius and his disciple Theognius were described, respectively, by Theodore, bishop of Petra, and Paul of Elusa, former members of the monasteries in question.[17] Thus the descriptions are based on personal acquaintance with the two communities. These two works complement Cyril's short biographies of Theodosius and Theognius.

The brief biography of "the Senator's daughter" provides some insight into the monastic movement in the Jordan valley in the sixth century.[18] But other information directly concerning the monks of the Judean desert is very meager. Most of the monasteries mentioned in the pilgrimage literature and depicted on the Madaba map (the sixth-century mosaic map of Palestine found in a church in Madaba, Jordan) were located near the baptismal sites along the Jordan River. The Church histories of Sozomenus, Evagrius Scholasticus, and others contain only a few references to the monasteries in the Judean desert. Unusual in this respect is Procopius's work, which mentions monasteries that were constructed or restored by the emperor Justinian, among which are monasteries in the Judean desert.[19] Other information of value is provided by sources postdating the Byzantine period, such as the biography of Stephen Sabaites, written toward the end of the eighth century, and the story of the monks who were killed in Saracen attacks on the Great Laura in the late eighth century. But despite their importance, these sources are not within the chronological framework of this study, and therefore I have made minimal use of them.

The archaeological remains also contribute greatly to our knowledge of Judean desert monasticism. The dry desert climate and the remoteness of the monasteries have helped to preserve their walls in relatively good condition. Some of them, rebuilt at the end of the nineteenth century and still functioning, offer a vivid picture of monastic life in the Byzantine period.

Archaeological research in the area began at the end of the nineteenth century, with the surveys by Titus Tobler, Victor Guérin, Charles Conder, Jean Louis Féderlin, and a group of German scholars (Karl Marti, K. Furrer, J. P. van Kasteren, and M. von Riess). These surveys were predominantly of sites known to earlier pilgrims and travelers, although the explorations of Conder and Féderlin also reached a number of new, remote monastic sites.[20]

Excavations of the monasteries of the Judean desert began in 1928 with the British historian Derwas Chitty's work at the monastery of Euthymius.[21] The next scholar to conduct excavations at monastic sites was Virgilio Corbo, who concentrated on the monasteries in the vicinity of Bethlehem. Together with another member of the Studium Biblicum Franciscanum, Bellarmino Bagatti, he also surveyed several sites elsewhere in the Judean desert.[22]

After 1967, Israeli scholars began to explore the area systematically, starting with a survey by Pesach Bar-Adon.[23] This was followed by surveys conducted by Joseph Patrich and by me. These were comprehensive surveys, carried out with the aid of modern equipment, and every site was mapped and measured. So we now have a complete picture of the monastic presence in the Judean desert. A number of excavations were also carried out, most significantly at Khirbet ed-Deir, the monastery of Martyrius, and the laura of Marda.[24]

THE PHYSICAL ENVIRONMENT

The Judean desert is a long, narrow strip bounded by the Judean hills and the Dead Sea (map 2). Its width ranges from 20 to 25 km, and its maximum length, from the Phasael valley in the north to the southern end of the Dead Sea, is about 90 km.[25] Compared with other desert regions, such as the Negev or Sinai, the Judean desert is very small. However, its climate varies dramatically from one part to another. The drop in altitude from the Judean hills to the Dead Sea ranges from 1,000 to 1,300 m over a distance of only 20 km. As a result, the annual precipitation declines from 700 mm in the region of the Judean hills to only 50 mm or less in the Dead Sea region, and temperatures rise from an annual average of 17.7°C in the Jerusalem area to 25.4°C in the Jericho region.[26] The climate becomes hotter and drier from north to south as well as from west to east. Consequently, the southeast corner of the Judean desert is its most arid and desolate part. This may explain the complete absence of monasteries south of Masada.

The Judean desert has a relatively large number of water sources (springs and natural depressions in the rock that collect rainwater), as well as enough precipitation to allow collection and storage of rainwater. The major springs of the Judean desert emanate mainly from the canyons of the main wadis and the cliffs that line the Dead Sea. In addition, several small springs are found along the desert fringe. These springs attracted monks, and monasteries were established alongside some of them during the Byzantine period.

The landscape is divided lengthwise into strips, as conditions change from

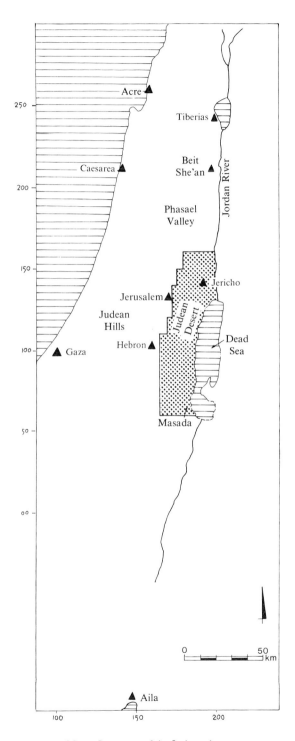

250 — Acre ▲

Tiberias ▲

Beit
She'an ▲

Caesarea ▲

200 —

Phasael
Valley

Jordan River

150 —

Jericho ▲

Jerusalem ▲

Judean
Hills

Judean
Desert

Hebron ▲

Dead
Sea

100 — ▲ Gaza

Masada

50 —

00 —

0   50
├──────────┤ km

▲ Aila

100   150   200

Map 2 Location of the Judean desert

west to east. Here it will be sufficient to distinguish four main units: the desert fringe, the desert plateau, the fault scarp, and the Jericho plain (map 3).

The desert fringe takes in the eastern slopes of the Judean hills, and its character varies with the extent of the slope. In the south it is narrow and steep, whereas in the north it becomes more moderate and extends to a width of several kilometers. It is dissected by several deep riverbeds. Annual precipitation is 250–500 mm, and this relatively high rainfall permits cultivation of crops without irrigation, including winter cereals, fruit trees such as olives, and deciduous trees.

The desert plateau comprises most of the Judean desert. The chalk rocks and the layers of flint between them create both a hilly landscape and more prominent elevations. Precipitation is scanty (100–250 mm), and temperatures are quite high. This region is used by nomads and by the inhabitants of the desert fringe for grazing in winter and spring.

The fault scarp marks the end of the desert plateau; in some places it reaches a height of 200 m over a horizontal distance of 1.5 km. The scarp region is almost completely barren and arid. A thin, flat strip ranging in width from less than 1 to 5 km lies between the foot of the scarp and the Dead Sea. In the nineteenth century, the sea touched the foot of the cliff at ʿEin Fashka, and this was probably the case in ancient times as well. Thus, no coastal road linked the southern and northern shores of the Dead Sea.

The Jericho valley and the Phasael valley are both part of the Jordan valley, but the monks saw them as belonging to the Judean desert. The Jericho valley is a flat, wide region lying between the fault scarp and the Jordan valley. The rock consists of Lissan marl, with thin, alternating layers of chalk, gypsum, clay, sand, and pebbles. The soil was formed partly out of Lissan marl and partly from the large amounts of erosive material carried along the riverbeds from the western hills. These fertile alluvial soils (enriched by copious springs) are utilized for various agricultural crops.

The Jericho oasis is the largest oasis in the Jordan valley. Jericho has flourished throughout history owing to its warm climate and plentiful water, which have created unique agricultural conditions. Its historical importance stems from its location across from the most convenient ascent to the plateau. The city was a factor in the establishment of monasteries in the Jericho valley, just as the desert fringe settlements attracted monasteries to that area. The main concentration of monasteries developed around a small spring called ʿEin Hajla, about 6 km southeast of Jericho, along the Jordan River.

Because the Judean desert is quite small, it is possible to travel from its center to any of the settlements along its edges in a day, and it is relatively easy to walk from the desert to the desert fringe. However, the steep landscape, and

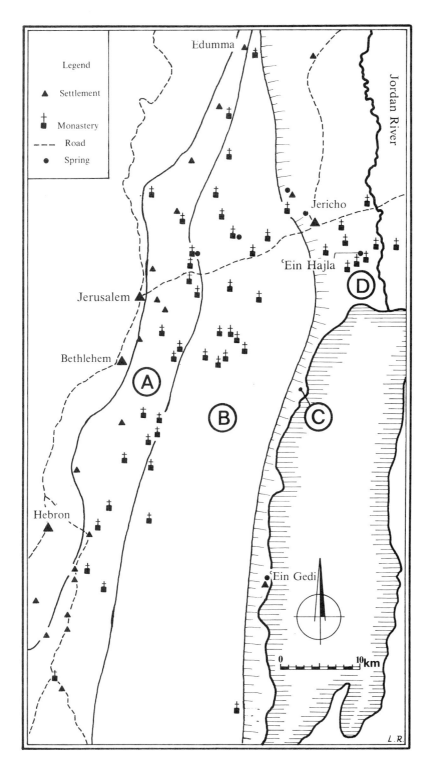

Map 3 Landscape units in the Judean desert: (A) Desert fringe (B) Desert plateau (C) Fault scarp zone (D) Jericho plain

especially the fault scarp, make it difficult to build roads for wheeled vehicles between regions. In fact, except for the Jerusalem–Jericho road, which utilizes the drainage basin of Wadi Qilt, hardly any major roads cross the Judean desert. This was one of the factors that attracted monks to the region. On the one hand, it was a relatively desolate, little traveled region; on the other, it was near major settlements, particularly Jerusalem, which allowed the monks to develop close ties with the residents of these settlements. The name given to the desert by the monks, "the desert of the Holy City," expresses their perception of Jerusalem as a spiritual and administrative center.[27]

At the peak of the monastic expansion in the Judean desert, approximately sixty-five monasteries were functioning in the region, from Phasael in the north to Masada in the south (see map 1). This number includes only the sites in the desert area to the east of the line of settlements on the desert fringe: from Duma (Byzantine Edumma) in the north, through Mukhmas (Machmas), Abu Dis (Beth Abudison), Tuquʿ (Tekoa), and Bani-Naʿim (Capar Baricha), to Khirbet Maʿin (Maon) in the south. The urban area of Byzantine Jericho, with its churches and monasteries, is not included.

Most monasteries were concentrated in two areas: the desert plateau, with about forty monastic sites, and the Jericho plain, where about twenty monasteries have been identified. On the desert plateau, the monasteries were distributed mainly along the desert fringe, the distance between them averaging 4–5 km, while on the Jericho plain, the density was much higher—only 1–2 km between sites. The presence of isolated hermitages, which are not included in the above count, added to the extreme density. A network of paths linked the monasteries to each other.

HISTORICAL BACKGROUND

Four chronological stages can be distinguished in the development of monasticism in the Judean desert: the founding stage during the fourth century; the expansion stage in the fifth century; the zenith, from the end of the fifth century to the beginning of the seventh century; and the stage of decline, during the seventh century.

Despite the lack of historical information on this period, the fourth century appears to have been a formative period. During this time, three monasteries—Pharan, Douka, and Souka—are known to have been established in the desert. All three were founded by Chariton, and all three were of the laura type.

A laura may be defined as a community of recluses. It offered the advantages of living in solitude in individual cells most of the time, but of meeting for communal prayer and Mass on weekends. The community provided for the material and spiritual needs of the solitary cell-dwellers, but without interfering in their daily routine or self-discipline. The word *laura* means "lane" in Greek and probably refers to the path linking the hermits' cells with the church.[28] Monks were accepted into a laura only when they were mature and experienced and had developed strong self-discipline. From the fifth century on, the preparatory years were usually spent in a coenobium—with a group of monks living a communal life in an enclosed complex, working, praying, and eating together according to a fixed schedule. The word *coenobium* derives from the Greek *koinos bios* ("communal life").[29]

Chariton was born into a well-known family in Iconium, in southern Asia Minor (today Konya, in Turkey). At the beginning of the fourth century, after the persecution of Christians in the empire had ceased, he made a pilgrimage to the Holy City. According to his biographer, he was captured by bandits, who took him to their cave in Pharan, near the spring of 'Ein Fara, 9 km northeast of Jerusalem. Miraculously rescued, he inherited the cave and the treasures hoarded in it and founded his first monastery there.[30] The second, Douka, he established in the cliffs of Mount Quruntul to the west of Jericho; and the third, Souka (also known as the Old Laura, or the monastery of Chariton), he built in a deep ravine, northeast of Tekoa.

The fact that Chariton came to the Judean desert as a pilgrim is significant, for it provides the first indication of the link between the monastic movement in this region and the stream of visitors to the Holy Land.[31] Most of the Judean desert monks went to Jerusalem as pilgrims initially and settled in the desert only after viewing the holy places. In this respect, Chariton can be described as a typical Judean desert monk.

The characteristics common to his three monasteries reflect a clear understanding of the necessities of monastic life. All three were built on cliffs near perennial water sources, not far from the settlements of the desert fringe. The steep and broken terrain offered a number of advantages to the monks: natural shelter from the harsh climate and desert predators in caves and recesses in the rock, solitude (on account of the difficulty of access), and minimal friction with locals, since the cliff areas were—and are—of little interest to the residents of the desert fringe (by contrast with the grazing and arable lands in the temperate zones of the desert).

Sources also indicate that a number of those who went to the desert refrained from establishing monasteries and lived as hermits on the Jericho plain.[32] The geographical characteristics of the Jericho plain suited their needs well. Water was available from the Jordan River and a number of smaller streams. The soft Lissan formation was rich in caves. The abundant palm groves provided the monks with food and raw material for their livelihood—the twining of rope and the weaving of baskets. The area was also very close to Byzantine Jericho, which, like other settlements on the edge of the desert, gave the monks a supply base, a market for their product, and a sense of security, all of which were vital to their survival in the desert.[33]

The monastic presence in the Judean desert grew considerably in the fifth century under the leadership of Euthymius the Great. Between the death of Chariton ca. 350 and that of Euthymius in 473, the number of monasteries increased from three to fifteen. The new monasteries spread from Jericho in the north to Masada in the south. It was during this period, apparently, that the custom of going into the interior of the desert for Lent was established. This practice was observed by experienced monks and had a deep impact on the monastic movement, since it gave the monks an intimate knowledge of the desert and what it took to survive there. During these peregrinations, new monastic sites were chosen, including those of the monasteries of Theoctistus, Castellion, and Spelaion.[34]

Euthymius was born in 377 into a noble family in Melitene, the capital of Armenia (today Malatia, in central Anatolia). He took part in church life from an early age and was eventually ordained as the priest responsible for the monks on the periphery of his city. At the age of twenty-nine, he decided to make a pilgrimage to the holy places in Jerusalem and to settle as a monk in the nearby wilderness. In 405, he reached the laura of Pharan, and there he began his monastic life in the Judean desert.[35]

Euthymius's monastic career was characterized by experimentation. The first monastery he founded, together with his friend Theoctistus, was a cliff monastery in Wadi Mukallik. The monastery of Theoctistus, as it was called, was the first coenobium in the Judean desert. Next he left the monastery and opted for the solitary life; then, later, he founded another coenobium—the monastery of Caparbaricha—near the villages in the Hebron hills. His last project was a laura named after him in the level area of Mishor Adummim.

Euthymius devised a model of monasticism that integrated aspects of the laura with those of the coenobium. Under his leadership, partial cooperation developed between his laura in Mishor Adummim and the "Lower Coenobium," the monastery of Theoctistus. The two monasteries had one steward and common possessions, including lands in Mishor Adummim and a hostel in Jerusalem. This sort of cooperation was subsequently adopted by founders of other monasteries, including Gerasimus, John of Choziba, and Sabas, all three of whom appear to have been influenced directly or indirectly by Euthymius.

Unlike Egyptian or Syrian monasticism, which mostly involved local monks, monasticism in the Judean desert was from its inception an international movement. The laura of Euthymius reflects this trend. Four of its first members, including Euthymius, came from Melitene; three were from Cappadocia; three from Rhaithou, in Sinai; one from Antioch; and only one from Palestine.[36] According to the writings of Cyril, Moschus, and others, many of the men who came to live as monks in the Judean desert were born in various districts of Asia Minor, such as Lycia, Galatia, Cilicia, and Armenia. Others came from Cyprus, Greece, or Italy. Numerous monks came from the eastern provinces of the empire, such as Mesopotamia, Syria, Arabia, and Egypt (map 4).[37] Of course, there were also monks from Palestine, like Cyril of Scythopolis, but they were in the minority.

The period of Euthymius's leadership was marked by an increasing involvement of desert monks in the Church establishment. Many of his followers were appointed to various offices, especially in the Church in Jerusalem.[38] It seems that just a few monasteries, particularly the laura of Euthymius, provided most of the monks for ecclesiastical service in Palestine. This may be due to the fact that Euthymius supported the orthodox patriarchs of Jerusalem against the anti-Chalcedonian opposition, which was also led by prominent monks. The result was a close relation between the Church in Jerusalem and the desert monasteries and a steady flow of financial assistance for building and maintaining monasteries.

Parallel to this development among the monasteries in the upper part of the Judean desert, a development along different lines was taking place in the monastic organization of the Jordan valley, under the leadership of Gerasimus. A native of Lycia, already experienced in monastic life, Gerasimus was one of a long line of Judean desert monastic founders from Asia Minor. According to the sources, Gerasimus was considered "the founder and patron" of the Jordan valley. This title, which was given to only two other monks, Euthymius and Sabas, underscores the importance of Gerasimus in shaping the monastic movement in the Jordan valley.[39]

Gerasimus founded a new kind of laura, which consisted of two elements: a central coenobium, surrounded by hermits' cells. As in every communal type of monastery, the coenobium included a church, a storeroom, a refectory, a kitchen, and living quarters for the staff, including cells for the abbot, the steward, and the priest. The coenobium centralized the service functions of the laura and was also the dwelling place of the novices. Both the physical plant and the inner organization of the laura of Gerasimus became models for other monasteries in the Jericho area, such as the laura of Calamon and the monastery of Choziba.[40]

When Euthymius and Gerasimus were at the peak of their activity, two young monks from Asia Minor, Sabas and Theodosius, arrived in the Judean desert and were educated by disciples of Euthymius: Theodosius by Marinus

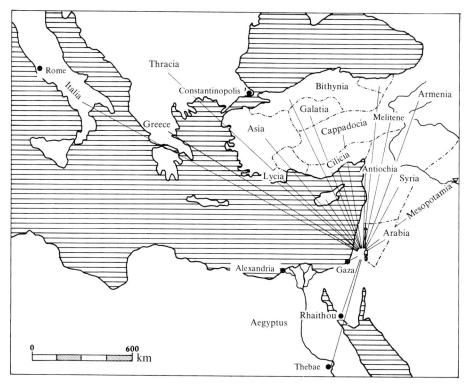

Map 4 Places of origin of the Judean desert monks

and Lucas, two of the first members of the monastery of Theoctistus, and Sabas under the guidance of Theoctistus. They became the leaders of Judean desert monasticism at its peak. Already in the first half of the fifth century, the office of archimandrite existed in the Church of Jerusalem. The archimandrite was a monk and head of an urban monastery but was also in charge of the desert monks. He gave a certain amount of economic assistance and spiritual guidance to the monasteries but had no real control over their internal affairs. In 494, Theodosius and Sabas were elected to this office; Theodosius was responsible for the coenobia of the Jerusalem region, and Sabas for the lauras and the hermits.[41] This was the first time that monks from the desert itself were elected to this post, and the appointments indicate that both the monasteries and the ecclesiastical establishment recognized the leadership of Theodosius and Sabas in Judean desert monasticism.

The strength of their personalities imbued the office of archimandrite with new significance. They had a great deal of influence over the patriarchs and were able to lead the Church of Jerusalem in a struggle against the anti-Chalcedonian policy of Emperor Anastasius from 511 to 518.[42] Even after their deaths, the office of archimandrite, of both the coenobia and the lauras, remained in the hands of desert monks.

Theodosius was born in 423 in the district of Caesarea, the capital of Cappadocia (today Kayseri, in central Anatolia). He reached Jerusalem about 451 and then made his way to the Judean desert. Theodosius represents the pure coenobitic concept of monasticism. His monastery, built ca. 479 on the southern bank of the Kidron valley, was the largest coenobium in the Judean desert. Its founding and operation were directly influenced by the rules set forth by Basil of Cappadocia, which gave priority to the coenobitic way of life and to social welfare activities.[43] This influence was evident in the help given by the monastery to elderly and infirm monks, peasants from the nearby villages, and pilgrims. The four churches of the monastery of Theodosius, which served Greek, Armenian, Bessian-speaking, and mentally ill monks, reflect the tolerant atmosphere and international character of Judean desert monasticism.

Sabas was born in a village near Caesarea, in Cappadocia, in 439. At the age of eighteen, he decided to settle in the Judean desert. He was received by Euthymius but, because of his youth, was sent to the monastery of Theoctistus. In about 478, after a period of wandering, he settled in a small cave in the cliff section of the Kidron valley. Many hermits gathered round him, and toward the end of his fifth year there he decided to build a laura on the site; it later became known as the Great Laura. According to Cyril, the Great Laura of Sabas was "the leader of all the lauras in Palestine."[44] Sabas, who had himself lived as a hermit in the interior of the desert, revived the lauritic concept developed by Chariton and Euthymius. His refusal to be ordained a priest, at least at the beginning, can be explained as part of a desire to return to a purer form of monastic life.

Although the monasteries of Theodosius and Sabas were completely separate from one another, the relation between the coenobitic and lauritic forms became most fruitful under their leadership, and the collaboration between their monasteries continued after their deaths.

Sabas was renowned for his prolific building activity. He initiated or participated in the establishment of ten monasteries, eight of which were in the Judean desert. Cyril lists the Great Laura (built in 483), the Nea Laura (507), the laura of Heptastomos (510), and the coenobia of Castellion (492), Spelaion (508), Scholarius (509), and Zannus (511). The laura of Jeremias, founded by Sabas in 531, a year before his death, can be added to the list.[45] Sabas's desert monasteries were united along the lines of a federation, but without strict rules binding them to each other. Apart from the Nea Laura, they were all built near the Great Laura in the Kidron valley.

His dominant personality aroused strong opposition. Some of his own monks rebelled against his leadership and founded the nucleus for the Nea Laura in 507. Immediately after Sabas's death in 532, a dispute arose between the Origenist monks of the Nea Laura and the monks of the Great Laura. This dispute, which centered on the theology of the third-century Church father Origen, divided the monks of the Judean desert into two camps and erupted periodically over the next two decades.[46] It continued until the emperor Justinian's condemnation of the Origenists in 553.[47]

The Origenist controversy appears to have weakened the power of the monasteries in the desert plateau, and there is no record of any new monasteries being founded in that region after the death of Sabas. The reverse is the case in the Jordan valley, however. Moschus gives the names of seven monasteries in the vicinity of Jericho and the Jordan River that are not mentioned by Cyril.[48] It can be assumed that some of these were founded during the sixth century. This great expansion was apparently caused by the growing number of pilgrims visiting the holy places near the Jordan River during the Byzantine period.

The influx of pilgrims also increased the number of monasteries located on the road between Jerusalem and the Jordan River. Four memorial churches, each with a monastery, were established along this route. Unlike a parochial church, a memorial church was not built to serve a community—a town, a village, or a monastery—but to commemorate a sacred event or to perpetuate the memory of a holy person. It was a destination of pilgrimage and functioned as a way station. Generally, a staff of monks was attached to the church to serve the pilgrims, and a small monastery to house them was built nearby.

The most notable memorial church was the church of St. John the Baptist on the west bank of the Jordan River, where Jesus's baptism is traditionally said to have taken place. The emperor Anastasius built the church there and endowed a monastic community attached to it; the monastery of St. John the Baptist was built near the church.[49]

The stream of pilgrims on the Jerusalem–Jordan road led to changes in monasteries already existing along the road, among them the monastery of Choziba. Toward the end of the fifth century, it was converted from a laura into a coenobium, the gates of which were open even to female visitors.[50] This transformation points to the readiness of the monks to show hospitality to travelers.

The growth and prosperity that continued uninterruptedly through the beginning of the seventh century were terminated by the Persian invasion of 614 and the Muslim conquest of 638. The Persian invasion was accompanied by pillage, mainly on the part of the Saracens, who took advantage of the turmoil. It seems that the physical damage was not extensive, however, and in most of the monasteries, normal life resumed after the conquest.[51]

The negative effects of the Arab conquest, by contrast, were profound and far-reaching, even if the Muslim rulers were reasonably tolerant. The monasteries were cut off from the centers of the Byzantine Empire, and the flow of pilgrims was radically reduced. Archaeological evidence suggests that most of the monasteries in the Judean desert were abandoned at this time.[52] The monastic movement, which at its peak could boast dozens of monasteries, was now confined to the most central of them and to those located close to the Jerusalem–Jericho road. Monasticism in the Judean desert did not cease to exist, but it never regained the scope and vigor of the Byzantine period.

The few monasteries that withstood the crisis remained in existence until the Middle Ages and continued to play an important role in the history of the Eastern Church, particularly those of Sabas and Chariton (Souka), which produced famous monks and a wealth of literary work.[53]

In the nineteenth century there was a revival of Judean desert monasticism, and several monasteries were restored by the Greek patriarchate of Jerusalem. The locations of these monasteries—the Great Laura and the monastery of Theodosius in the Kidron valley and Choziba, Douka, Gerasimus, and St. John the Baptist in the Jericho and Jordan River area—give some idea of how widespread the monastic movement was in the Judean desert during the Byzantine period.

CHAPTER ONE

Types of Monasteries

The appointment of two monks to share the position of archimandrite, with each one responsible for a different group of monks, underscored the clear distinction made between the two main types of monastery in the Judean desert: the laura and the coenobium.[1] Besides these classifications according to life-style and the concomitant differences in physical structure, two further subgroups can be distinguished: monasteries built on the ruins of desert fortresses from the Second Temple period (first century B.C.E. to 70 C.E.) and monasteries built beside memorial churches. While the fortress monasteries are also divided into lauras and coenobia, their general layout reflects the structure of the fortresses on which they were built. Monasteries established near memorial churches are dominated structurally by the church.

THE LAURA

As noted earlier, a laura is a community of monks who live in separate cells, spend most of the week in solitude, and assemble on Saturdays and Sundays for communal prayer and to receive provisions for the following week.[2] It consists of two elements: a core, which includes a church and service buildings, and the monks' cells. The abbot (or hegumen) generally lived in the core, together with the steward (*oikonomos* in Greek) and probably any other monks whose work required it, such as the priest and the manager of the hospice. The rest of the monks, known as "cell-dwellers" (*kelliotai*), were dispersed around the core.[3] A network of paved footpaths between the cells and the core buildings made the scattered buildings of the laura into an integral architectural unit.

During the week, each monk divided his time between prayer and meditation on the one hand and a craft demanding neither concentration nor assistance,

such as basketry, on the other. In the silence of the desert, the monk in his
cell would hear the sound of the *symandron,* the wooden board that hung near
the church and was struck to give the signal for prayer.[4] The monks could also
hear each other's voices raised in prayer, and this contributed to the feeling of
community among them.

At least two buildings could be found in the center of each laura: a church
and a bakery.[5] It seems likely that the bakery was part of a larger structure with
rooms for storing utensils and food. Cyril mentions a "pantry," where the food
supplies of the laura of Euthymius were stored, and a storeroom called "the
steward's office" in two other lauras: the "laura of the Towers," near the Jordan
River, and the Great Laura of Sabas.[6] Other buildings, such as a hospice or an
infirmary, are seldom mentioned and were probably found only in the larger
lauras.

The church and related buildings seem to have been deliberately kept apart
from the bakery and the service buildings. Cyril points out that the church of
the Great Laura was built "above" the bakery and the infirmary (*V. Sab.* 32,
117. 8)—which seems to indicate that the church was on a higher topographical
level. There is also much archaeological evidence of this tendency to separate the church from the service buildings. Such a separation appears to stem
from practical considerations: it removed the church from the noise, commo-
tion, odors, and dirt generated by the service activities. But this can only have
been part of the reason, since the church was used only at weekends, when the
service buildings were not in use. The separation primarily reflects the classical approach to architectural design, which deemed it unthinkable to combine
spiritual and practical activities in one place.

In the sources dealing with most of the lauras of the Judean desert, there is
no mention of either a kitchen or a refectory[7] though some cooking obviously
had to be done for the weekly communal meal. But, since the fare was very
simple, the meal may have been prepared in a corner of the service buildings, at
least when the community was small.[8] Larger communities must have had some
more formal arrangement for cooking and for storage of kitchen utensils. From
the sources, we know of two such cases. In the laura of Gerasimus, the cooking
was done in the coenobium of the laura, presumably in a proper kitchen, since
meals had to be prepared daily for the monks living in the coenobium itself.
In the Great Laura, the cook's work area was in the hospice and was equipped
with tables; we have no indication, however, that the monks themselves ever
dined there.[9]

Not only is there no mention of a refectory in descriptions of lauras: in
the account of the conversion of the laura of Euthymius into a coenobium, we
are told that a refectory was built, which means that there must not have been

one at the laura stage.[10] The venue for the cell-dwellers' communal meals thus remains a mystery.

Since the cells were scattered around the core buildings, sometimes at a considerable distance, the laura could not have an enclosing wall. Nevertheless, the borders of its territory were not left unmarked. The area occupied by each laura was determined by the positions of its most distant cells. In lauras situated along cliffs and ravines, the cliff marked the border. Sometimes a tower was erected in a prominent place to signify the monks' claim to the adjacent ground, as we find in the description of the founding of the Great Laura: "First, wishing to establish a claim on the place, which was unoccupied, he (Sabas) built a tower on the hill at the northern end of the ravine, beyond the bend. Then he began to organize the laura" (*V. Sab.* 16, 100. 8). The beginning of the area occupied by the Cells of Choziba is marked by a stone gate.[11] In lauras established in flat areas, such as the lauras of Marda and Heptastomos, the border was marked by a long stone fence.

This brings us to another way of classifying Judean desert monasteries according to whether they are built on cliffs or on level ground. In the case of lauras, there is a clear difference between the two types in the external form of the core complex and in its relation to the cells. The first type is built close to the cliff face or on a slope, with a small, somewhat irregular core and cells scattered at random in caves or natural shelters in the rocks; whereas in the second type, the core building is constructed according to a well-conceived plan and the cells are arranged in a more orderly fashion.[12]

The archaeological findings show that no less than nineteen lauras existed in the Judean desert during the Byzantine period.[13] Ten were situated on or near cliffs, and nine on flat land, a ratio that undermines the image of the typical laura as among cliffs.[14] All the cliff lauras are located on the desert fringe and the desert plateau, whereas most of the level lauras are in the Jericho area—as might be expected from the topographical character of each of these regions. Nevertheless, three lauras of the level type were located on the high desert plateau: the laura of Euthymius, on the plain known as Mishor Adummim (later converted into a coenobium), the laura atop Masada (Marda), and the laura of Heptastomos, north of the Kidron valley.

The Cliff Laura

Chronologically, the cliff laura precedes the level type. The first three monasteries established in the Judean desert were cliff lauras. The first level lauras in this region—the laura of Euthymius and the laura of Gerasimus—were not founded until about a century later.

The laura of Pharan The first monastery in the Judean desert was the laura of Pharan, founded by Chariton ca. 330. Its remains were discovered in the canyon section of Wadi Fara, near the spring of ʿEin Fara, about 9 km northeast of Jerusalem.[15] It is no coincidence that the first monastery was founded in the vicinity of ʿEin Fara, one of the most prolific springs in the Judean desert, and was situated between two impressive cliffs 30–40 m high, offering many caves suitable for dwellings (fig. 1). The core buildings and the monks' cells occupy the area between the two cliffs. All told, the laura covers an area of about 30,000 m². Entry to the laura was via a path from the south, which forks near the southern cliff, one branch descending to the wadi, the other turning west toward the core buildings (fig. 2). The monks' cells are scattered along these two paths. A survey of the site located fifteen cells, six on the south bank and nine on the north bank, each cell an average of about 35 m from the next.[16]

The core of the laura was at the foot of the southern cliff. Its remains were partially damaged in the course of the construction of a small (now deserted) Russian Orthodox monastery at the site in the early twentieth century. The remains of four structures from the Byzantine period can still be seen here. Most

Figure 1 The laura of Pharan, situated between the cliffs (looking east)

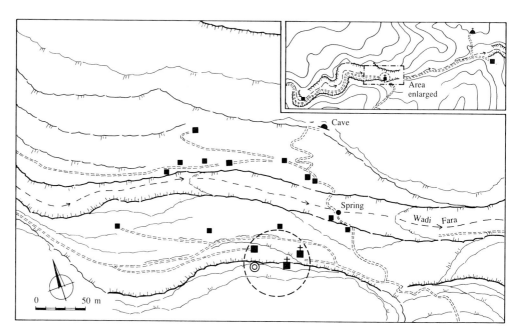

Figure 2 Sketch plan of the laura of Pharan

prominent is a cave church, about 12 m above ground level. This is the church that was consecrated by Chariton when he first arrived at the spot. In the sixth century, it was called "the Old Church" (*V. Char.* 11, 24. 20), which probably means that after Chariton's time, another church was built in the laura.

The archaeological evidence supports this conclusion. Just below the cave church, a small chapel, built of cut stone, was excavated in the late nineteenth century.[17] About 25 m west of the chapel, the remains of a large Byzantine structure were found; they include sections of walls and a large area with a white mosaic floor. The structure probably housed the laura's bakery and storerooms. Another element found among the core buildings was a large water reservoir carved out of the bedrock of the cliff about 35 m west of the cave church. Its capacity has been estimated at about 600 m³.

The laura of Pharan was originally concentrated near the spring, but remains of cells and buildings have also been found to the west and the east of it. One cell was particularly isolated, located about 1,000 m west of the spring, on the northern bank of the wadi. This may have been the cell of Euthymius, who, according to Cyril, "lived in a solitary cell outside the laura" (*V. Euth.* 6, 14. 10).

About 1,200 m east of the spring lie the remains of two large edifices, one opposite the other. Within the northern structure, the remains of a small chapel have been uncovered.[18] The dozens of Byzantine burial caves surrounding the northern building may have comprised the laura's cemetery. The southern structure is a large, square building whose function is not clear.

The laura of Pharan is one of the smaller lauras. The small number of cells indicates that the community consisted of no more than twenty monks. In that respect, it is representative of several lauras in the Judean desert, such as the laura of Jeremias, the Cells of Choziba, and the laura near 'Ein el-Fawwar.[19]

The monastery of Chariton The large lauras in the Judean desert had two or three times as many cells as the laura of Pharan. The oldest of the bigger lauras is the monastery of Chariton, also known as the Old Laura, or Souka. The identification of the monastery as Khirbet Khureitun, 15 km south of Jerusalem and 2.5 km northeast of Tekoa, is universally accepted.[20] The remains of the laura are scattered over the steep slope of Wadi Khureitun, covering an area of about 450,000 m² (fig. 3). Two paths lead to the site: one from Tekoa, to the west, and another from Bethlehem, to the north.

The remains of at least thirty-five cells have been found at the site, most of them concentrated south of the core complex. The cells are 20–80 m apart and

Figure 3 Aerial view of the monastery of Chariton (looking west)

usually face south, as in many other lauras, such as the Nea Laura, the laura of Firminus, and 'Ein el-Fawwar. The northernmost point of the laura is marked by the remains of the core complex, while the southernmost point is the "Hanging Cave" of Chariton. The structure of the monastery underwent additions and changes after the Byzantine period.

The core complex is triangular, with a tower at each apex (fig. 4). The base of the triangle is formed by massive retaining walls that were designed to provide level areas for construction. The prominence of the northern tower and the thickness of its walls show that it was meant to demarcate the northernmost point of the laura. The other two towers are at lower levels. Fragments of a chancel screen found on the site show the existence of at least one church within the core of the laura.

The Great Laura The largest laura in the Judean desert in terms of number of monks was the Great Laura, in the Kidron valley, where the monastery of

Figure 4 Reconstruction of the monastery of Chariton

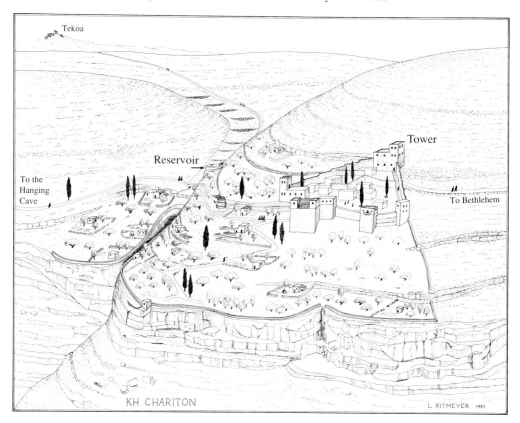

Figure 5 Present-day monastery of Mar Saba, alongside the Great Laura
(looking west)

Mar Saba stands today (fig. 5). When the Great Laura was founded by Sabas in 483, it had about 150 monks.[21] The remains of the cells are dispersed along the cliffs on both sides of the valley, and about forty-five of them have been surveyed.[22] The distance between the cliffs ranges from 200 to 250 m, and the northernmost and southernmost cells are about 2 km apart (fig. 6). The total area of the laura was therefore about 400,000 m². The northernmost ruin is a small structure on a hill west of the valley and would seem to be the remains of the tower built by Sabas to mark the boundary of the laura. Some of the cells are traditionally linked with the monks mentioned in the sources dealing with the monastery.

The core of the laura was located where the present monastery stands and covered an area of about 6,000 m².[23] From the gate of the present-day monastery, a flight of stairs descends to a central courtyard flanked by the two churches that were built by Sabas. One is a cave church, today named after St. Nicholas,

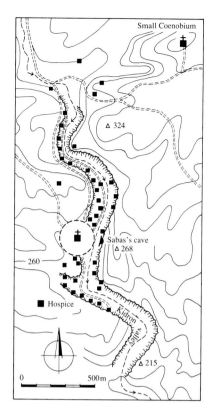

Figure 6 Sketch plan of the Great Laura.
Numbers refer to height above sea level.

and the other is dedicated to the Virgin Mary. Sabas's grave is in the courtyard between the two.

On the hill to the south of the monastery of Mar Saba stands a ruin, Deir Maqtal el-Ghuweir, which is thought to have been the hospice of the Byzantine monastery.[24] The "Small Coenobium," whose remains were found on top of the hill about 1,600 m northeast of the present-day monastery, was an integral part of the Great Laura and was connected to it by a well-paved path.[25] The existence of a hospice and a coenobium in the Great Laura distinguishes it from most other lauras in the Judean desert.

The Nea Laura I discovered the Nea Laura in 1982 in a rocky section of Wadi Jihar, 2.5 km south of Tekoa. The overall area of the laura is about 600,000 m². Within this area, more than forty cells have been found, as well as a good number of cisterns, garden plots, sections of paved paths, and so forth. Most of the cells, as well as the core buildings, are situated on a slope north of a small wadi descending steeply to the main wadi (fig. 7). The choice of a slope facing south was apparently motivated by practical considerations: for in that direction, the doors and windows of the cells were sheltered from the prevailing northwesterly winds. The average distance between the cells is 35 m.[26]

The core buildings are easily identified by their dimensions and the quality of their construction. They comprise two separate complexes: the church complex and another complex about 150 m to the west. The church complex includes a small chapel (identified by the many fragments of roof tiles and marble) built in a prominent position adjacent to the cliff on a natural rock step. The western complex is larger and consists of a building with several rooms, cisterns, and agricultural facilities arranged around an interior courtyard. Judging from its dimensions and interior organization, it seems likely that this compound was the service area of the laura.

Other large, cliff lauras in the Judean desert include the laura of Firminus and Khallet Danabiya, both in the northern part.[27]

Figure 7 Sketch plan of the Nea Laura

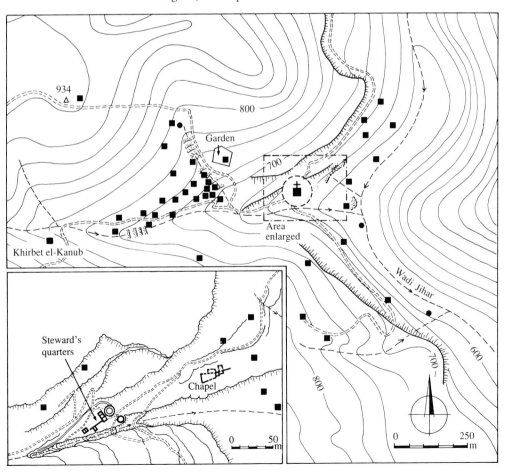

The Level Laura

The laura of Gerasimus Lauras of the level type are found mainly in the Jericho valley. I surveyed only one in that area, the laura of Gerasimus. Its remains surround the present-day monastery known as Deir Hajla, which lies about 5.5 km southeast of Jericho (fig. 8). The remains of the core of the laura were discovered 350 m east of the existing monastery.[28] They consist of a small mound of ancient building stones and a large quantity of mosaic tesserae (including colored ones).

The remains of the core building and the monks' cells are situated between two parallel riverbeds, the northern of which is called Wadi en-Nukheil, "Valley of the Little Palm" (fig. 9). The distance between the two wadis is about 400 m, and that between the westernmost and easternmost cells is about 950 m; the total area covered by the laura is thus approximately 380,000 m². To date, the remains of only seven or eight built cells have been found, and these are minimal: a small mound, some fieldstone, and a few potsherds from the Byzantine period. It seems likely that there were once a lot of cells here, but no material

Figure 8 Present-day monastery of Deir Hajla, which, according to tradition, occupies the site of the Byzantine laura of Gerasimus (looking northeast)

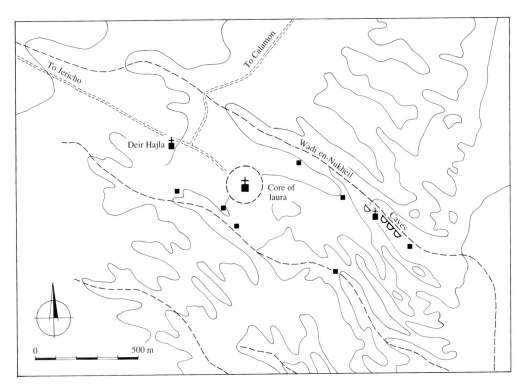

Figure 9 Sketch plan of the laura of Gerasimus

evidence has been found. Apart from cells that were obviously built, an impressive compound of four cave cells and a chapel was found at the northeastern
end of the laura, 650 m from the core. The compound is carved into the southern cliff of Wadi en-Nukheil. Along the cliff are traces of other cave dwellings,
which explain the other name by which the laura of Gerasimus was known—
"The Caves."

The laura of Heptastomos Two level lauras that are in better condition are
found on the desert plateau. One is the laura excavated at Masada, which will
be discussed in the section on fortress monasteries; the other is the laura of
Heptastomos, founded by Sabas in 510. Both are relatively small, and they could
not have housed more than twenty monks.

The laura of Heptastomos is identified as Khirbet Jinjas, in the gentle hills
north of the Kidron valley, about 4 km northwest of the Great Laura.[29] Its remains are marked out with a 50-cm thick fence, which is preserved to a height
of one or two courses. The fence consists of two extremely straight sections:
one extending southward for 330 m, the second extending eastward for 480 m
(fig. 10). Beyond those points, the fence was contoured to the topography, as

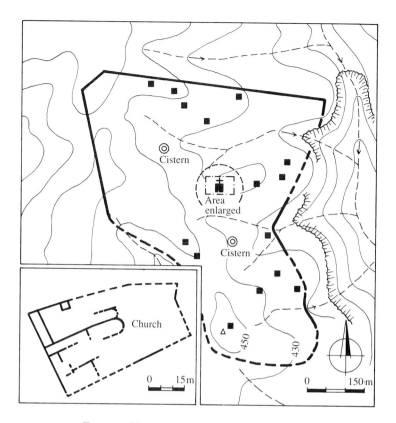

Figure 10 Sketch plan of the laura of Heptastomos

can be seen from a number of sections discovered to the south and east. The function of the fence was to delimit the area belonging to the laura; its good state of preservation allows us to determine the area of the monastery with relative precision: 250,000 m².

The remains of fifteen cells have been counted: eight north and east of the core and seven south of it. The average distance between cells is about 65 m. A reservoir was built in the center of each group of cells; since few of the cells surveyed have been found to contain cisterns, it is assumed that the reservoirs were shared by the monks in the nearby cells. The core buildings occupy an area of at least 2,000 m². They are surrounded by a wall measuring 38 × 20 m. The remains include a church and sections of its adjoining rooms, arranged around two inner courtyards. The existence of two courtyards suggests a functional separation between the church and its annexes (centered around the western courtyard) and the service buildings (centered around the eastern courtyard).

Most of the characteristics typical of a level laura are found in the laura of Heptastomos: it has a symmetrical structure, with a clear division between the two groups of cells, and a regularly shaped fence, as indicated above. The core consists of a large central block whose form resembles that of a coenobium.

The layouts of the various lauras of the Judean desert are compared in figure 11. Seeing them on a uniform scale allows us to note the differences in size and shape. Table 2 provides a summary of information regarding lauras in the Judean desert that have been studied. From the table and the comparative chart, we can see that the lauras of the Judean desert had a number of characteristics in common:

1. Each occupied a large area.
2. Their boundaries were delimited either by topographical features (cliffs or wadis) or by a stone wall.

TABLE 2

Lauras in the Judean desert that have been surveyed

Type	Size	Name	Area (m²)	Number of cells	Average Distance between cells (m)	Comments
Cliff	Small	Pharan	30,000	15	35	Single cell to the west of the laura, two separate complexes to the east
		Jeremias	27,000	12	33.2	
		'Ein el-Fawwar	30,000	12	34.6	
		Cells of Choziba	15,000	12	33.5	Laura annexed to coenobium
	Large	Old Laura	450,000	35	43	
		Great Laura	400,000	45	small	Densely built
		Nea Laura	600,000	40	35	
		Firminus	1,200,000	40	45	2 or 3 concentrations of cells at a great distance from the core
		Khallet Danabiya	220,000	35	34	
Level	Large	Gerasimus	380,000	12[a]	?	State of remains makes investigation of site difficult
		Calamon	240,000	40[b]	45	
		Heptastomos	250,000	15	65	Enclosed by stone fence
	Small	Marda (Masada)	80,000	13	60	Enclosed by stone fence

a. According to the written sources, there were 70 cells.

b. Approximate number of modern cells built on the old foundations.

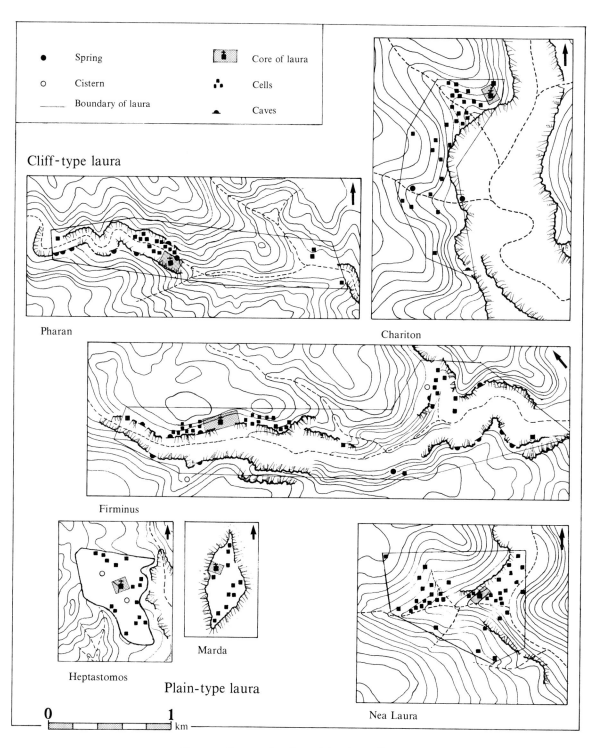

Figure 11 Comparative chart of the plans of Judean desert lauras

3. The core buildings in the center of the laura were separate from the cells scattered around the core.
4. The church compound tended to be separate from the service buildings.
5. In the level type of laura, the core tended to be bigger and to be like a small coenobium.
6. Large courtyards were built in front of the church.
7. The cells were usually scattered haphazardly around the core.
8. A network of paths consolidated the laura into one integrated unit.

THE COENOBIUM

A coenobium is a monastery in which monks live a communal life, with a daily routine of communal prayer, work, and meals.[30] Typically, coenobia are square buildings surrounded by a wall and range in size from modest to vast. The smaller coenobia are reminiscent of late Roman agricultural villas, in being built around a closed inner courtyard, which provided air and light and served as a unitive element.[31] The large coenobia, by contrast, were like small towns, containing everything needed for their sustenance, including workshops, hospices, and hospitals.

The most striking example of a large coenobium in the Judean desert is that founded by Theodosius. It has not been excavated, but according to Theodore of Petra, it had two workshops, various hospices and hospitals, and a home for aged monks. Theodosius also included a "place of seclusion," which was a kind of "monastery within the monastery" for monks who had lost their sanity and for their attendants. The monastery of Theodosius had four churches. Later, in the time of Sophronius (Theodosius's successor as abbot), a fifth church, dedicated to the Virgin Mary, was built.[32] The present-day monastery of Theodosius (fig. 12) reflects its appearance in the Byzantine period.

Another coenobium whose original structure is known from the sources is the monastery of Choziba in Wadi Qilt, which was described by Anthony of Choziba. Entry was through two gates and a passageway leading to an inner courtyard. The courtyard gave access to the church, behind which, on a higher level, stood the refectory and the kitchen.[33] The monastery of Choziba provides a good example of a departure from the classical square coenobium, resulting from the need to adapt the shape of the monastery to the rocky terrain of the wadi.

Like the lauras, the coenobia of the Judean desert can be divided on the basis of topography into two main types: a cliff type and a level type.[34] The first includes coenobia attached to steep cliffs, the second, coenobia built on hilltops or slopes in relatively flat areas.

Figure 12 Aerial view of the present-day monastery of Theodosius
(looking east)

The Cliff Coenobium

To date, forty-four coenobia have been studied in the Judean desert.[35] Of these, thirty-nine are of the level type and five of the cliff type, indicating a clear preference for building the coenobia in level areas or on moderate slopes. Nevertheless, the first coenobium to have been established in the Judean desert was a cliff coenobium, the monastery of Theoctistus, founded by Euthymius and his friend Theoctistus in 411.

The monastery of Theoctistus The remains of the monastery of Theoctistus were discovered in a canyon section of Wadi el-Mukallik, about 15 km east of Jerusalem.[36] The monks had originally intended to build a laura like that of Pharan, but because of the steepness of the cliffs and the difficulty of access to the mouth of the cave that they had designated as a church, they decided to build a coenobium (*V. Euth.* 9, 16.25–17.3).

The monastery of Theoctistus is indeed in one of the steepest places in the Judean desert (fig. 13). The cave church is on the cliff face, 9 m from the ground, and to this day access is possible only with the aid of ladders, ropes, or other climbing gear.[37] In order to create a broad, flat area on which the monastery could be built below the cave church, a huge retaining wall was built on the riverbed. Long sections of that wall survive, and in some places it is intact to a height of about 5 m; a massive support pier (1.5 m wide) can be seen along the wall (fig. 14). Most of the remains of the monastery are found in the 25 m between the retaining wall and the cave church, in an area of approximately 2,200 m². The retaining wall, the monastery itself, and the cave church form a pyramid, with the apex at the top of the church.

The entrance gate to the complex is to the west. From the gate, a narrow passage leads to a small interior courtyard, bounded by a stone railing to the south and the cliff to the north. A spacious cave in the cliff (17 m long, an average of 9 m wide, with a 5-m-high ceiling), was probably used as a stable, since holes for hitching up pack animals can be seen in protrusions in the rock wall. On the eastern side of the courtyard there was probably another gate leading to the interior of the monastery. The existence of interior gates in coenobia is often

Figure 13 Aerial view of the monastery of Theoctistus (looking northwest)

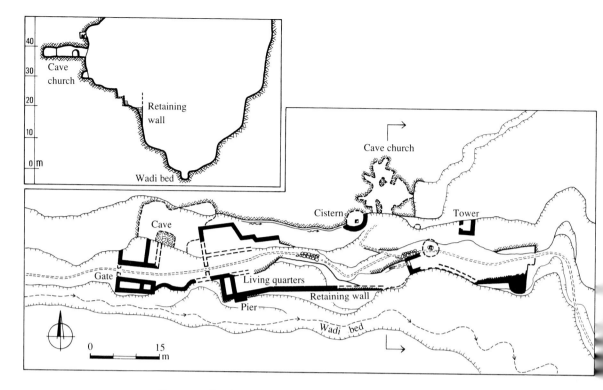

Figure 14 Sketch plan and cross-section of the monastery of Theoctistus

mentioned in the sources (as in the description of the monastery of Choziba) and is attested to by archaeological findings (at Khirbet ed-Deir, for example). From the point at which the inner gate is assumed to have stood, a paved stone path, flanked by various buildings, led toward the center of the monastery. In the center, a well-constructed stairway led to the cave church. To the east of the stairway is an almost completely intact two-story tower with a vaulted stone ceiling. The tower and the frescoes found in the cave church have been dated to the Middle Ages.[38]

It is difficult to estimate the population of the monastery of Theoctistus. The impressive scale of the complex might suggest that it was a community of several dozen monks. However, many of the remains are retaining walls and various other structures designed to solve the problem of construction on precipitous terrain, which greatly limited the area available for living quarters. It is more likely, therefore, that the community was of medium size, numbering no more than forty monks.

The monastery of Choziba The cliff coenobia of Choziba and Khirbet ed-Deir are similar to the monastery of Theoctistus in size and layout. The monastery of Choziba (today, Deir Mar Jariys, also known as St. George's Monastery) in Wadi Qilt is a classic example of a coenobium built next to a cliff. The present-day monastery lies in a canyon section of the wadi, about 5 km west of Jericho.

According to Anthony of Choziba, the site was originally used as a hermitage, in which five Syrian monks lived in succession in the first half of the fifth century. Later a coenobium was built there, with a laura-like community of hermits living alongside it, in the Cells of Choziba, as they are called in the sources. The massive building was traditionally thought to have been constructed by John of Thebes (also called John the Chozibite), who joined the monastery in the late fifth century.[39] The present structure, built on the foundations of the original monastery, hugs the natural wall of the cliff behind it. Its appearance exemplifies the unique character of coenobia built next to cliffs (fig. 15).

The first systematic description of the site, given by Conder and Kitchener, is most important, since it is the only one that predates the rebuilding of the monastery.[40] According to their report, the monastery was built on a long, narrow shelf at the foot of an immense cliff on the northern bank of the wadi. The entrance gate was in the eastern part of the rock shelf. From the gate, an exterior passageway (40 m long and about 10 m wide) leads to the present monastery

Figure 15 Present-day monastery of Choziba, now known as St. George's Monastery (looking northwest)

Figure 16 Reconstruction of the monastery surrounding ʿEin es-Sakhari

building. The cliff face above the passageway contains large traces of plaster, as well as two parallel rows of carved sockets designed to support the wooden beams that provided the framework for a structure at least two stories high. The present monastery is also built on several levels.

Judging from the plan supplied by Conder and Kitchener, the original monastery was about 90 m long and 10–30 m wide. Its area was therefore about 1,800 m². (In calculating its overall area, account must be taken of its high, multilevel structure. Precise measurements of the site have never been made.) Remains of a smaller cliff-side coenobium surrounding ʿEin es-Sakhari, not far from the monastery of Chariton,[41] give an indication of what the monastery of Choziba probably looked like during the Byzantine period (fig. 16).

Khirbet ed-Deir One of the most remote monastic sites in the Judean desert is Khirbet ed-Deir. It is situated on a ridge bordering a small ravine that branches off from Wadi er-Ghar about 13 km southeast of Tekoa and about 28 km south of Jerusalem. I have carried out systematic excavations at this site, in the course of which most of the components of the monastery were uncovered.[42]

As with other coenobia, the complex was surrounded by walls. The monastery covered an area of about 4,000 m² and probably housed no more than forty monks. It was built on three separate levels: the lowest level, the ravine, was taken up by the garden; the middle level—that is, the cliffs—was the locus of the communal areas of the monastery; and the upper level, on top of the hill, comprised the monks' living quarters (fig. 17). The three levels were connected by a paved path that began at the main entrance to the monastery.

The small finds of the excavation, especially two coins from Justinian's reign and several oil lamps, suggest that the monastery was founded at the beginning of the sixth century and was in use for more than 140 years, until the Muslim conquest of Palestine in the middle of the seventh century.

From the external gate-house of the monastery, a monumental stairway

Figure 17 Aerial view of Khirbet ed-Deir (looking northwest)

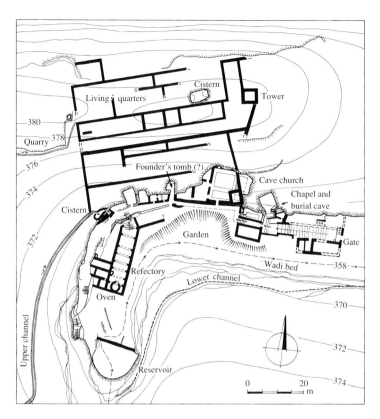

Figure 18 Sketch plan of Khirbet ed-Deir

with twenty completely intact steps leads to an inner gate (fig. 18). In front of
the inner gate is a small courtyard (4.5 × 6 m) with a stone bench, probably
meant for visitors. In the cliff wall behind the bench is a large, partially hewn
cave, with a small chapel at its entrance. A Greek inscription in the mosaic floor
informs us that the complex was a burial place for the priests attached to the
monastery. Thus visitors and pilgrims could visit the graves and pray, as the
inscription says, for the intercession of the sainted priests, without having to go
all the way into the monastery.

A path from the inner gate leads to the entrance of the main church. The
church, built into a large cave (25 m long, 13 m wide, and 4 m high), consists
of a large prayer room, a small chapel, and three additional rooms in the rear.
The prayer room has a colorful mosaic floor, in which the fourth and fifth verses
of Psalm 106 are featured in Greek (see ch. 5). Next to the western wall of the
cave church, a cell was cut into the rock; it has a bench and a low, narrow entrance. In front of the cell, a mosaic floor decorated with two crosses and a
Greek inscription referring to the resurrection of the dead were uncovered. The
cell appears to have been the burial place of an important figure in the history of
the monastery, probably the founder, and may originally have been his abode.

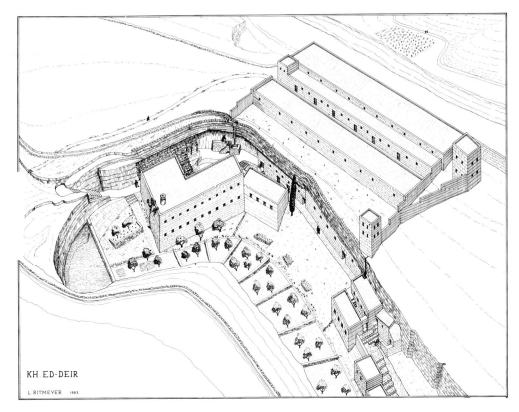

Figure 19 Reconstruction of Khirbet ed-Deir

Thus he continued to hold his central place in the daily life of the monks, who would pass his grave on their way from the church to the refectory.

The paved path continues westward to the refectory complex, which is separate from the church and the burial caves. The refectory and ancillary rooms were conceived as one unit, surrounding a small courtyard. The long narrow dining hall (26 × 7 m) was built above the kitchen. Fragments of a mosaic floor found among the debris on the ground floor attest to the existence of this second story, since the kitchen and service rooms on the ground floor were paved with plain stone slabs. An oven was discovered at the southern end of the kitchen.

The passageway continues up a flight of stairs to the living quarters of the monastery (fig. 19). This complex is quite imposing, some two and a half times the combined area of the church and the refectory. Since it has been excavated only partially, its inner divisions are unclear. It probably surrounded a courtyard, however, and the eastern end, on the ridge, contains the remains of an annex that may have been a tower. Another tower was built above the cave church. Walls delimit the living area to the east and the west, giving it the shape of a large rectangle (about 30 × 50 m, or 1,500 m^2). A sizable quarry to the west served the needs of the monastery's builders.

In the monastery at Khirbet ed-Deir, we find in the right-angled walls of the living area the orthogonal plan typical of coenobia. The adaptation of the church and refectory area to the contours of the cliffs shows the monks' ability to cope with the difficult topographical conditions of the Judean desert.

The Level Coenobium

The level coenobia vary considerably, some being erected on the plain, others on a slope or atop a steep hill with a flat summit. They can thus be divided into two subgroups: those built on plains and those built on slopes. As we will see, both the appearance and the size of the monasteries reflect this division.

The monastery of Martyrius One of the earliest monasteries to be built on an open plain with easy access was the monastery founded by Martyrius before he was appointed to the clerical staff of the Church of the Holy Sepulchre in Jerusalem in 474 (*V. Euth.* 32, 51. 20–1). The site of the monastery has been identified as Khirbet el-Murassas, about 6 km east of Jerusalem.[43] Its structure, which has been entirely uncovered, is an excellent example of a coenobium built on an orthogonal plan (fig. 20). The monastery is surrounded by a massive stone

Figure 20 The monastery of Martyrius after excavation (looking west)

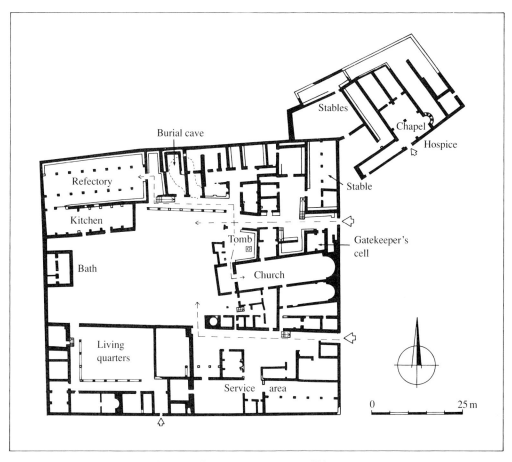

Figure 21 Plan of the monastery of Martyrius

wall, which delimits an area 78 m long from east to west and 67 m long from
north to south, a total of 5,200 m². A building just outside the northeast corner
of the monastery is thought to be a hospice; its area, about 1,200 m², brings the
total size of the monastery to about 6,400 m².

Two entry gates were cut through the eastern wall; according to the excavators, the more southerly of the two was sealed during the sixth century.
There was another, smaller, posternlike entrance in the south wall. Two parallel
paved passageways led from the eastern gates to the central court of the monastery (fig. 21). The monastery church and its annexes were in the area between
the passageways, and on the outer sides of the passageways stood the service
buildings (stables and storerooms). This functional division of the monastery by
means of longitudinal passageways is typical of the large monastery complexes
of the Byzantine period.[44]

A central courtyard occupies about a quarter of the overall area of the monastery. To its south was a large residential building (23 × 37 m) surrounding a
spacious inner courtyard. There was a chapel on the ground floor, and the living
quarters were on the upper story. The refectory and kitchen complex was across

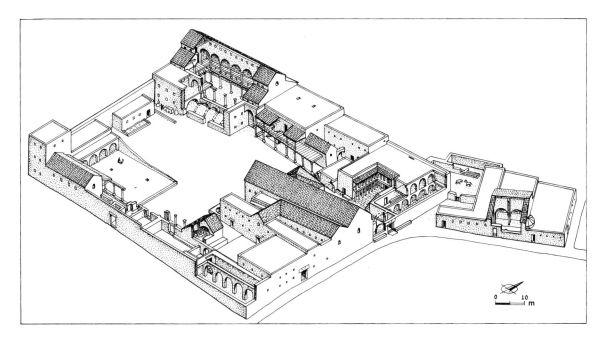

Figure 22 Reconstruction of the monastery of Martyrius

the courtyard (fig. 22). An unexpected feature discovered by the excavators is a small complex of bath installations, including a heating system, located between the living quarters and the refectory. Since the ascetic lifestyle precluded such luxuries as baths, this complex was probably intended only for the use of ailing monks.

The central structure of the monastery was the tomb of Paul, who headed the monastery after Martyrius, and his successors, which was discovered in the northwest corner of the church compound.[45] The site of the tomb was chosen very carefully. Near it, the northern passageway of the monastery interesected the path to the church. Visitors passed this point on their way from the gate to the church, while the monks passed it on their way from the church to the refectory.[46]

Another tomb situated between the church and the refectory was originally the cave in which Martyrius used to seclude himself. A Greek inscription near the cave indicates that it was later converted into a burial cave for the priests attached to the monastery. Later still, a small chapel was built next to it.

A substantial portion of the monastery was occupied by the service wings, situated on the east side north and south of the church complex. Their location near the gates permitted efficient loading and unloading of goods and kept the associated noise and dirt away from the center of the monastery. The service wing in the northeast corner housed stables for pack animals and various storage rooms. The living quarters of the monks working in this service wing appear to have been on an upper story, judging from the remains of a stairway. The opposite wing, in the southeast corner of the monastery, consisted of a large hall, storage rooms, and a chapel. Here, too, the quarters of the monks working in this wing were probably on an upper story. Similar to the monastery of Martyrius are the monastery of Theodosius, the largest monastery in the Judean desert, and that of Euthymius.[47]

The monastery of Gabriel Gabriel, one of Euthymius's disciples and later hegumen of St. Stephen's Church in Jerusalem, built a "small monastery" in a valley east of the Mount of Olives (*V. Euth.* 37, 56. 8–9). The monastery, founded in the second half of the fifth century, has been identified with the remains in Qasr er-Rawabi, about 6 km northeast of Jerusalem.[48]

The plan of the monastery, like that of other coenobia built on plains, is rectangular, 20.3 m long (not including the apse) and 14.1 m wide—an area of only about 286 m² (fig. 23). Its small size reflects its declared purpose as a place

Figure 23 Plan and cross-section of the monastery of Gabriel

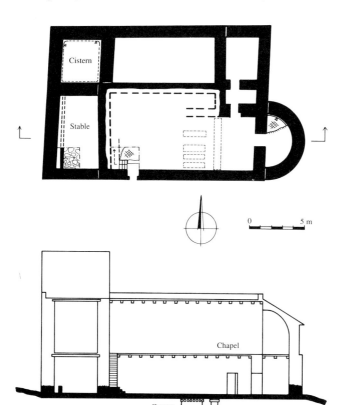

of retreat for Gabriel during the period of Lent (*V. Euth.* 37, 56. 10). It probably housed no more than a few monks throughout the year. The entrance, in the south wall, leads to a chapel-like room whose external dimensions are 8.8 × 15.4 m. An external apse protrudes from the east end. The floor is of coarse white mosaic; but near the apse, fallen fragments of colored mosaic were found, which may indicate that the chapel was on an upper story of the monastery. Well-built tombs were found below the ground floor, and their quality and central position would seem to support Cyril's statement that the founder of the monastery, Gabriel, was buried there.

The remains of a stone staircase near the entrance to the monastery also point to the existence of a second floor. West of the stairs is a long narrow room, which was used as a stable (judging from the trough installed against one wall and the coarse stone slabs of the floor). North of the stable is an underground cistern, later used as a limekiln. The archaeological evidence indicates that the ground floor of the monastery was used for utilitarian purposes, and that the living quarters, the chapel, and the parts of the monastery connected with the daily life of the monks were on the upper floor.

The distinctive feature of this monastery is the limited area of its inner courtyard. The compact plan of the monastery leaves little space for an interior courtyard. (It would be unreasonable to assume that the building was entirely devoid of a courtyard, though that is by no means impossible.)

Other small coenobia Several other relatively small coenobia were surveyed in the Judean desert, including Khirbet el-Quneitira, Khirbet et-Tina, Castellion (see below), the monastery of Severianus, and El-Qasr. Khirbet el-Quneitira is perhaps the best example of a coenobium built on a slope. The reconstruction shown in figure 24 demonstrates the way in which the various elements of the coenobium were incorporated into the slope.[49]

The layouts of the Judean desert coenobia are compared in figure 25. Table 3 provides a summary of a selection of the coenobia in the Judean desert that have been studied. On the basis of the table and the comparative chart, we can note the following common characteristics of these monasteries:

1. Their construction was compact, with connected architectural elements.
2. They were at least two stories high.
3. The monastery was enclosed within solid stone walls (occasionally using the cliff face).
4. The design was orthogonal in flat areas but departed from that plan where the topography was steeper.
5. They were built around an inner courtyard.

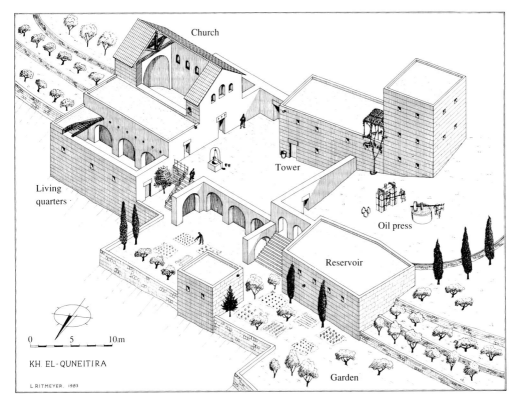

Figure 24 Reconstruction of Khirbet el-Quneitira

6. The entrance wall usually faced the courtyard.
7. The public, common buildings (church, refectory, service buildings) were separate from the living quarters.
8. The living quarters were remote from the entrance gate.
9. The larger monasteries contained a hospice, built just outside the gates.

THE FORTRESS MONASTERY

This is not really another type of monastery, but rather a subgroup deriving from a phenomenon typical of Judean desert monasticism: the settlement of monks in fortresses erected during the Hasmonean and Roman periods. Traces of coenobia or lauras have been found in six of the eight desert fortresses built by the Hasmoneans or by Herod: Masada, Hyrcania, Doq (Dagon), Herodium, Cypros, and Nuseib el-ʾAweishireh.[50] No evidence of monasteries has been found in Alexandrion and Machaerus, which are beyond the geographical boundaries of the Judean desert. Two Roman Byzantine fortresses, Khirbet el-Qasr and Khirbet el-Kilya, were also used for monastic purposes.[51]

Settlement of monks in abandoned fortresses is not peculiar to the Judean

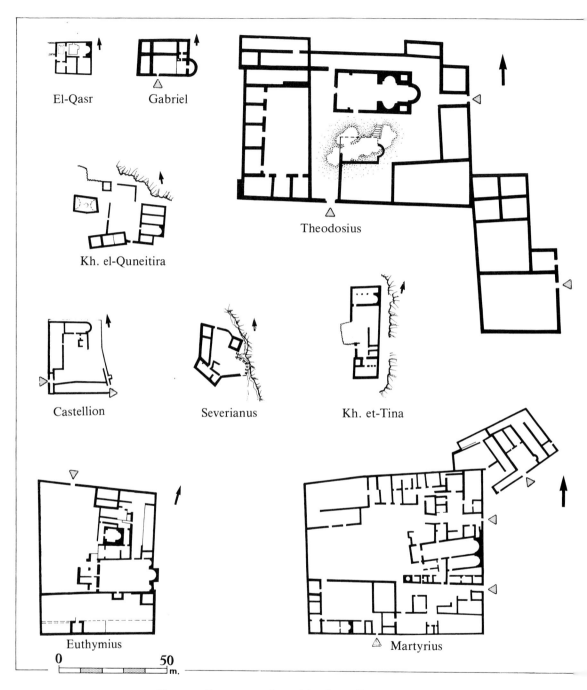

El-Qasr

Gabriel

Theodosius

Kh. el-Quneitira

Castellion

Severianus

Kh. et-Tina

Euthymius

Martyrius

0   50 m.

Figure 25 Comparative chart of the plans of Judean desert coenobia

desert; it is also known in Palestine and the neighboring countries. Antony, father of Egyptian monasticism, lived for years in an abandoned fortress. In Palestine, the monastery of Kathisma was built among and within the abandoned buildings of the Romans' Tenth Legion encampment south of Jerusalem.[52] A similar phenomenon, on a larger scale, occurred in Syria, where the many fortresses erected in the border regions were occupied by communities of monks during the Byzantine period.[53]

Settlement in abandoned fortresses was convenient for monks. The siting of fortresses in isolated spots on peaks suited their reclusive way of life. Moreover, such sites were already equipped with buildings—or at least walls—and with water systems that could be put back into action with relatively little effort. Finally, the absence of any private claim of ownership meant that monks could settle in such places without fear of eviction.

The monastery of Marda (Masada) The assumption that the forts were vacant is based on Cyril's description of the arrival of Euthymius at Marda: "He . . . arrived at a lofty mountain, set apart from the other mountains, called Mount Marda, and having found a collapsed well, he restored it and stayed there, feeding on the wild herbs he could find and on mallow" (*V. Euth.* 11, 22. 4–6). The

T A B L E 3

Selection of Judean desert coenobia

Type	Name	External Dimensions (m)	Dimensions of the Hostelry (m)	Total Area (m²)	Second Story
Cliff	Khirbet ed-Deir	50 × 70	—	4,000	yes
	Theoctistus	25 × 90	—	2,200	yes
	Choziba	20 × 90	—	1,800	yes
	'Ein es-Sakhari	?	—	?	yes
Level	Theodosius	70 × 100	30 × 68	9,000	yes
	Martyrius	67 × 78	28 × 43	6,400	yes
	Euthymius	54 × 65	?	3,500	yes
	Gabriel	14 × 20	—	286	yes
	Khirbet el-Quneitira	30 × 50	—	1,500	yes
	Castellion	30 × 40	—	1,200	?
	Severianus	23 × 25	—	600	yes
	Khirbet et-Tina	14 × 20	—	560	yes
	El-Qasr	11.4 × 13.7	—	225	?

existence of the collapsed cistern indicates that the place had been inhabited in the past and had been abandoned for some time when the monks arrived.

The systematic excavations carried out at the site under the direction of Yigael Yadin yielded a great deal of information regarding the appearance and functioning of the monastery.[54] The plan of Byzantine Masada puts the monastery in the category of lauras of the level type (fig. 26). Though Masada is surrounded by sharp, rocky peaks, its top is flat. It is about 600 m long, and its width ranges from a narrow point to 300 m at the center; the total area is about 80,000 m². The hill's steep slopes give it its familiar shiplike form.

During the Herodian period, a casemate wall (a wall with rooms along its inner periphery) was built around the perimeter of the summit; and this wall was restored by the Byzantine monks. In fact, the only building that the monks erected themselves from the foundations up was the chapel and its annexes. All the other buildings were constructed from Second Temple period remains. The monks chose relatively well-preserved remains, such as the western palace gate and the eastern wall of the bathhouse, and also made use of smaller remains. For example, sections of columns supported tables or were used as thresholds at the entrances of buildings.

The entrance gate of the monastery was placed at the western end of the summit, opposite the Roman ramp. It was a solid stone gate with double arches. The upper arch is pointed, one of the earliest examples of its kind. From the gate, a path leads to the core of the laura, which included a church and service buildings. The church compound consisted of a large prayer room, a narthex, and two annexes to the north. To the east of the church and its annexes lies a courtyard surrounded by a stone wall, marking out an area measuring approximately 18 × 20 m.

The service wing of the laura seems to have utilized the rooms of the casemate wall, about 50 m west of the church. Several tables and a large supply of Byzantine storage vessels were found in the rooms. The service wing opened onto a walled courtyard. If this was indeed the location of the service buildings, we have here one more example of the division of the core of a laura into two parts: a church compound and service buildings, as at Pharan, the Nea Laura, and the laura of Firminus.

Thirteen cells were found on the summit, at an average of 56 m from each other, a distance close to the average for other lauras in the Judean desert. All the cells were placed within or among the ruins of Herodian buildings— for example, one was built next to the bathhouse, and another in the entrance gate. Some cells were located in abandoned water cisterns, and others in an underground cave whose walls were marked with red crosses. Judging from

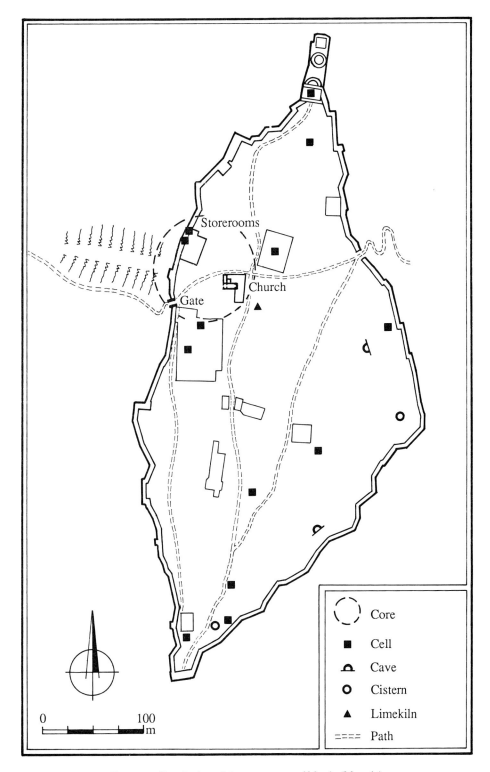

Storerooms

Church

Gate

Core

Cell

Cave

Cistern

Limekiln

Path

0   100
           m

Figure 26 Sketch plan of the monastery of Marda (Masada)

the number of cells, the laura of Marda must have housed between fifteen and twenty monks.

The monastery of Castellion The description of the founding of the monastery of Castellion illustrates the characteristics of monasteries built among or within the ruins of abandoned desert fortresses. Sabas arrived there during Lent of 492, and during that time he purified the place with his prayers. After Easter, he brought a group of monks to the site "and began to clear the place and build cells with the material that was found there." The first of the monks' tasks was to remove the debris of earlier ruins. The work had useful consequences, for, according to Cyril, "under the debris they discovered a large vaulted structure made with wonderful stones. They dug it out and set it in order, then Sabas made it into a church and from that moment he set his mind to making the place into a coenobium—and this was done by and by" (*V. Sab.* 27, 111.19–22). From the description, it would appear that this was one of the Herodian vaults discovered in the course of excavating the foundations of the monastery.[55]

The monastery of Castellion is identified as El-Mird. It is situated atop a conical hill 3.5 km northeast of Mar Saba and was built among the abandoned remains of the fortress of Hyrcania (fig. 27). Its location on the flat hilltop permits us to include it among the level coenobia. The influence of the fortress on the layout of the monastery is seen both in its plan and in the use made of the building stones, the remains of walls, and the underground vaults from the Herodian period (fig. 28). Most parts of the surrounding wall, the church, and the large hall (perhaps a refectory) adjoining the church to the west were built on foundations from the Second Temple period.[56]

Khirbet el-Qasr As mentioned above, monks in the Judean desert in the Byzantine period also made use of two fortresses from the early Byzantine period (fourth to fifth centuries). One of these sites, Khirbet el-Qasr, lies southeast of the village of Bani Na'im, in the southern part of the Judean desert. The most prominent structure is the large fortress, consisting of a square tower (11 × 11.2 m) and a courtyard (33.5 × 42 m).[57] The tower is surrounded by a sloping stone rampart, preserved to a height of 4 m. The courtyard, to the east of the tower, is enclosed by a massive stone wall. Judging by its structure, this fortress belonged to a chain of strongholds erected in the fourth century along the eastern border road of the Hebron hills.[58]

The findings of a survey of this site indicate a second stage of use. The southeast corner of the courtyard was found to contain a few walls with a different orientation, as well as a large quantity of mosaic tesserae and broken roof tiles. The survey also uncovered two large stone lintels decorated with crosses and the remains of an oil press. On the basis of these findings, it may be as-

Figure 27 Aerial view of the monastery of Castellion (looking east)

sumed that the fortress was handed over for civilian use during the Byzantine period. While it is possible that it was given to the sixth-century settlers known as "limitanei," the presence of the lintels decorated with crosses strengthens the assumption that the fortress was occupied by a community of monks and was used as a monastery. The same pattern of settlement can be discerned in Khirbet el-Kilya, in the northern part of the Judean desert.[59]

Cave hideouts Another noteworthy phenomenon is the settlement of monks in caves which had been used as hiding places in the Second Temple period. Patrich and Rubin first noted this type of monastic site in the course of their survey of the laura of Firminus in Wadi Suweinit.[60] In the "El-ʿAleilyat caves," on the northern bank of the wadi (fig. 29), they found inscriptions, crosses, and potsherds indicating two periods of use: first, the Second Temple period and the time of the Bar-Kokhba revolt (first and second centuries C.E.), when Jews used the caves as hiding places, and second, the Byzantine period, when the caves were used as hermitages by Syrian and Greek-speaking monks.

Figure 28 Sketch plan of the monastery of Castellion

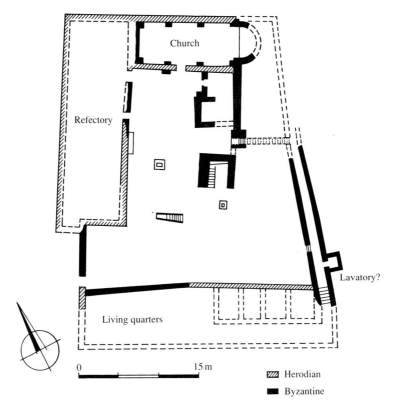

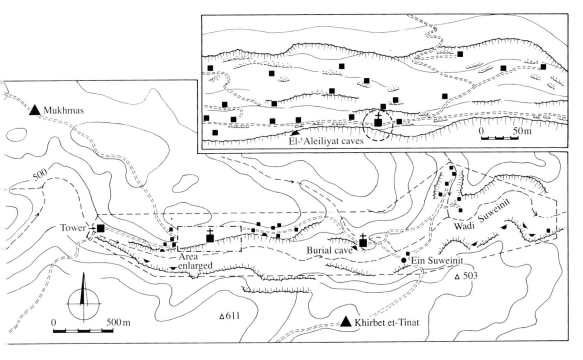

Figure 29 Sketch plan of the laura of Firminus

This discovery prompted a search for similar caves in other parts of the Judean desert. The survey of the laura of Firminus was expanded and turned up more than twenty such hideouts, some of which were also used as hermitages by the monks of the laura.[61] A similar phenomenon was noted at the laura of Pharan, which was found to contain dozens of caves that had been used as hiding places by Jews in the Second Temple period.[62]

In the rocky cliff to the south of the monastery of Gabriel, two complexes of caves were explored, and were found to be similar in character to the caves near the lauras of Firminus and Pharan. Accordingly, it is surmised that they too may have been carved out as hiding places by Jews during the Second Temple period.[63] It seems likely that in the Byzantine period these caves were used as dwellings by monks attached to the monastery of Gabriel.

MONASTERIES NEXT TO MEMORIAL CHURCHES

The monasteries erected next to memorial churches were all coenobia. Although monasteries of this kind are found throughout Palestine, they were generally intended to serve the needs of pilgrims coming to the holy places from all over the Byzantine Empire, so were usually situated near the roads taken by pilgrims. An example of a monastery built at the end of a pilgrim route is the monastery of St. Catherine, next to the Church of the Holy Bush in southern Sinai.[64] Another example, closer to the Judean desert, is the monastery attached to the Kathisma Church, south of Jerusalem, which was erected at the place where the Holy Family rested on their flight to Egypt.[65] The monastery lies halfway between Jerusalem and Bethlehem and was set up to provide services for the faithful who wished to rest or pray on their way from one place to the other. The Kathisma complex was erected by a Roman noblewoman, Icelia, in the mid-fifth century (*V. Theod.* 236. 20).

Remains of four monasteries of this type are known in the Judean desert, all of which are situated along the pilgrim road from Jerusalem to the site traditionally associated with Jesus's baptism in the Jordan River. The first is the monastery of St. Peter's Church (Qasr 'Ali), on the descent from the Mount of Olives. The second is the monastery of St. Adam's Church (Khan Saliba) on the descent to the Jericho valley. The third and fourth are the monasteries of Galgala (Ghalghala) in the Jericho valley and St. John the Baptist (Qasr el-Yahud) on the Jordan River.[66] It is noteworthy that the distances between the sites are more or less equal (5–10 km) and geared to the pace at which the pilgrims would have advanced.

St. Peter's Church At the last three of these sites, the archaeological picture is unclear, which only serves to increase the importance of the monastic remains at Qasr 'Ali, which is identified as St. Peter's Church.[67] The site is located on top of a small hill beside the ancient road from Jerusalem to Jericho.

According to Cyril, the church dedicated to St. Peter and a large reservoir near it were built by the empress Eudocia in 459, a year before her death (*V. Euth.* 35, 53. 8–10). The reservoir was intended to quench the thirst of wayfarers, among them many pilgrims descending to baptismal sites on the Jordan River or coming up from the river to the Holy City.

Cyril mentions only the church and the reservoir; knowledge of the existence of the monastery came only from archaeological finds. Following a test excavation, it became clear that this monastery was a complex consisting of four detached elements that together created an architectural entity (fig. 30). The four structures occupy an area measuring 80 × 45 m, or about 3,600 m².

The central element is the church building, on the highest point of the site. Its external dimensions are 15.1 × 29 m, which suggests that it was a basilica. On its western side are the remains of an atrium with a cistern in the center. East of the church is a nearly square wing, measuring about 24 m on each side. This

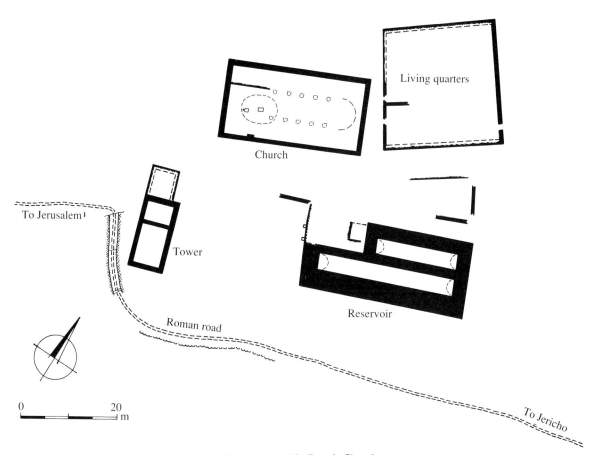

Living quarters

Church

To Jerusalem

Tower

Reservoir

Roman road

To Jericho

0   20
           m

Figure 30 Sketch plan of St. Peter's Church

was probably the monks' living quarters. Southeast of the church, on a lower level, are the remains of a huge water reservoir 33 m long and 15 m wide, one of the largest to be found in a monastery in the Judean desert. The fourth element was a well-built, towerlike structure, 14.3 m long and 7.4 m wide. It probably marked the southwestern extremity of the monastery area. South of the tower are remains of the main road between Jerusalem and Jericho.

The archaeological evidence uncovered at the site is sufficient to allow a reconstruction of the appearance of this monastery (fig. 31). The reconstruction emphasizes the character of the complex as a monastery beside a memorial church—that is, the dominance of the church building and its separation from the other elements of the monastery.[68]

This type of complex not only had a religious function; it also served as a way station, supplying shade, a place to rest, drinking water, and perhaps some

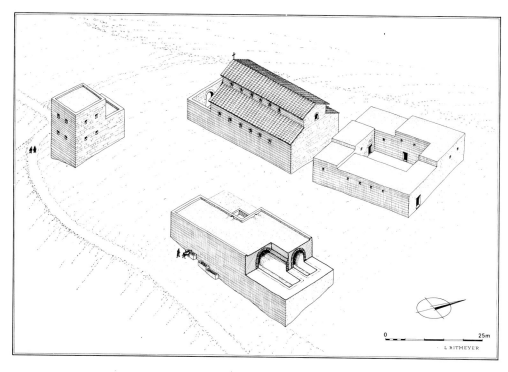

Figure 31 Reconstruction of the monastery of St. Peter's Church

other kinds of assistance to the pilgrims.[69] The combination of memorial church and monastery is typical of the holy places in Jerusalem; this type of monastery thus reflects the influence of urban monasticism. The influence of the city on the desert is also reflected in the construction and decoration of the monasteries, as we will see later.

CHAPTER TWO

How Monasteries Were Built

The building process varied from one monastery to another. In small monasteries, most parts were completed quickly. The monastery of Castellion is typical in this regard. Sabas reached the site with a group of monks from the Great Laura soon after Easter of 492. The construction work began in late April or early May and was difficult and fatiguing. Around August, when the builders were near collapse from lack of food and water, assistance came from Marcian, head of a monastery near Bethlehem, who was archimandrite of the Jerusalem district monks (both lauritic and coenobitic). Marcian sent the pack animals of his monastery, laden with provisions, to Sabas and his monks on the hill of Castellion. The monks managed to complete the construction of the monastery by November (*V. Sab.* 27. 111–12).

Pack animals actually played a very important role in the building of monasteries.[1] It is said that Theodosius bought "two small donkeys" and with them began constructing his monastery. The building of the Nea Laura was also made possible by pack animals brought by Sabas. That laura was built in only five months.[2] But short construction periods were not always the rule for small monasteries. Sabas built the coenobium of the Cave (Spelaion) "gradually."[3] Zannus and his brother Benjamin turned a hermitage into a coenobium, later named the monastery of Zannus, slowly; and a church was built there only at the last stage, and then at Sabas's initiative.[4] The monastery of Theognius was also built a bit at a time: first a small tower, then a few structures and a small church, which was later enlarged.[5]

The construction of large coenobia could also take a long time. The transformation of the monastery of Euthymius from a laura to a coenobium took three years (*V. Euth.* 44, 65. 10). The monastery of Theodosius, which was the largest in the Judean desert, grew in stages. According to Theodore of Petra,

various "wings" were gradually added, and indeed the ruins include several
wings built next to each other but with different orientations, which generally
indicates construction in stages.[6]

Another example is the Great Laura. Sabas first lived in the ravine there as
an anchorite. By his fifth year there (ca. 483), about seventy monks had gathered
around him, and he decided to build a laura on the site. Two buildings were
erected: a tower in the northern bend of the ravine, to mark off the property, and
a small oratory in the center of the laura for communal prayer (*V. Sab.* 16, 100.
8–12). The community grew rapidly (according to Cyril, the population then
reached 150), and Sabas converted a spacious cave into a church (this church,
now known as St. Nicholas's Church, is still functioning). At the same time,
many cells were built on both sides of the ravine, and beasts of burden were
acquired (*V. Sab.* 18, 102. 10–12). The consecration of the cave church in 490
marks the end of the first stage of the construction of the Great Laura, which
had continued for seven years (483–90).

The second stage began in 491. At that time, Sabas's mother, Sophia, died
and left him a large sum of money. He used it to build a hospice at the laura.[7] A
year later (492), he built the Mikron Coenobium ("Small Coenobium"), which
was a branch of the Great Laura. In 494, a third stage began, with the arrival
of the two brothers Theodolus and Gelasius, who had been professional architects in their home district of Isauria, in Asia Minor. A bakery, a hospital, and
water reservoirs were built, as well as a large new church dedicated to the Virgin Mary. The dedication of this church in 501 (*V. Sab.* 32, 117. 6–19) marked
the close of the third stage of construction.

The monastery of Martyrius provides excellent archaeological evidence of
the gradual expansion typical of the coenobia and lauras. Excavations have
revealed three stages of construction: an original building from the time of Martyrius (mid-fifth century); a main stage of construction from the time of Paul,
Martyrius's successor as head of the monastery (late fifth century); and a later
stage dating from the second half of the sixth century. The end result was a
generously proportioned monastery, one of the largest in the Judean desert.[8]

The proportions and complexity of the larger monasteries indicate considerable planning, a process rarely mentioned in the sources. Cyril, describing the
monastery of Euthymius, specifies that an engineer (*mechanikos*, the term used
to describe the chief architect) took part in the building project, and that the
work was coordinated so as to ensure that the funeral chapel would stand in the
center of the new complex: "So Fidus [the deacon, who was sent by the patri-
arch] took an engineer, a multitude of craftsmen, and much building material,
descended to the laura and built the coenobium, surrounded it with a wall and
fortified it. Also [Fidus] transformed the old church into a refectory and built

the new church above it, and he also erected a tower inside the coenobium, very strong and very graceful, and coordinated the work so that the funeral chapel would stand in the middle of the coenobium" (*V. Euth.* 43, 64. 15–21). According to Cyril, Euthymius himself had given instructions for the plan of the coenobium which was to be built after his death.[9] But the best evidence of planning lies in the remains themselves. The excavators of the monastery of Martyrius noted the organization of the various parts of the building around a central courtyard, with each wing intended for a different purpose.[10]

Smaller monasteries were also planned, as can be seen in the division of the wings of Khirbet el-Quneitira into separate service and residential areas and in the builders' repeated use of the same dimensions.[11] The layout of the building shows a clear division between the living quarters, including the chapel and the tower, south and east of the courtyard and the service area, including the oil press, the reservoir, and the garden, on a lower level, west and north of the courtyard. Thus the northern side of the courtyard remained open to the landscape beyond it. Further investigation of the monastery shows that in the three main elements—the tower, the chapel, and the reservoir—the builders used the same length, 12.4 m, which is equivalent to 40 Byzantine feet (1 Byzantine foot = 31 cm). Two of the structures, the tower and the chapel, were identical in width: 6.2 m, or 20 Byzantine feet. The use of round numbers and a constant length–width ratio are prime indications of prior architectural planning.[12]

Another example of a planned monastery is provided by the ruins of the laura of Heptastomos, identified as Khirbet Jinjas. There is a clear division between the core and the two groups of cells, and the area of the laura is entirely enclosed by a straight wall.

Water systems offer additional evidence of a master plan. In many monasteries, reservoirs and subterranean cisterns are found, fed by a network of drainage canals installed in the foundations of the monastery building. The water for these networks was drained from the balconies and roofs of the monasteries, and the proper functioning of the system depended on a general plan, as in the monastery of Martyrius. All these elements, together with the fact that different categories of monastery had typical features, indicate that builders followed specific models in constructing monasteries.

The main source of funding for the construction and subsequent maintenance of monasteries was donations from pilgrims and other visitors. Sometimes bequests helped the monks to build, and often the monks themselves contributed money and property to the monastery (see ch. 4).

Various construction projects initiated by church dignitaries or the imperial authorities were, of course, financed by them. John, a patriarch of Jerusalem, financed the construction of a reservoir, presumably for the monks, in the Jeri-

cho area (*Pratum* 134, 2997C). The empress Eudocia ordered the construction
of a church and a cistern on the road from Jerusalem to Jericho. The emperor
Anastasius erected the Church of St. John the Baptist on the Jordan River with
money from the treasury and allocated 6 solidi per year in perpetuity for the
sustenance of each monk there.

The monks' supporters among the local population gave money and even
assisted in the construction work. Aspebet, chief of a Saracen tribe, brought
masons and built the laura in Mishor Adummim for Euthymius and his first disciples (*V. Euth.* 15, 24. 17). Euthymius's supporters from the village of Aristobulias and other nearby villages built him the monastery known as Caparbaricha.[13]
But the bulk of the actual building was done by the monks. This was only natural: the monks constituted a pool of cheap, available, and enthusiastic labor. For
the most part, they performed the relatively simple tasks that did not demand ex-
pertise or previous experience. John Hesychast, for example, helped the builders
of the hospice at the Great Laura by bringing stones (*V. John Hes.* 5, 205. 18–19).
Another monk from that laura was sent to Jericho to fetch wooden beams.[14]

Generally the monks limited themselves to the construction of small, modest buildings, such as the cells common in the lauras of the Judean desert.[15]
Building a cell of this type required neither skill nor special equipment (such
as cranes and hoists) and thus could be accomplished by the monk who was to
live in the cell, with the help of his brother monks. Of course, where monks had
been masons or architects before entering the monastery their skills could be
utilized. The most famous example is the case of the above-mentioned architects
Theodolus and Gelasius.[16]

The dimensions of most of the monasteries and the high quality of their
construction show that professional builders were employed. This conclusion is
consistent with the sources, which mention builders who worked in the service
of the monks. Usually the sources mention the profession of "builders" only in
general terms—as in the case of the workers brought to construct the laura of
Euthymius or the Small Coenobium in the Great Laura.[17] We are rarely given
precise details regarding the personality or specialization of the builder. An exception is the mention of a plasterer from Bethlehem named Mamas, who was
hired by the monks of the Great Laura to install a cistern in their monastery and
who worked with his young apprentice Auxentius (*V. Sab.* 82, 187. 9–11). Research has shown that Byzantine architecture in provincial areas was influenced
most by the rural masons who lived in the towns and villages near the building
site.[18] It is likely that a number of monasteries were built by hired craftsmen like
Mamas of Bethlehem.

Some monasteries in the Judean desert are particularly large and well built
—a direct result of a different kind of financing, by the imperial treasury or the

Church of Jerusalem. One such project was the conversion of the monastery of Euthymius from a laura into a coenobium. According to Cyril, it was Martyrius, the patriarch of Jerusalem, who financed the project. As we have already seen, he chose Fidus, the deacon, as supervisor, and Fidus brought an "engineer" with him, along with a large number of workmen. Monks, including Cyriac, were also employed in the project. The work took three years, in the course of which the original cells were demolished, the monastery was surrounded by walls, and a refectory, a church, and a tower were added.[19]

The monastery of Martyrius may have been an imperial construction project (probably through the patriarch of Jerusalem). The dimensions, splendor, and appearance of the monastery complex are similar to those of the monastery of St. Catherine in southern Sinai, which was erected by Justinian.

Another possible example of a project that had imperial backing is Bir el-'Uneiziya, the large reservoir of the monastery of Chariton (fig. 32). Evidence of imperial interest includes not only the excellent execution of the reservoir but also the two elaborate embossed crosses on its interior walls (fig. 33). Clearly their placement inside the reservoir had purely symbolic significance, for when

Figure 32 Well-constructed reservoir at the monastery of Chariton

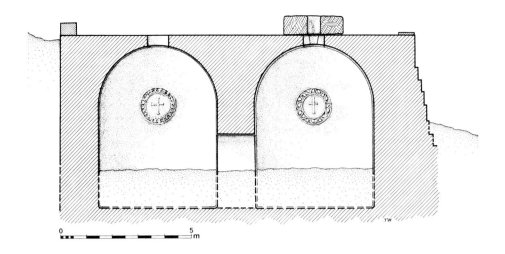

Figure 33 Cross-section of the reservoir at the monastery of Chariton, showing the two elaborate crosses on its interior wall (looking east)

the construction was complete they were completely invisible.[20] A similar cross with an inscription above it was discovered in the water reservoir beneath the Nea Church complex in Jerusalem.[21] This inscription states that the construction was due to the efforts of the emperor Justinian, a fact known also from the sources. No such inscription was found in the reservoir of the monastery of Chariton; nevertheless, it is conceivable that the monks received an imperial grant for its construction.

The principal building material used in Judean desert monasteries was the limestone plentifully available in the area.[22] It was used for walls, floors, terraces, cisterns, and other elements. Stone arches were often the chief means of supporting the ceiling. Similarly, maximum use was made of the by-products of limestone–lime and mosaic tesserae.

The stones were generally quarried and dressed near the building sites. A quarry has been identified to the west of Khirbet ed-Deir. The excavators of the monastery of Martyrius raised the possibility that many of the stones used in the construction may have been quarried from the huge cisterns while they were being dug.[23] In support of this theory is the fact that the type of limestone used in the construction of the monastery of Martyrius is identical with the stone on which the monastery stands. Within the confines of the monastery of Chariton, a small quarry has been located, in which a cut stone prepared for construction still lies. In the Jericho area, on the other hand, the monks had to bring stones for building from the quarries of Khirbet Samra, north of Jericho, or from another quarry south of Wadi Qilt.[24] This was because most of the monasteries in this region were built on the soft, crumbly Lissan formation, which cannot be used for construction. In building the monasteries, much use was made of fieldstone. Small unhewn stones were used to level off the courses of blocks, and medium-sized stones were used as filler between the courses and were incorporated in the arches. It can be surmised that one of the most fatiguing tasks in building a monastery was the gathering of a sufficient quantity of fieldstone. As noted earlier, one of John Hesychast's tasks was to bring stones to the builders of the hospice of the Great Laura (*V. John Hes.* 5, 205. 18).

The second most important building material was wood, mainly used for roofing. In church buildings, a tile roof was supported by wooden scaffolding like the rafters found at the monastery of St. Catherine in Sinai.[25] The wooden beams brought from Jericho for the hospice of the Great Laura were probably palmwood, which has always been common in the area around Jericho.[26]

Extensive use was also made of plaster and cement, for binding the courses of masonry, roofing the buildings, and finishing the walls. The main ingredients of the plaster then in use were loam, lime, and water. Loam is widely available and needs no processing. Lime, however, requires a long process involving the slow burning of limestone. Evidence for the use of lime is found in the biography of George of Choziba, which relates that the monks carried lime from the kiln to the monastery of Choziba (*V. Geor.* 26, 125. 8). The monks actually made the lime themselves at the monastery of Marda, where a pit for the local manufacture of lime was discovered east of the church building.[27]

The use of plaster required large quantities of water. We know from the sources that it was also John Hesychast's job to draw water from the stream for the masons. Dependence on water obliged the monks to invest great effort in the production of hydraulic plaster for sealing cisterns. This differs from regular plaster in that it contains larger quantities of crushed pottery, which serve as binding materials and give the plaster its characteristic reddish tint. The use of reddish hydraulic plaster is known throughout Byzantine Palestine, but it is particularly common in the Judean desert, where a large number of plastered cisterns and reservoirs can be found.

The public buildings of the monastery were usually coated and decorated with stucco. Red painted inscriptions on stucco were found in the refectories of the monasteries of Khirbet ed-Deir and Martyrius. Sometimes the stucco served as a base for frescoes. Remains of frescoes in colorful geometric patterns have been found in the chapels of Khirbet el-Quneitira, the Nea Laura, and the Great Laura.[28]

The most common type of floor in the monasteries of the Byzantine period was the mosaic floor. The coarsest white mosaic stones were usually made at the building site, as can be seen in the rubble left from the manufacture of the mosaics at the monastery of Marda.[29]

Some use was made of fired bricks, generally in installations connected with cooking and baking. At Khirbet ed-Deir, for example, a large oven made of fired bricks was discovered, and next to it stoves of the same material.[30] The use of sun-dried mud bricks was noted only in the Jericho area, mainly for building cells.[31]

Fragments of tile are almost always found at monastic sites in the Judean desert. The churches of the monasteries were usually roofed with terra-cotta tiles, as were large structures like the refectory at the monastery of Martyrius.[32] It seems likely that the tiles, like the fired bricks, were produced in some manufacturing center near the Judean desert.

Glass panes, also a local product probably, were used to seal windows in the monasteries of the Judean desert. Broken glass was found in the refectory of the monastery of Martyrius, as well as in the cave church at Khirbet ed-Deir. The cells of the monks were also fitted with glass windows, as attested by broken panes found during the excavations at Masada.[33]

In the monasteries, marble was used mainly to decorate various parts of the church. The chancel screen and the altar table were usually made of marble, as in churches in other parts of Palestine. An impressive example of an altar made of marble has been found at Khirbet ed-Deir.[34] Sometimes local limestone was used instead of marble. The tombstone of Paul, abbot of the monastery of Martyrius, found in situ, was made of local reddish limestone; it is carved simply, but the workmanship is good, and it is perfectly polished.[35] A chancel post made of local limestone, polished and well shaped, was found in the vicinity of the Nea Laura.[36]

For the most part, the monasteries used the same construction techniques. The wall foundations were usually placed on bedrock (except in the Jericho area), and stones as large as 1–2 m long were included in them. On sites with steep topography, the builders were obliged to erect huge retaining walls. In the monastery of Chariton, for example, retaining walls 6–7 m high were erected, and the space between them and the hillside was filled with a mixture of cement and small fieldstones. In this way, the builders leveled off sizable areas for construction.[37]

Monastery walls typically consisted of an outer vertical surface composed of hewn stone and an inner vertical surface was made of fieldstone and cement.[38] Walls built in this fashion were about 0.7 m thick. The doors and windows were more or less uniform, varying in size according to the dimensions of the monastery. The threshold and lintel stones were usually large, heavy, and well finished.

The lintels of the main entrances to the church or to the whole complex were often decorated with crosses.

The remains of monastery gates always contain a groove for the door and sockets for the hinges and the bolt. Another means of securing the entrance was discovered near the main gate of the monastery of Martyrius: a roller stone (a round stone that can be rolled into place) 2.5 m in diameter.[39]

The windows of the monasteries were generally small and few in number. Judging from the stone window frames found in monasteries like Khirbet Umm el-ʿAmed and Khirbet el-Quneitira, their width did not exceed 30–40 cm.[40] A narrow window, widening toward the interior, was found intact in the church of the monastery of Marda.[41] In monasteries built on slopes, the doors and windows, as well as the balconies, were oriented toward the open landscape, a practice that can be found in monastery construction to this day—for example, at the monastery of Douka (fig. 34). Cyril recounts that the cook at the hospice of the Great Laura would throw scraps of food out of the window to the bottom of

Figure 34 Aerial view of the present-day monastery of Douka, known as Deir el-Quruntul (looking west)

the ravine (*V. Sab.* 40, 131. 1). Orienting the openings toward the slope assured the maximum penetration of light into the inner recesses of the monastery.

Roofs in the monasteries were usually flat. Layers of plaster were embedded in a matrix of reeds or wooden planks, supported by a lattice of wooden beams. The beams were laid at regular intervals along the building. This method was the cheapest and simplest one. Ceilings of this kind needed constant reinforcement by rolling a heavy cylindrical stone over the surface to compress the plaster. One such roller was found in excavations at the monastery of Martyrius.[42] Vaulted stone ceilings are rarer and were generally used for subterranean buildings like crypts and cisterns.

Another method of roofing was to use arches to support the lattices along the length of the building, with shorter wooden planks or stone slabs laid on top of them. A good example of this kind of roofing is the cistern at Khirbet el-Qasr. It is also found in the refectories of the monasteries of Martyrius, Theognius, and Khirbet ed-Deir.

It was customary to use gabled tile roofs for churches. The diagonal lines and the reddish color of the roof made the church stand out against the other buildings of the monastery, with their flat roofs. Contrast of this sort is also typical of nonmonastic settlements during the Byzantine period: on the Madaba map the roofs of churches or monasteries are gabled and red, while the roofs of other buildings are flat and gray or yellowish.[43] Thus the gabled tile roofs of churches distinguished the cultic buildings from buildings put to more mundane use.

Both in conception and plan and in the quality of the masonry and construction, the desert monasteries resemble the mansions of well-to-do families in Byzantine Palestine. In many areas, it is not easy to distinguish between a monastery and a villa, aside from location.[44] It is not surprising, therefore, that people from the lower classes were attracted to monastic life. But the appearance of the monasteries also hinted at a more spiritual and meaningful life-style than the average laborer outside the monastery might expect. The monks' daily routine will be the subject of the next chapter.

CHAPTER THREE

The Daily Life of the Monks

THE BIRTH OF A MONASTIC COMMUNITY

Most monastic communities in the Judean desert came into being in accordance with what might be termed "the guru pattern." An experienced, prestigious monk would leave an organized community and go into seclusion in an isolated spot. After a while, he would find himself surrounded by disciples; and together they came to constitute the core of a new community.

This process is described repeatedly in the hagiographic literature of the Judean desert. According to Cyril, Euthymius spent five years in the laura of Pharan. He then went with his friend Theoctistus into the interior of the desert, where they took up residence in a cave. Cyril writes: "In a short time, Euthymius's fame spread; many came to him and, hearing the word of God, desired to remain with him . . . [and then] step by step they built the place into a coenobium, keeping the cave as a church" (*V. Euth.* 8–9, 15–17). We are not told precisely how long it took to convert the hermitage into a coenobium (the monastery of Theoctistus), but it would appear to have been relatively short.

The same process seems to have been operative in the founding of Euthymius's second monastery, Caparbaricha, in the Ziph desert region, east of Hebron. Euthymius arrived in this area after about ten years at the monastery of Theoctistus. He settled near several villages and soon became well known among the local residents. After he had miraculously cured the son of a resident of Aristobulias, "people came to Euthymius from Aristobulias and the nearby villages and they built him a monastery; a few brothers gathered together to live with him, while God provided for their bodily needs" (*V. Euth.* 12, 22. 19–22). We see the same "guru pattern" in the case of Euthymius's third monastery, as well as in many other monasteries, such as the three founded by Chariton and those founded by Theodosius and Theognius.

It should be noted that sometimes the interval between the arrival of the founding monk at the place of seclusion and the conversion of the hermitage into a monastery was as long as four or five years. Such was the case with the founding of the Great Laura in a ravine in the Kidron valley. Sabas arrived at the spot after four years of wandering in the interior of the desert and settled in a cave. Cyril writes: "Sabas spent five years in this ravine all alone . . . and then, in the forty-fifth year of his life . . . [he] began to receive all those who came to him. Many of the anchorites and grazers [monks who lived off the edible wild plants] scattered [in the desert] came and settled with him . . . to each of those who came to him [Sabas] gave a suitable place, consisting of a small cell and a cave, and by the grace of God his community reached seventy men" (*V. Sab.* 16, 99–100).

A sizable group of monasteries was founded far less "organically," in a more deliberate, organized fashion, in which monks from a mother monastery would leave and found a new monastery. Typical examples are the monasteries founded by Sabas and the monks of the Great Laura. The first was the monastery of Castellion, built in 492 near the Great Laura. It was Sabas who determined the location of the monastery, and later "he took some fathers [from his laura], went to the Castellion and began to clear the place and build cells with the material that was found there . . . then Sabas made [the site] into a church and from that moment he set his mind on making the place into a coenobium—and this was done by and by" (*V. Sab.* 27, III. 16–24).

Sabas followed the same pattern in founding his other monasteries, among them the New Laura, the monastery of the Cave, and the monastery of Scholarius. The act that marked the founding of a new monastery was usually the dedication of the church. (As we saw above, in monasteries founded around a place of seclusion, the church was used by the founder even before the monastery was formed.)

A smaller group of monasteries were established with external assistance, usually from the emperor or his representatives. As we have already seen, these monasteries were usually located at strategic points or at pilgrimage sites: for example, the monastery of St. John the Baptist at the site traditionally associated with Jesus's baptism in the Jordan River (Theod., *De Situ* 20, 121) and the monastery founded near the Church of St. Peter near the pilgrims' road from Jerusalem to Jericho (*V. Euth.* 35, 53). These monasteries served an imperial propaganda function, and their location near sites of pilgrimage was not accidental. It should be noted, however, that relatively few monasteries of this kind were established in the Judean desert.

JOINING A MONASTERY

As noted in the introduction, most of the monks in the Judean desert came
from places outside Palestine. In fact, there was a strong link between the
monastic movement and the thousands of pilgrims who came to Palestine every
year.[1] Pilgrimage was encouraged by the emperors as a way of maintaining the
unity of the Byzantine Empire, and the holy places of Palestine, particularly in
Jerusalem and Bethlehem and on the Jordan River, were especially venerated. It
is not surprising, therefore, that foreigners en route to the desert first went to
Jerusalem to pray at the holy places. Euthymius, for example, arrived in Jerusalem in 405 at the age of twenty-nine and, after visiting "the Holy Cross, the
Church of the Holy Resurrection and the other venerable places," went to the
laura of Pharan, about 10 km from Jerusalem (*V. Euth.* 6, 14. 3–10). Like many
other Judean desert monks, he had already had a taste of monastic life before
arriving in Palestine, and his journey was for the express purpose of joining
a monastery in the desert. Cyril was himself introduced to monasticism while
growing up in Scythopolis (Beit She'an) and had joined a nearby monastery at
the age of eighteen. He then made a pilgrimage to Jerusalem and went down
into the Judean desert.[2]

According to the sources, most of those wanting to join a monastery had
decided on doing so before they arrived in Palestine. However, there are also
tales of pilgrims who decided not to return to their homes and settled instead in
one of the desert monasteries. Epiphanius, a boxer from Constantinople, went
on a pilgrimage to the holy places of Jerusalem and the Jordan River, in the hope
of being healed of an illness. On his way to the river, he visited the monastery
of Choziba and met the venerated George. He then decided to remain there as
a monk. The same thing happened with the Senator's daughter, who arrived in
Jerusalem as a pilgrim from Constantinople, left her escorts, and fled into the
desert of the Jordan valley, where she lived as an anchorite for a long time.[3]

Monasteries were inhabited, then, by people of various types. Men who
were already monks who arrived at a monastery and asked to join it were immediately incorporated into the community. They handed over the few possessions they had brought with them to the abbot and promptly began doing their
share of the heavy chores that were usually assigned to the new monks. Cyril
describes the situation graphically: "Coming under blessed Theoctistus's guidance, our father Sabas devoted himself completely to God. What [money] he
had from his family he surrendered into the hegumen's hands, and he stripped
for the contest, spending his days in physical toil and his nights without sleep
in giving praise to the Lord" (*V. Sab.* 8, 91. 29–92. 4).

Those who were not already monks went through an admission ceremony.

Such a ceremony was held at the monastery of Choziba when George was admitted and is described thus by Anthony: "After a short time, the hegumen, noticing George's great dedication and his monastic discretion, shaved his head and clothed him in the monastic habit. Then he called one of the recluses, a man already advanced in asceticism, who was entrusted with the care of the so-called 'new garden,' and gave him George as a helper" (*V. Geor.* 4, 99. 1–5).

This account indicates that there was a certain length of time (not long) during which the applicant lived in the monastery as a lay person. Only after he had been deemed suitable was he clothed in the habit. The admission ceremony constituted formal recognition of his desire to withdraw from the world and devote himself to the monastic life. After this, he had to prove his devotion. For this reason, monks who had recently joined the community were given the most arduous tasks, such as helping the gardener in George's case or the duties assigned to John Hesychast at the Great Laura, where he "acted in full obedience to the steward and to the other fathers, serving with complete submission and zeal" (*V. John Hes.* 5, 705. 15–19).

INTERNAL ORGANIZATION

The monastery was meant to provide an organizational framework for those choosing to live in seclusion. This framework was based on a hierarchy and on obedience to rules. The most senior post in the monastery was that of the hegumen (from *hegoumenos,* Greek for "leader" or "chief"), the abbot—or, as he was called, the *abbas* ("father" in Aramaic, the tongue then spoken by the inhabitants of Palestine and Syria). The hegumen was appointed for life and was regarded as a direct successor of the founder of the monastery, inheriting his power and authority. Along with the abbot, there was often a staff of senior monks, the "elders" of the monastery, who had a voice in important decisions, including the appointment of the abbot's successor.[4]

Discipline and obedience to the commands of the abbot took precedence over everything. The monks were required to receive the abbot's blessing whenever they left the monastery, for example. Many of the stories told by Cyril are about monks who did not obey the hegumen's orders and received divine punishment. Cyril tells of a monk from Asia Minor called Auxentius, who refused to serve as mule-driver for the laura of Euthymius. He was stricken with convulsions and, after being healed by Euthymius, finally accepted the job (*V. Euth.* 18, 28–9). A similar story is told of two monks in the same laura, Maron and Clematius, who planned to leave the monastery at night without obtaining Euthymius's permission. As in Auxentius's case, one of them had an attack of convulsions, and only after the fathers' entreaties did Euthymius heal him (*V. Euth.* 19, 31–2). The monk Jacob disregarded Sabas's opposition to the building of a new laura on the property of the Great Laura. He was taken ill and recovered only after he asked Sabas's pardon.[5]

Among the tasks of the abbot was the admission of new monks to the monastery. Thus, as already mentioned, we hear of George being received into the community of Choziba only after the abbot was convinced of his diligence and readiness to lead an ascetic life, and the abbot presided over the ceremony of admission.[6] The abbot also had the authority to decide where the members of the monastery would live; for example, Theognius received his cell at Calamon from the head of the laura, and Sabas would assign places to new monks arriving at his monastery in the Kidron valley.[7]

The abbot was usually chosen by his predecessor. Thus we are told that, before leaving the laura of Pharan, Chariton chose an outstanding monk and appointed him abbot in his place (*V. Char.* 18, 30. 4). Sometimes, however, the abbot was elected by the elders of the monastery, as described by Cyril.[8] Moschus tells of an old monk in the laura of the Towers whom the elders asked to become abbot. We also hear of a dispute that arose in the laura of Calamon following the death of an abbot who had died before appointing a successor.[9]

The living quarters of the abbot, usually called the *hegoumeneion,* were generally in the center of the monastery near the church.[10] Sabas chose to live in the tower he built above the church of the laura, and Theodosius lived in a cell from which he could look out at the church and oversee the prayers.[11]

The status of the abbot is evident from inscriptions found at monastery sites. Several dedicatory inscriptions mention the name of the abbot in office at the time of construction, indicating that the authority to decide upon and execute the project was in his hands. In the monastery of Martyrius, for example, a dedicatory inscription in the refectory's mosaic pavement states that the construction was completed in the days of the "priest and archimandrite" Genesius. A mosaic inscription at the eastern entrance of the monastery of Theognius blesses the abbot Eglon, who was apparently responsible for building this wing of the monastery.[12]

In coenobia, the abbot was usually assisted by a deputy (*deuterarios*). The deputy's task was to assist the abbot in all financial and administrative matters. His term of office was indefinite, and if he proved to be capable and worthy, he could end up as the abbot's successor. Sophronius was deputy of the monastery of Theodosius for fourteen years (515–29) before becoming Theodosius's successor as abbot.[13]

In lauras, the abbot was assisted in administrative and financial affairs by a steward (*oikonomos*). Since the steward's duties prevented him from leading the life of a cell-dweller, his term of office was limited to three years.[14]

The steward and the deputy were appointed by the abbot, as was customary also in the monasteries of Egypt.[15] Except for the abbacy, these were the highest appointments a monk could have. Cyriac, at the Old Laura, was assigned to four different jobs in succession: baking bread, caring for the sick, receiving guests, and finally, administering the monastery. John Hesychast had a similar career at the Great Laura. As mentioned previously, he initially worked at various manual tasks such as bringing water, cooking for the masons who were building the hospice, and even helping with the actual construction. In his second year at the laura, he was placed in charge of the hospice. At the end of that year, Sabas permitted him to live in seclusion in a cell for three years and then appointed him steward. Once John had completed his term of office, Sabas decided to recommend him for the priesthood.[16]

In general, each monastery had its own deputy or steward. In two exceptional cases, the monasteries of Euthymius and Theoctistus and those of Elias near Jericho, there was a common administration for two monasteries. In both cases the arrangement was temporary and lasted only a short time. The monasteries of Euthymius and Theoctistus cut their ties after a conflict broke out between them (*V. Cyr.* 6, 226. 3–22), and one of the monasteries of Elias was subsequently sold to a group of eunuchs from Constantinople (*V. Sab.* 69, 171. 23–5).

Among the tasks of the steward was the purchase of food and various other items, including beasts of burden. He was also responsible for job assignments and work schedules, as we learn from Cyril's story about a monk at the laura of Euthymius who was asked by the steward to take the job of driving the animals.[17] One of the most important jobs of the steward was to supply the monks with raw materials—palm fronds and canes—for their livelihood—for example, basket weaving and rope twining—and to sell their finished products (*V. Sab.* 44, 135. 4). When a monk died, the steward had to transfer the dead man's possessions to the service building (*oikonomeion*).[18]

The service building apparently included the storerooms and larders of the monastery; Cyril mentions food supplies brought to the Great Laura from Jerusalem and stored in the oikonomeion (*V. Sab.* 58, 160. 6). It is likely that the steward's cell was located near the service building and was reassigned when the post changed hands. This would suggest that the monks had some mobility with regard to living quarters in the monastery.[19]

Ritual offices, as opposed to service posts, were usually filled by monks who had been ordained before their arrival at the monastery. Only if he was found worthy and suitable to assist at the liturgy would a monk be proposed for ordination and appointed to a ritual office. Such appointments also depended on the monastery's needs and policy. A large monastery, with more than one church, would require a large number of priests, whereas a small community would need few.

Some monasteries would provide for the ordination of the worthy, even if their services were not needed in the community. Thus the laura of Euthymius and the coenobium of Theodosius "exported" the monks most fit for spiritual leadership, who would then serve as deacons, priests, and even bishops throughout Palestine and abroad.[20] Sabas, however, was initially opposed to ordaining monks at all and even refused to provide his community with a resident priest, his motive being to discourage ambition and a thirst for power.[21] Hence, although the Palestinian clergy had many monks in its ranks, attaining even the lowest level of priesthood was not an ordinary event in a monk's career.

The first stage of clerical advancement could be a minor post in the church, such as sexton. Such was the case with Cyriac. After four years at the Old Laura, Cyriac, who had been ordained a deacon while still at the monastery of Euthymius, was made sexton, treasurer of the church, and leader of the prayers. Only after he had served in these posts for thirteen years was he ordained a priest, and he continued to serve as church treasurer and leader of the prayers for another eighteen years (*V. Cyr.* 7–8, 226–7).

The church was the most important part of the monastery; therefore a number of monks were involved in work related to it. As mentioned above, every monastery had at least one priest, who celebrated Mass and administered Communion to the monks; and the priest was assisted by a deacon. The posts held by Cyriac—treasurer of the church and leader of the prayers—are frequently mentioned in the biographies of Judean desert monks.[22] Another ritual office was the lighting of candles in the church, a job held by Anthony of Choziba.[23]

According to Cyril, the service staff was rotated every year on a fixed date, such as the beginning of the fiscal year (1 September).[24] For example, Domitian, Euthymius's favorite disciple, was appointed steward of the laura for the "first year" (*V. Euth.* 17, 27. 7), and John Hesychast was in charge of the Great Laura's hospice for one year.[25]

The sources allude to the job of refectory worker (*V. Euth.* 48, 69. 17), and the post of cook is often mentioned.[26] Another food-related job was that of the monk "responsible for the storeroom." He would give out the daily rations of oil, wine, and bread and see to it that the monastery had a stock of provisions for a long period. On the day Theognius died, "an immense crowd rushed [to his monastery], and the storeroom-keeper had only two batches of bread, which had to suffice for the consumption of our ascetes alone for fourteen days."[27]

The baker is mentioned too (*V. Cyr.* 7, 226. 23). It is not clear, however, whether this was a special post or if the baking was done by the cooks or the storeroom-keepers, since bread was made in great quantities and stored so that a plentiful reserve could be on hand for guests.[28] The baker availed himself of the help of brothers who had no fixed job and would volunteer for the most tiring duties, such as gathering wood for fuel, lighting the oven, and cleaning it. Anthony of Choziba relates that "the old man [George of Choziba] would ask the men who were in charge of the store-room, never to bake bread without him" (*V. Geor.* 23, 122. 8–9).

Since wood is scarce in Palestine, especially in the desert, gathering it was a basic part of the monks' daily routine. It was a job for the youngest and strongest, so is often mentioned as among the first jobs held by the leading monks, such as Sabas and Cyriac.[29] Some monks would go out every day before dawn to bring in fuel as an exercise in diligence (*V. Geor.* 19, 119. 2–3).

Lighting the oven was a hot, uncomfortable job. George of Choziba would volunteer for it in spite of his advanced age, as a way of practicing the virtue of hospitality, since most of the bread was given to guests. ("The brothers would say: 'This old man is made of iron.'" *V. Geor.* 23, 123. 4.) The oven had to be swept between batches, and Moschus tells the story of George the Cappadocian, a monk notable for his diligence, who entered the hot oven and cleaned it with his cloak after the other helpers had hidden the brooms and rags in order to try his patience. His dedication was rewarded, and he came out unharmed by the fiery heat (*Pratum* 92, 2949B).

One last kitchen duty: Cyril paints a charming picture of monks sitting outside the monastery gate and chatting as they wash edible "saltbushes" (*V. Euth.* 56, 77. 14–15).

The mule-driver played a key role in the monastery: he was charged with the transport of goods and the performance of errands in the outside world. Sabas served as mule-driver in his early days at the monastery of Theoctistus.[30] This was considered very trying work, since it involved leaving the monastery frequently and coming into contact with lay men and women (*V. Euth.* 18, 28. 26).

Another essential job was that of the gardener, who took care of the kitchen garden that provided the community with fresh vegetables. Anthony of Choziba tells stories about the gardener, and we have already noted that in George's early days as a monk, he was appointed assistant to the monastery gardener.[31] In one of Moschus's stories, the gardener of the monastery of Marda is mentioned as being in charge of a garden near the shore of the Dead Sea (*Pratum* 158, 3025D).

Lauras were usually without a surrounding wall, hence the sources never mention gatekeepers in reference to them; but in coenobia, the position was crucial. The gatekeeper at the monastery of Choziba is frequently mentioned in Anthony's writing.[32] To visitors, the gatekeeper represented the monastery; so a mature monk with a great deal of self-discipline was needed. Since his work brought him into contact with all kinds of people, he had to be skilled in a special kind of diplomacy, combining caution and firmness with charity and good manners. Anthony tells of a gatekeeper who was rude to a poorly dressed woman who turned out to be a wealthy matron or even the Virgin Mary in disguise.[33]

Caring for the sick, welcoming guests, and the other social welfare activities of the Judean desert monks were inspired by the teachings of Basil the Great of Cappadocia. Hospices and hospitals could be found in the larger monasteries of the Judean desert. These facilities required workers. John Hesychast was appointed "warden and cook of the hospice" in his second year at the Great Laura.[34] The doctor of the Great Laura is mentioned in the sources. One of Cyriac's jobs at the Old Laura was to look after the sick. The hospitals in the central lauras like those of Calamon and the Towers served also the hermits living in their vicinity.[35]

At the monastery of Theodosius, some monks specialized in the care of mentally ill brothers, who had their own separate wing (Theod. Petr., *V. Theod.* 17, 41–2). Other monasteries may also have provided some care for unbalanced members of the community, though in at least one case we learn of someone being sent to another monastery, where there was a chance of his being cured by the intervention of a holy man.[36]

We have little evidence of literary activity in the Judean desert monasteries. Cyril mentions a calligrapher at the Great Laura (*V. Sab.* 84, 189. 17–18), and this is the only direct evidence of such a post; but copying books was an important monastic task from the earliest times.[37] We do not know if the Palestinian monks produced books for the public, as monastic scribes did in medieval Europe. But the writings they copied were certainly needed for internal use, in order to teach novices the Psalms and the rest of Scripture, to promote the study of the doctrine of the Church Fathers among the more learned monks, and to enable the monks to keep in touch with the latest developments in theology.

Some original writing was also done in the monasteries—especially, it seems, in the lauras, since the cell-dwellers were by definition mature monks with a penchant for meditation and were freer from routine duties than their colleagues in the coenobia. Cyril wrote his work while he was at the Nea Laura and the Great Laura.

The Sabaite monks (followers of Sabas) played a major role in the Origenist dispute from the sixth century on, writing letters and sending booklets to other monasteries and Christian centers. Analysis of these works reveals an intensive use of patristic and polemic literature, so there is no doubt that the larger monasteries, especially the lauras, had a library as well as an archive.[38] The job of librarian probably existed in these monasteries, although this office is not mentioned in the sources from the Byzantine period.

SIZE OF THE MONASTIC COMMUNITY

Most studies of Judean desert monasticism fail to touch on the number of monks living in the various communities. The only scholar who does address this question, though only in a general way, is Rehav Rubin. On the basis of the historical data, Rubin surmised that in the smaller communities there were only a dozen or two monks, whereas in the larger monasteries the population ranged from several dozen to several hundred.[39] This conclusion is supported by other historical data and by new archaeological information based on field studies in the Judean desert.

My estimate of the number of monks in each monastery is based on the assumption that the physical size of the monastery reflects the maximum size of its population.[40] Thus, the largest monastery in the Judean desert, that of Theodosius, accommodated the largest community. Theodore of Petra reports that at the time of Sophronius, Theodosius's successor as abbot, the population was 400.[41] This figure is in keeping with the physical size of the monastery, whose area, excluding the hospice, comes to 7,000 m^2.

Yitzhak Magen, who conducted excavations at the monastery of Martyrius, estimates the size of its community as between 100 and 120.[42] This number strikes me as too low. Judging from the size of the monastery—5,200 m^2, not including the hospice—its capacity would have been somewhere between 150 and 200. At any rate, it is clear that the monastery of Martyrius was one of the larger coenobia of the Judean desert.[43]

By contrast with the coenobitic monasteries of Theodosius and Martyrius, the communities in the larger lauras probably never numbered more than 100–150 monks. The Great Laura had 150 monks at its peak during Sabas's lifetime, and the Nea Laura had up to 120 monks.[44]

In other words, the populations of the larger Judean desert monasteries ranged from 100 to 400 monks. Since the monastery of Theodosius was exceptional in size, it appears likely that the average number of monks in the larger monasteries was about 150. The middle-sized monasteries usually had populations of about 50, a size that is typical of monasteries in Syria and Asia Minor.[45] Cyril mentions that the laura of Euthymius already had 50 monks at an early stage of its existence, while the biographer of Gerasimus states that the cell-dwellers in the laura of Gerasimus numbered 70.[46] Since these two lauras enjoyed special status during the lifetime of their founders, it is reasonable to assume that the average population of the middle-sized monasteries of the Judean desert did not exceed the somewhat smaller number of 50.

The sources provide no information on the smaller monasteries, which were in the majority in the Judean desert, but they do indicate that their populations must have been quite small. "Although many desired to join him," says Paul of Elusa, "Theognius absolutely refused to have a crowd, but accepted only a few men" (Paul. El., *V. Theog.* 9, 88–9). The original population of the laura of Euthymius was twelve, and the coenobium of the Cave initially housed only four monks.[47]

Archaeological research has supplied further data. Fifteen cells were found at Khirbet Jinjas, identified as the laura of Heptastomos. Assuming that the number of monks living in the core of the laura came to about a fourth of this figure, it seems likely that a total of between eighteen and twenty monks lived in the laura. Similar figures emerge from studies of the laura of Pharan, the laura of Marda (Masada), the coenobium of the Cave, and Khirbet et-Tina.[48] Judging from these findings, the average population of the small monasteries in the Judean desert was about twenty monks.

Assuming, then, that the small monasteries had about 20 monks, the middle-sized ones 50, and the large ones an average of 150, it is possible to compute the approximate number of monks in the Judean desert monasteries during the Byzantine period. The 35 small monasteries housed a total of about 700 monks, the 12 middle-sized monasteries about 600 monks, and the 6 large monasteries about 900 monks,[49] giving a total number of monks living permanently in the desert monasteries as about 2,200. To this estimate we must add the hermits scattered all over the desert, as well as the inhabitants of several "ghost monasteries"—that is, monasteries mentioned in the sources but not identified in the Judean desert itself.[50] It appears, then, that there were never more than 3,000 monks in the Judean desert, even at the zenith of the monastic movement.[51]

THE DAILY ROUTINE

Maruta, a fifth-century bishop in northern Syria, composed seventy-three rules for monastic life. One of them states: "The day shall be divided into three parts: one part shall be for prayers and reading, one for work, and one for eating and rest (peace)." Another rule attributed to Maruta stipulates: "In the summer, when the days are hot, they shall work early as long as it is cool. When the day becomes hot, they shall read until the time of the midday service. After the service, they shall eat and rest until the end of the day. When the day becomes cool, they shall go out for work until the evening meal, and they shall eat after the service."[52]

These regulations reflect the strict daily schedule of a monastic community. Originally oral and only later committed to writing, they were necessary for maintaining life within the collective monastic framework. Basil the Great of Cappadocia also set down a rule of life for monks; Theodosius would often read Basil's regulations to his community (Theod. Petr., *V. Theod.* 20, 50. 15–16). Sabas gave his monks "The Regulations of the Great Laura," which are mentioned by Cyril several times.[53]

The daily schedule of a monastic community was dictated by the times of prayer. The monasteries of the Judean desert, lauras and coenobia alike, adopted the Cappadocian routine of seven daily offices (though in the lauras the cell-dwellers prayed alone most of the week).[54]

The schedule of daily prayer was as follows:

1. A nocturnal vigil, which began at cockcrow (after midnight) and ended before dawn.
2. Morning prayer (*matins*), which began at sunrise.
3–5. The prayers of the third (*tertia*), sixth (*sexta*), and ninth (*nona*) hours (about 9:00 a.m., noon, and 3:00 p.m.).
6. Evening prayer (*vespers*), after (or sometimes before) the evening meal, before sunset.
7. Night prayer (*compline*), after sunset, before going to sleep.

The cell-dwellers recited these offices—consisting of various psalms and hymns—in their cells, while the coenobites prayed them together in the church of the monastery. Before prayers, the designated monk, usually the one leading the office, would strike the *symandron,* a wooden board hung near the church by means of ropes or an iron chain.[55]

The symandron can be seen to this day in Greek Orthodox monasteries—for example, in the monastery of St. Catherine in Sinai.[56] Although this is a late example, it is probably not too different from a symandron of the Byzantine period. It is not difficult to imagine Cyriac, when he was leader of the office, striking the wooden board to wake the monks of the Old Laura for the nocturnal vigil (*V. Cyr.* 8, 227. 5). In the silence of the desert night, the banging of the wooden board would resound throughout the laura. In the coenobia, the symandron would also remind the monks to open the gate so that caravans could make an early departure (*V. Euth.* 44, 65. 23 and 59, 82. 2).

Meals were considered a direct extension of the prayer ceremony. Among the instructions given by Euthymius to the monks of the monastery of Theoctistus was a rule against conversing "in the church during prayers and in the refectory when the brethren eat."[57] A story told in the biography of George of

Choziba indicates that the monks dined in the refectory after they had prayed *sexta* together—that is, at about 1:00 p.m.—and that after dining, they took a nap (*V. Georg.* 24, 123. 5). It seems that work resumed in the afternoon.

But according to the same source, on some occasions another meal was served at 10:00 a.m. to monks engaged in heavy work outside the coenobium (*V. Geor.* 14, 110. 5); we do not know if this was the general rule or an exception. Moschus tells of a monastery in Raithou in Sinai where the monks ate at the ninth hour—that is, at about 3:00 p.m. (*Pratum* 153, 3021C). Thus it may be assumed that the time for the meal was not fixed, but varied from one monastery to the next. It is also not impossible that two meals a day were served in the same monastery, as was the custom in Egypt.[58]

The monks' day ended early, at "the second hour of the night" (before 8:00 p.m.), as attested by Anthony in his biography of George of Choziba:

> One Sunday [George] happened to prolong his conversation with one of the brothers until the second or third hour of the night. The second hour had already gone by when the old man—who had the habit of never spending the night in the coenobium—went out to the gate-house and asked the gatekeeper to unlock the door and let him out [so that he could go to his cell]. The gate-keeper tried to stop him, saying: "But the hour is late, Reverend Father . . . you had better lie down and sleep, and leave at daybreak" (*V. Geor.* 20, 119. 19–120. 3)

It should be remembered that the first office, the nocturnal vigil, began soon after midnight. Thus the monks would sleep for about four hours before the vigil and about two hours after it. The division of the night into six hours of prayer and six hours of sleep was recommended by Chariton to his disciples in the laura of Pharan (*V. Char.* 16, 28. 19–20).

Mass (*eucharistia*) was celebrated on the weekends. At the monastery of Theoctistus, the laura of Pharan, and—until 482—the monastery of Euthymius, it was celebrated on Sundays only. In other monasteries, such as the lauras of Gerasimus and Sabas and the monastery of Choziba, it was celebrated twice a week, on Saturdays and Sundays.[59]

The monks used sundials to determine the hours for prayer and work. A sundial found at the monastery of Castellion is made of a single stone 38 cm wide and 30 cm high (fig. 35). Ten slots, each labeled with a carved Greek letter, are incised in a round depression carved into the stone, which is decorated with a cross.[60] Two sundials were found at the monastery of Martyrius. In both, the day is divided into twelve hours.[61] One of the sundials was found in the refectory. The monks in charge probably made use of it to plan daily work schedules in the refectory and kitchen.

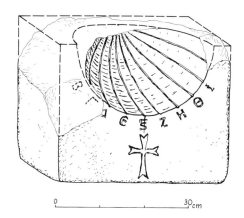

Figure 35 Sundial found at
the monastery of Castellion

THE MONKS' DIET

It is impossible to calculate the average life span of the monks, but there is ample evidence that many of them lived to a ripe old age. Among the latter were some of Cyril's heroes, including Cyriac, who died at 107, and John Hesychast, who lived to the age of 105. Euthymius reached the age of 97 and Sabas 94.[62] Moschus tells of a monk from the monastery of Theodosius who lived to the age of 113 (*Pratum* 95, 1953B). Even taking into account the natural tendency of the sources to make the monks seem as remarkable as possible, it seems that life expectancy in the desert was extremely high. The longevity of some of the Desert Fathers can be explained not only by the wholesome climate of the desert and the tranquility of the monastic way of life, but also by the well-regulated diet and the freshness of the food.[63]

Judging from the sources, the staple of the desert monks' diet was bread, even for the most ascetic monks, as can be seen from Chariton's instructions to the cell-dwellers of the laura of Pharan: "One must partake of food once a day, toward evening, and in any case moderately, so that the belly might not be heavy . . . that is, bread with salt for food, and for drink, water . . . from natural springs or fallen from heaven as rain."[64]

Gerasimus instructed the cell-dwellers in his laura to eat nothing but bread, water, and dates (*V. Ger.* 2, 3). Moschus tells a story about a monk in the laura of the Towers who had only one loaf of bread in his cell (*Pratum* 9, 2860A) and also mentions a monk in the laura of Pharan who managed with only a single piece of bread every four days (*Pratum* 42, 2896C). Another would content himself with the holy bread eaten at Mass at church on Sundays.[65]

Bread was the staple food for guests as well. We are told, for example, of four hundred Armenian pilgrims who, on their arrival at the laura of Euthymius, received pieces of bread, wine, and oil.[66] Large quantities of bread were needed at the monastery of Theodosius to provide for the many visitors who came. At first, the monks in charge wanted to limit the portions of bread to one litra (327 g) per person. However, Theodosius ordered that bread be served freely at the tables.[67]

The leftover bits were carefully gathered up and used later, as is evident from a story told by Theodore of Petra about the monastery of Theodosius. On the day commemorating the death of the Virgin Mary (15 August), "many people had gathered . . . so that the brothers . . . had nothing to set before them, except one loaf of bread for each table; nevertheless, they gathered so many baskets of leftover morsels that not only the need of the brothers was satisfied . . . but the surplus of the remnants, dried in the sun, even sufficed them for several days" (Theod. Petr., *V. Theod.* 15, 38).

Bread was generally dried before being stored to reduce its bulk and make it easier to carry. Dry bread was also the food that the monks would take into the interior of the desert for Lent, as we learn from the story of Sabas and his disciple Agapetus, who took "a sack with ten loaves of dry bread" with them for provisions (*V. Sab.* 24, 107. 25). Even a hermit like Cyriac, who grew a few vegetables for his sustenance, ate bread he brought with him. This bread probably came from the bakery of his mother monastery, the Old Laura.[68]

The monks' reluctance to give away bread in unlimited quantities was due to a very real problem: grain was often scarce, and sometimes the community itself had to go without bread and be content with vegetables. This was the case at the monastery of Marcian when Theodosius went there to visit.[69]

Since grain production was difficult in Palestine, where conditions were more suitable for orchards, the monks of the Judean desert apparently had to import wheat from Transjordan for their bread. Cyril's writings provide information about the purchase and delivery of wheat to the Great Laura. He relates that the steward of the laura hired Saracens to transport the wheat from the Dead Sea by camel (*V. Sab.* 81, 186. 17). The wheat was purchased in Machaerus, on the eastern shore of the Dead Sea, and was apparently transported to the west bank by boat. The two boats shown crossing the Dead Sea in the Madaba map may have been bringing wheat to be sold in Palestine.

Wheat was transported via camel caravan not only because of the distance involved, but also because of the great quantities needed by the monastery. In ancient times, transportation was expensive, doubling the price of the wheat.[70] Nevertheless, grain was vital, and purchase of it, at least in the larger monasteries, became an established routine. The monastery of Choziba had a permanent agent in Transjordan.[71] The need for a special agent demonstrates the large scale of the purchases as well as the monks' dependence on imported grain. Part of the supply also came as donations from devout Christian villagers; Cyril relates that the people of Madaba, who venerated Sabas, contributed wheat and kidney beans to the Great Laura and Sabas's other monasteries (*V. Sab.* 45, 136. 4).

The wheat supply, purchased after the harvest for the entire year, was stored in granaries built at the monasteries. When Theodosius visited the monastery of Marcian and was served only vegetables, he plucked out a small seed that was entangled in Marcian's beard and jokingly gave it to his friend, who ordered that it be placed in the granary. The next day, when the monks came to open the doors of the granary, they found it overflowing with wheat.[72]

This story shows that the grain was kept in closed storerooms with doors that could be locked. A good example of a storeroom of this kind was uncovered at Khirbet ed-Deir (fig. 36). The room (2.2 × 2.5 m) was part of a warehouse next to the monastery refectory. It stands at the southern end of the complex, near the kitchen. This location, facing the sunlight and close to the heat of the oven, was meant to ensure the aridity necessary for prolonged storage of wheat.

Figure 36 Granary at Khirbet ed-Deir

Its floor and walls were coated with a thick layer of grayish plaster, not the waterproof kind, but of a high quality nonetheless; the other floors of the monastery were made of mosaic or polished stone slabs. Assuming that the wheat was piled 1 m high, 5.5 m^3 of wheat could be stored there. The assumption that this room was used to store grain, not liquids, is based, among other things, on a similar installation used to this day to store grain at the monastery of St. Catherine in Sinai.[73] To date, this is the only granary that has been found in the monasteries of the Judean desert.

The wheat was ground locally, with hand-operated flour mills.[74] The monks generally baked their bread in the monastery—hence the bakery as one of the constant features of monasteries. The bakery was one of the first buildings erected at the laura of Euthymius, Mishor Adummim, and the bakery and the church were the first two buildings at the Nea Laura.[75]

The principal installation in every bakery was the oven, which the monks fueled, as already noted, with wood gathered in the desert.[76] The story of George the Cappadocian climbing into the oven of the monastery of Theodosius and cleaning the floor with his cloak (*Pratum* 92, 2949B) shows that the oven, at least in a community like the monastery of Theodosius, was large enough for a person to enter. The oven was heated by sticks of wood placed against its walls. After the fire had been kindled, the center of the oven had to be cleared of the remains of previous fires.

These details from the sources are confirmed by the remains of the oven found at Khirbet ed-Deir. This oven, discovered at the southern end of the kitchen, has been preserved to a height of 1.5 m and stood on a round stone pedestal 0.7 m high (fig. 37). The interior of the igloo-like oven is 2.4 m in diameter. The floor, where the loaves of bread were placed while baking, was made of wedge-shaped tiles with the wide end facing outward. The ceiling was domed, as in the sixth-century oven that has remained entirely intact at the monastery of St. Catherine in Sinai.[77] Figure 38 provides a reconstruction of the oven at Khirbet ed-Deir.

The bread was baked in quantities sufficient to last for several days. On the day of Theognius's death, there were two oven loads of bread in his monastery, meant to supply the needs of the community for two weeks (Paul. El., *V. Theog.* 22, 105. 15). The bread baked by the monks was apparently round, of the type frequently depicted in Byzantine mosaics.[78] The loaves, at least those used for Communion, were decorated with a cross, which was imprinted on the bread with a special stamp.[79]

The reverential atmosphere that surrounded the baking of bread is evident in the rules of Pachomius: "No one shall speak when kneading is done in the evening, nor shall those who work at the baking or at the boards [of dough] in

Figure 37 Oven at Khirbet ed-Deir

the morning. They shall recite together until they have finished. If they need anything, they shall not speak, but shall signify it by knocking."[80]

The vegetables eaten by the monks were served either raw or cooked. One of Cyriac's jobs in the laura of Gerasimus was to "clean vegetables for the brethren" (*V. Ger.* 5, 6). Anthony of Choziba informs us that in the monastery of Choziba, vegetables and pulse were served to the community as well as to guests (*V. Geor.* 12, 108. 9–10). He recounts that leftovers, including "bones" (meaning fruit or olive pits), were taken by George of Choziba to his cell.[81]

Pulses were a staple food of the peasants, and they were usually found in the monks' diet as well. The relative ease of growing and storing them made them suitable for a monastic diet, especially in the desert.[82] Thus, every year a monk at the laura of Pharan would bring bread and "soaked pulse" to his friend at the laura of Calamon.[83]

One leguminous plant whose seeds are edible after soaking is the lupine. Its seeds were a common food of the very poor and are also mentioned as the only nourishment of a cell-dweller at the laura of the Aeliotes, near the Jordan River (*Pratum* 134, 2997C). Other foods were *pisarion,* probably peas (the Latin name

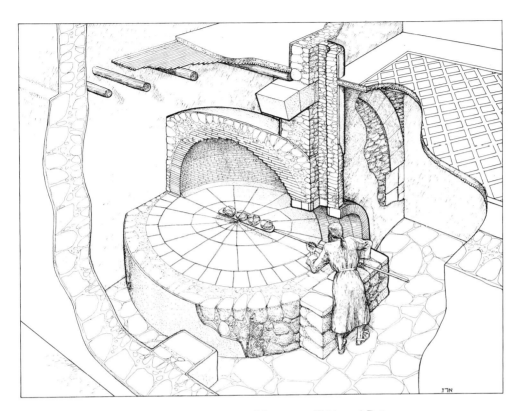

Figure 38 Reconstruction of the oven at Khirbet ed-Deir

for "pea" is *pisum*), and cooked pumpkins (*phakos*), a dish served to masons working at the Great Laura.[84]

Along with vegetables, the monks ate carobs and dates. These fruits could be stored for a long time and thus added variety to the monks' diet throughout the year. After Sabas's death, the monks found only dried carobs and dates in his cell, although he had been ill for some time.[85] Theognius ate only bread and a few carobs, and at the laura of Gerasimus the food supplied to the monks consisted of bread and a small quantity of dates.[86] Date palms grow well near springs and have many uses. The cultivation of dates at the laura of Calamon both for the fruit and for various raw materials is mentioned in the writings of Anthony of Choziba.[87]

Another tree that nourished the monks of the Judean desert was the fig. One of Cyril's most beautiful stories is about John Hesychast's fig tree:

> The place where this holy elder [John Hesychast] dwelled had a lofty cliff . . . which supported the roof of the cell. . . . One day, this holy elder took a seed of a dried fig and . . . plastered the fig to that unbroken wall. God . . . ordered

this unbroken and dry rock to sprout. . . . The old man, seeing the shoot, tearfully gave thanks to God. The shoot grew higher and higher until it reached
the roof and covered it. . . . Finally it bore three figs. The old man took them
and tearfully kissed them and . . . ate the figs, giving a little to his disciples as
well. . . . The tree loudly testifies to the old man's virtue.[88]

Needless to say, the Judean desert monks abstained from meat and probably also from fish. Meat and fish were eaten only by ailing monks (*Pratum* 65,
2916A). Fish is mentioned as a food for the ill in the monastery of Abba Seri-
dos in southern Palestine (Doroth. 11, 140. 9–10), and it was also eaten by the
brothers there if some was left. It may not have been forbidden to the monks,
but it was simply too scarce to be part of the diet of the poor. Further, it was
difficult to preserve even salted fish in the hot climate of the desert. In the biography of the post-Byzantine monk Stephen Sabaites, pickled fish is mentioned
as a delicacy that could be offered to visitors on the rare occasions when it was
on hand.[89]

Wine and olive oil were available to all monks in the coenobia, as well as to
monks in the cells of the lauras, and not availing oneself of them was considered
a sign of great asceticism.[90] Wine and oil presses have been discovered in several
monasteries, especially those on the desert fringe. Vine growing was common,
even in the monasteries of the inner desert. In his *Historia Lausiaca*, Palladius
relates that a monk of the monastery of Douka, west of Jericho, planted a vine
shoot on the rocky edge of the mountain, and that after some time, the vine
grew and covered the church.[91] Vines were important not only as a source of
grapes, but also as shelter from the sun in and around the central courtyard of
the monastery.

Oil and wine are mentioned several times among the foods served to visitors
at the monasteries. At the monastery of Choziba, George performed a miracle
by causing the vat of oil in the storeroom to remain full even though it was in
use for three weeks (*V. Geor.* 37, 136. 11). When Sabas was visiting the Great
Laura's hospice in Jericho and met an important guest at supper, he asked for
wine. No wine was left, but only vinegar, which had been brought to the table in
order to season the pulses. Sabas proceeded to bless the vinegar, and thereupon
it was transformed into wine (*V. Sab.* 46, 136. 27).

In addition to water and wine, monks would drink *eukration* ("mixture"),
hot water flavored with pepper, cumin, and anise.[92] It may be assumed that hot
drinks were an important addition to the monks' diet, especially during the
winter and during the cold desert nights. An anecdote told about Gerasimus
relates: "Some of his anchorites came to him, saying: 'Give us permission to
make ourselves a hot drink, to eat cooked food, and to light a lamp during the

nocturnal office, so that we can read.' But he answered: 'If you even desire to drink *eukration,* eat cooked food, and read under a lamp, you had better stay in the coenobium'" (*V. Ger.* 4, 4).

Another source of sustenance for monks in the Judean desert consisted of edible wild plants. The written sources mention three plants that were gathered systematically by the monks: a wild herb called *manouthion,* the saltbush, and the caper. Two other plants—*melagria* and canes—were eaten primarily by the hermits. The monks' ability to identify edible plants seems to have been acquired over long years of residing in the desert. They probably obtained some of the necessary information from their neighbors on the desert fringe (to this day wild plants are an important component of the diet of peasants in the Judean hills).

The plant most commonly gathered by the monks was the *manouthion.* The monks would form groups and search the desert, bringing large quantities back to their monasteries. Sabas, while living as a novice at the monastery of Theoctistus, would gather three loads of manouthia daily, although the other monks gathered only one.[93] According to Anthony of Choziba, the monks would gather the plant in a particular season. To that end, they would mobilize all the monks, including cell-dwellers and visitors (*V. Geor.* 14, 110. 2). In view of this intensive effort to gather the plant, it would appear that manouthion had a short season.

Anthony mentions the plant quite often. In one of his stories, a monk is blown off the mountainside by a strong wind while bringing manouthion bushes back to the monastery of Choziba (*Miracula* 3, 363. 16). In another story he tells of a particularly hard-working monk who would go out to gather manouthia after the nocturnal office and return to the monastery at dawn, laden with the bushes (*V. Geor.* 19. 119. 2–3). It seems that the plant was thorny, judging from Anthony's mention of a monk who was pricked until he bled while gathering it (*V. Geor.* 14, 110. 2). Manouthion bushes were gathered and stored in the monastery storerooms. In the monastery of Choziba, the monks would keep it near the oven (*V. Geor.* 24, 123. 14).

What, then, was manouthion? Judging from the description of it in the sources, it may have been the tumble thistle (*Gundelia tournefortii* in Latin, ʿaqub in Arabic). This plant is found widely on the desert fringe in Palestine. When it first sprouts in February or March, all its parts—stems, leaves, roots, flowers, and seeds—are edible.[94] Toward the summer, the leaves turn yellow and become prickly. Indeed, if manouthion is tumble thistle, it may have been eaten shortly after being harvested, with whatever was left over or gathered out of season being used for fuel.

Cyril mentions that he and his comrades from the monastery of Euthymius would sit together and clean the "*malwa* bushes" (*V. Euth.* 56, 77. 14). The word *malwa* is no doubt a corruption of the Hebrew word *maluah* (which literally means "salty"), which refers to an edible plant mentioned in the Bible.[95] The saltbush (*Atriplex halimus*) grows everywhere in Palestine, including the desert. Its leaves are edible, both raw and cooked.[96]

The monks of Choziba would gather "caper seeds." Anthony's mentor, George, told him that the caper bushes near the monastery were formerly so prolific that a whole basketful could be gathered daily (*V. Geor.* 42, 143. 8–12). The caper (*Capparis spinosa*) grows throughout Palestine and is known to favor stony ground, cliffs, and walls. The edible parts are the buds of the flowers and the young fruits. In the cliffs along the banks of riverbeds in the Judean desert, caper bushes are found in abundance.[97]

The difficulty of growing cultivated plants such as vines and olive trees made manouthia, saltbushes, and capers important constituents of the diet of the Judean desert monks, judging by the frequent mention of these plants in the hagiographic literature.

The monks' diet sometimes underwent extreme variations: monks seeking mortification often ate bizarre preparations, while, on the other hand, high-quality food was occasionally brought to the monasteries as an offering. Anthony of Choziba relates that George "would ask the men whose turn it was to be in charge of the storeroom to keep for him . . . the waste wiped off the tables . . . be it vegetables, pulses, or kernels; then he would take these scraps, grind them in a stone mortar, and make them into balls, which he would put in the sun to dry for two or three days. If he wanted food at all, he would eat some of these balls, soaked in water, in his cell."[98] For many years, in the Great Laura, John Hesychast would mix ashes into the gruel that was his only food (*V. John Hes.* 19, 215. 25–216. 6).

By contrast, Cyril tells of a caravan of thirty pack animals that brought wine, bread, wheat, oil, honey, and cheese to the Great Laura—a gift from a guild of publicans in Jerusalem (*V. Sab.* 58, 160. 5). This was indeed an exceptional event, viewed as miraculous by the monks; but the detailed list of commodities provides an idea of the various types of food found in monasteries from time to time.

On Saturdays and Sundays, offerings of food were brought by the local people to the laura of Gerasimus in the Jordan valley (*V. Ger.* 4, 4). In the fourth century, before the founding of monasteries in the Jericho area, when there was only a scattering of hermits in the vicinity, a resident of Jericho would bring them dates and vegetables (Palladius, *Hist. Laus.* 52, 145. 1–5). When Sabas was living as a hermit in the interior of the desert, a few local Saracens visited him twice and brought him loaves of bread, cheese, and dates (*V. Sab.* 13, 96. 18). John Hesychast, during a spell in the desert, was visited by an old man who brought him freshly baked bread, wine, oil, cheese, eggs, and honey.[99] Eggs, fish, and even meat were given in exceptional cases to ailing monks (e.g. *Pratum* 65, 2916A).

Thus it seems that animal products (cheese, honey, eggs, and so forth) were not available as a rule in the monasteries, nor were they purchased from outside; but the monks would sometimes receive them from the local villagers. On such occasions, a feast would be held, and the offerings consumed,[100] for it must be kept in mind that some of these provisions were not easily preserved.

THE MONKS' DRESS

The monk's habit was bestowed on the novice at the ceremony admitting him to the monastery, as we are told in the story of Sophronius's admittance to the monastery of Theodosius.[101] A regulation of the Syrian monasteries explains the wearing of the habit: "Before all things it is right for those who wear this holy and angelic garment of our father, the blessed Aba Antonios [of Egypt], that they emulate his asceticism and humility."[102]

Additional details about the admittance of monks and their attire are found in the biography of Simeon "the Fool," who was admitted to the monastery of Gerasimus in the early seventh century. Only after he had sat in his cell dressed in the "holy habit" for a week was he allowed to remove his ceremonial habit and dress in a rougher garment made of sackcloth, which was meant for the daily activities of the monastery.[103]

The garments of the Judean desert monks were probably dark in color. In one of Cyril's stories, a monk wears a black hood, and further on Euthymius is described as being dressed in a black cloak.[104]

The classic monk's attire was a tunic without sleeves. George of Choziba wore this type of tunic for Mass, but a patched tunic for daily use. The garb of the cell-dwellers in the laura of Gerasimus included a tunic, a cloak, and a hood.[105]

The hood was the most conspicuous garment peculiar to monks. In frescoes found in a cave tomb in the monastery of Castellion, monks are shown wearing hooded cloaks. Although these drawings probably date from the Middle Ages, they reflect the appearance of the Judean desert monks from the Byzantine period.[106]

In addition to the tunic and the hood, the monks wore a capelike garment. Anthony of Choziba relates that George had to remove his clothing in order to draw water from a stream which was hidden under a tangle of reeds and wood, and that the gardener told him to put his cape around his loins.[107] It is not clear how this article looked. It may have been a sash worn over the shoulders and crossing on the back, whose purpose was to keep the tunic in place. Such a garment was used by Egyptian monks and is described by Dorotheus of Gaza as one of the four articles of clothing worn by the monks in southern Palestine (sleeveless tunic, belt, sash, and hood).[108] But it is not out of the question that this "cape" was a scapular—a long vest or apron covering both front and back—like the ones worn by Benedictine monks in the West.

Though the monks probably went barefoot inside the monastery, they wore sandals outside it. Sandals are mentioned among the items worn by Cyriac (*V. Ger.* 5, 6). The custom of wearing sandals is also mentioned in the rules of Syrian monasticism ("They shall not wear shoes upon their feet but sandals").[109] A pair of sandals was found in the monastic remains at Tel Masos, near Beersheba, in the grave of one of the monks.[110]

The mosaics of the monastery of St. Catherine in Sinai give us an idea of the appearance of the sandals typical of the Byzantine period. The mosaic decoration of the central apse shows Moses taking off one of his sandals in front of the burning bush.[111] It may be supposed that the sandals shown were like those worn by the artist's contemporaries, particularly the monks.

A monk's constant companion was his staff. On the wall of the cave tomb mentioned above, Euthymius is depicted in a black cloak and a black hood, holding a staff in his hand (fig. 39). Cyril also describes Euthymius as holding a staff (*V. Euth.* 50, 73. 21). Anthony of Choziba tells of a monk who used his staff to kill a serpent that was about to bite him (*Miracula* 4, 365. 8).

The following description of Stephen Sabaites, an eighth-century monk who lived in the Great Laura and continued the Byzantine tradition of periodic wandering in the desert, sums up the monk's personal effects:

Figure 39 Fresco
portraying Euthymius
(left), found in the
monastery of Castellion

Whenever he chose to go into the desert for seclusion, he would take with him neither food nor clothing but a hairy tunic, a sheepskin cape, a leather bag to carry a small Bible, a knife for cutting herb-roots, reeds, and hearts of wild palms, a small quantity of kidney beans, a staff decorated with an iron cross, a hairy hood on his head, a wide leather belt around his loins, and sandals on his feet (*V. Steph. Sab.* 15. 1, 362)

The monk's habit was provided by the monastery. The various articles of clothing were apparently purchased at nearby settlements (to date there is no evidence that the monks of the Judean desert engaged in spinning or weaving). According to Theodore, the monks of the monastery of Theodosius spent a donation of 100 gold pieces on articles of clothing for their monastery (Theod. Petr., *V. Theod.* 81. 4–6). Rule no. 22 of the Syrian regulations attributed to Maruta states: "They [the monks] shall receive [winter] clothing in the latter Tesri [November]; everyone shall write his name on the summer garments he has been wearing, and place them in the community. When the winter is over, they shall take their summer garments, everyone his [own] garments according to the names written on them, and again they shall write their names on the winter garments that they take off."[112] This rule suggests that there was some kind of clothing storeroom in the monasteries, although such a place is not mentioned explicitly in the sources.

PRIVATE AND COMMUNAL POSSESSIONS

The hagiographical literature offers several descriptions of the contents of a Judean desert monk's cell. Cyril writes of a monk named Aphrodisios from the Great Laura, who secluded himself for thirty years without once leaving his cell. To illustrate his asceticism, Cyril lists what Aphrodisios did not have in his cell, which provides a clue to the items ordinarily possessed by a monk: a mattress, a stove, and various cooking utensils such as a pot and a kettle. According to Cyril, Aphrodisios made do with a straw mat for sleeping and a bowl from which he would eat leftover food prepared at the laura (*V. Sab.* 44, 135. 2–8).

Another article often found in a monk's cell was a chair. Cyril writes that his cell in the Nea Laura was equipped with a chair, on which he sat when he began to write (*V. Euth.* 60, 84. 1). There was probably a writing stand as well, since no table is mentioned.

One set of Syrian monastic regulations stipulates that the monk must sleep reclining on a seat of stone or wood.[113] Sleeping in a seated position seems to have been the norm in the monasteries of the Judean desert. According to Cyril, Euthymius would sleep sitting down, supported by a rope suspended from the ceiling.[114] In an account of a robbery at the laura of the Aeliotes, the victim is described as having been asleep in a wicker chair or on a stool.[115]

But not every cell was so well equipped. In Anthony's cell there was not even a chair, and his master sat on a mattress on the floor (*V. Geor.* 40, 142–3). Sleeping on the floor of the cell without bedclothes was considered an expression of the monk's ability to mortify himself. Chariton is said to have liked sleeping on the ground (*V. Char.* 15, 27. 17–18). Anthony of Choziba says that he decided to begin sleeping on the floor of his cell as an act of self-denial. But he adds that it affected his health, and therefore George ordered him to gather straw or leaves and use them for a sleeping mat, though a very modest one, if he was determined not to use a mattress (*V. Geor.* 40, 142. 10–15). Each of the hermits in the laura of Gerasimus was permitted to use three articles of bedding: a straw mat, a rag blanket, and a pillow (*V. Ger.* 3, 4).

Actual beds and bedclothes were apparently reserved for elderly monks (*Pratum* 182, 3053D) and the sick, as we learn from the following story about Theognius. After he broke a leg, he was brought back to his monastery and laid on a bed. The bed must have been made of wood, judging from the doctor's instruction to make a hole in it and place a clay pot beneath it so that Theognius could perform his bodily functions while lying down (Paul. El., *V. Theog.* 15, 96. 15–16). Since it was summer, Theognius covered himself with a sheet; woollen blankets were probably used only in winter.

To date, no remains of wooden beds have been found, but a few monasteries contain the remains of stone couches. Several couches were found in a room at Khirbet Juhzum, east of Bethlehem. They were built of fieldstones and cement and coated with white plaster. At the southern end of each couch is a pillowlike projection.

Similar stone couches were found at the monastery of Martyrius, close to the inner gate, and at the monastery of Euthymius, in a small side room (fig. 40).[116] In structure and dimensions, the couches are identical to those found at Khirbet Juhzum. In some monasteries, then, or at least in some parts of them, proper beds were used.[117]

This evidence raises another, more fundamental question. Did the monks sleep in dormitories, or each in a cell of his own? The sources pertaining to Judean desert monasticism never mention shared sleeping quarters; on the other hand, they often mention private cells in coenobia, although only in connection with priests, elders, and monks appointed to specific posts.[118] However, Justinian's Codex, which set forth regulations for all conditions of Byzantine life, explicitly ordered that coenobitic monks sleep in dormitories, presumably so that they could keep an eye on each other.[119]

But was the Justinian Codex really followed? Judging by some other monas-

Figure 40 Stone couches at the monastery of Euthymius

tic regulations it established, it would appear that the law did not always have any real influence. The question has not yet been examined in the field, since very few monasteries have been fully excavated. In many instances, the findings of excavations and surveys indicate that the living quarters of the monks were on the upper story. However, in at least one case we have evidence of the existence of large halls, which must have been dormitories.

In a survey of Deir Qal'a in the western hills of Samaria, I found three large halls, which are thought to have been the living quarters of the coenobium. This monastery was probably built in Justinian's time, and its structure seems to follow Justinian's specifications, even to the extent of having only one gate. This may indicate that the Codex had practical influence on desert monastic architecture, though Deir Qal'a itself is outside the boundaries of the Judean desert (if not very far away).[120]

It seems that both arrangements existed at the same time: namely, accommodation in dormitories, probably for the younger and less experienced members of the coenobium, and private cells for the elders. This arrangement once again points up the hierarchic structure of coenobitic life.

Among the possessions kept by a monk in his cell was a sheepskin ruck-sack. Moschus tells of a monk at the monastery of Penthucla in the Jordan valley who took his rucksack and went out to seclude himself in the desert.[121] Monks also kept various ceramic vessels in their cells for the storage of food and water. Among the articles that Gerasimus permitted his monks to keep in their cells was a clay jug for water, both for drinking and for moistening the palm used in basketry (*V. Ger.* 3, 4). George kept a clay jug in the corridor of his cell, and Theognius, at the laura of Calamon, had a mug for drinking.[122] Vessels of this kind and others have been found in excavations and surveys of monasteries throughout the Judean desert.

Another article kept in the monk's cell was a broom. When sweeping, the monks would hang their possessions, such as mattresses, on the wall (*V. Geor.* 40, 142. 11–12). Work tools, mainly for agricultural purposes, were also on hand. Cyril mentions several by name, such as an axe, a hoe, and a sledgehammer. These tools were used by Sabas's opponents to destroy his tower in the Great Laura (*V. Sab.* 36, 122. 25–6). George and his brother Heraclides would chop down palm trees with an axe (*V. Geor.* 7, 102. 6). The scythe used by the gardener at the monastery of Choziba is also mentioned.[123] These tools must have been the property of the monastery and have been kept in the monastery storerooms when they were not needed for daily use by a particular monk.

To illuminate their cells, the monks used clay oil lamps of the kind common in the Byzantine period. Theodosius is said to have sat up at night reading holy books by candlelight. In public buildings such as churches, monks used glass and metal oil lanterns or chandeliers holding wax candles.[124] Typical clay oil lamps were found at Khirbet ed-Deir (fig. 41). Several pieces of bronze lanterns, as well as two torch-holders, were found in the church of the monastery of Martyrius.[125] Bronze lanterns were also used for liturgical purposes in the underground burial places, and one of the regular jobs in the monastery was their maintenance and lighting (*Miracula* 6, 368. 14).

A monk could keep books in his cell, but books were scarce and expensive. As mentioned earlier, Moschus tells of a hermit who worked as a mason for months in order to buy a Bible with his wages; he finally purchased it from a fellow monk for three gold coins (*Pratum* 134, 2997B). It was probably the well-off monks who owned one book or more; otherwise books were borrowed either from the owner or from the monastery library.[126]

A humble but most necessary object in the monasteries was the chamber pot. The sources do not discuss the manner in which the monks relieved themselves, except for the mention of the chamber pot used for the sick in the monastery of Theognius. It seems likely that each hermit kept a chamber pot in his cell. But in those monasteries in which the monks slept in communal dor-

Figure 41 Oil lamps found at Khirbet ed-Deir

mitories or slept two or three to a cell, a special place had to be allotted for this purpose.

A lavatory, if it existed, might conceivably have been just a room equipped with chamber pots. Thus it would not be easy to recognize even after its excavation. A more sophisticated lavatory was excavated at the monastery of Martyrius.[127] Built in the service wing, near the stables and storeroom of the monastery, it is a narrow room with a long, open channel beside one of the walls, to the right of the entrance (fig. 42). The liquid waste was probably washed away with water through a drain.

We do not know how the solid waste was discarded, but it is likely that beside every monastery there was a refuse heap, like the heaps near the monastery of Choziba that are mentioned in Anthony's writings.[128] It may safely be assumed that this was the place where the monks threw away their solid waste and organic garbage, later to be collected for secondary use as manure in the garden.

The communal activities centered mainly on the refectory and the kitchen. Food was served on tables; at the monastery of Theodosius the monks would set 100 tables for guests every day. It seems that the monks' tables were kept

Figure 42 Lavatory at the monastery of Martyrius, with a drainage channel
along the wall to the right

apart from those of the guests, a custom found to this day in the refectories of Greek Orthodox monasteries.[129]

A wide variety of ceramic food vessels was found in excavations of the monastery of Martyrius (fig. 43). They numbered in the hundreds—one of the largest concentrations of ceramics discovered at a Byzantine monastic site—and included wine goblets, plates, large storage vessels, and pots. Large marble trays and metal utensils were also found.[130]

In all the monasteries excavated so far in the Judean desert, relatively large quantities of a certain type of bowl have been uncovered.[131] The bowls have rounded sides that bend inward. Their height ranges from 4 to 6 cm, and their diameter from 11 to 15 cm. The great frequency with which these bowls are found suggests that they were the monks' main eating vessels. The dimensions and shape of the bowls apparently suited the cooked vegetables of the type mentioned in the sources. The uniform pattern of the bowls and the humble local materials of which they were made befitted the simple way of life of the monks.

Figure 43 Ceramic vessels found in the kitchen of the monastery of Martyrius

Large clay vessels were used to store wine and oil, like the "vat of oil" blessed by George of Choziba that remained full for three weeks (*V. Geor.* 37, 136. 11). Two vats of oil stand in front of the church of the present-day monastery of Choziba (St. George in Wadi Qilt) to commemorate George's miracle (fig. 44). Such vessels were also used to carry water. Moschus recounts that the monks at the laura of Gerasimus would bring back water from the Jordan River in four jars bound to a frame on a donkey's back.[132]

The church equipment included ritual vessels, lamps, and wooden seats or benches. The biography of Abramius mentions the wooden seat he used in the church.[133] In certain monasteries, a stand was placed before the altar for readings from holy books, as in the church at Khirbet ed-Deir, where eight triangular marble slabs with bronze nails were found in a pile. Each slab is numbered with one of the first eight letters of the Greek alphabet, and when they are assembled

Figure 44 Vats of oil in the monastery of Choziba (St. George's Monastery in Wadi Qilt), placed there to commemorate the miracle in which St. George caused a vat of oil to remain full for three weeks

Figure 45 Marble sections of
what was probably a reading
stand, found in the cave church
at Khirbet ed-Deir

in that order, a marble square, 38 × 38 cm in size, results. This was probably
affixed to a wooden frame with the bronze nails (fig. 45). A picture of a wooden
stand appears in a Byzantine manuscript from the mid-tenth century.[134] This
illustration is somewhat late, but it can be used to reconstruct the reading stand
whose remains were found in the church at Khirbet ed-Deir.

CHAPTER FOUR

Sources of Livelihood

Donations were the main source of income in Judean desert monasteries.[1] Contributions to the monasteries came in various forms: cash gifts, bequests, money and property brought by monks joining the monastery, and support from the Church and the imperial court.

Monetary contributions were generally used for construction. The construction of the monastery of Theodosius, for example, began with a contribution of 100 gold coins (*solidi*) from Acacius, a nobleman from Byzantium, who continued to send money to the monastery on a regular basis. Cyril reports:

> While [Theodosius] stayed hidden away in his cave . . . a Christ-loving man arrived from Byzantium. . . . Having heard of [Theodosius's] virtue . . . he went to see Theodosius in his cave . . . and being aware that [Theodosius] would not accept any gift from him, buried a purse of 100 gold coins in the cave without asking permission. . . . Great Theodosius . . . having found the above-mentioned purse of gold hidden in his cave on the morrow of the senator's departure, [used the money] to build a hospice above his cave, and began to welcome every visitor who came to him. Then he purchased two little asses, and would go out by himself to bring the necessary provisions. (*V. Theod.* 238. 9–13).

The average daily wage of a worker in the fourth to sixth centuries was ¹⁄₃₀ of a solidus, so the sum of 100 solidi was sufficient to employ 30 workers for a period of 100 workdays.[2] Contributions also made it possible to enlarge existing buildings. A sizable gift from Mamas, nephew of Theodosius's successor Sophronius, permitted Sophronius to enlarge the building and erect a new church (*V. Theod.* 240. 23–4). Cyril's parents sent an annual offering to the Great Laura (*V. John Hes.* 20, 217. 16). Moschus tells of a pilgrim who contributed to three monasteries in the Jordan valley: Soubiba of the Bessians, Soubiba of the Syrians, and Chorembe. Special generosity was shown by the Byzantine nobility who came to pray or to be healed in the holy places of Jerusalem and the Jordan River.[3]

Considerable income came from legacies. Sabas's mother, Sophia, left all her worldly goods to the Great Laura, thus giving Sabas the means to erect the hospice of the monastery and purchase another hospice in Jericho. Terebon, son of Aspebet the Saracen, left much property to the monasteries of Theoctistus and Euthymius.[4]

Income also derived from the monks themselves. Among them were wealthy men, who occasionally contributed their possessions to the community. For example, upon his arrival at the monastery of Theoctistus as a novice, Sabas gave all his money to the abbot (*V. Sab.* 8, 92. 1). The contribution of Maris the Saracen, Terebon's uncle, was even more significant. Upon joining the monastery of Theoctistus, he donated all his property to it, thereby providing the means for the expansion of the monastery.[5]

It seems that the abbots put pressure on prospective monks to bring a "dowry" when they joined the community. Sabas even demanded that his monks build their cells at their own expense if they had the means.[6]

The harmonious relations between the patriarchate and the monks of the Judean desert, particularly in the days of Theodosius and Sabas, also helped when it came to money. Thus Sabas turned to Elias, the patriarch of Jerusalem, when he wished to build the Nea Laura and received 72 solidi (*V. Sab.* 36, 123. 22–3).

An important source of financial support for the monasteries was the imperial court. Direct imperial support for holy places in general commenced with Constantine the Great and his mother Helena and continued with greater intensity under Theodosius II and his wife Eudocia. Later, under Justinian, certain monasteries in the Jerusalem district were renovated and enlarged with the support of the imperial treasury, as we see from Procopius's list of building projects in the monasteries of the area. Cyril tells of Sabas returning from a visit to Constantinople with a large amount of gold, which he distributed among his various monasteries.[7]

Most donations were in gold—that is, coins—but there were also contributions in kind, including the above-mentioned donations of real estate. Theodore of Petra tells of a woman who regularly donated food to the monastery of Theodosius; and later he mentions a whole village that regularly sent food supplies to the monastery.[8] The town of Madaba did the same for Sabas's monasteries.

The monastery of Theodosius is the only one in the Judean desert that is explicitly said to have received contributions in land. According to Theodore of Petra, Cyricus, commander of the Roman army in the Eastern provinces, gave two estates, Kourone and Antikourone, to this monastery in gratitude for a military victory won while he was wearing, for good fortune, a tattered garment belonging to Theodosius (Theod. Petr., *V. Theod.* 85. 13–15). These estates may have been located near Phasael in the Jordan valley, since we know from Moschus that the monastery owned a pig farm there. In that area, the abbot of the monastery built a church dedicated to St. Cyricus.[9]

Two other monasteries, those of Theoctistus and Euthymius, also received land, perhaps from the legacies of the above-mentioned Saracens, Maris and Terebon. Sabas's efforts to obtain a reduction in land taxation from Anastasius (494–518) (*V. Sab.* 54, 145) may also point to substantial land ownership among the larger monasteries, although the situation in Palestine was not comparable to that in Egypt, where the monasteries owned enormous parcels of land.[10]

Monastery funds were stored in a common coffer. Cyril writes that the monks of the monastery of Euthymius kept their money, totaling six hundred gold coins, in three purses in cabinets in the diaconicon (*V. Euth.* 48, 69. 15–25). The fact that the monks did not carry money explains the almost entire absence of numismatic finds at monastic sites (including those excavated thoroughly). At the monastery of Martyrius, where excavations produced plentiful finds of all sorts, only a few coins were found, in a pitcher buried on the eve of the monastery's destruction. This absence of coins does not demonstrate the "monks' modest way of life," as the excavators write,[11] but rather the custom of keeping the monastery's money in a common coffer that could be picked up and carried off.

Manual labor was considered an integral part of the monastic way of life, in coenobia and lauras alike. This emphasis on physical work derived from the goal of self-sufficiency. With the labor of their hands, the monks produced items for sale, using the income to purchase their daily necessities, such as grain and various implements and vessels. Similarly, the monks processed agricultural produce, manufacturing mainly oil and wine, which they used for their own sustenance and for sale in the nearby markets. Raising fruits and vegetables and gathering wild plants also helped them subsist in the desert.

Crafts traditionally pursued by monks in the Judean desert and throughout the Byzantine Empire were the weaving of baskets and mats and the twining of rope. The raw materials for these activities—reeds and palm leaves—were plentiful and cheap, especially in the oasis of Jericho and on the shores of the Dead Sea. There was a steady demand for the monks' handiwork, and the simplicity of the work permitted even those who were not expert at it to pray and meditate while they worked.[12]

Sabas was a prolific basket-weaver during the time that he lived in a cave outside the monastery of Theoctistus: "On Sunday toward evening [Sabas] would leave the coenobium, taking his weekly supply of palm-leaves, and he would spend the five days without any food. Then on Saturday morning, he would come back into the coenobium, carrying with him the product of his five days' work, fifty baskets" (*V. Sab.* 10, 94. 12).

Another monk, Aphrodisios, from the Great Laura, would receive a supply of palm branches from the steward at the beginning of each month and consign ninety finished baskets to the monk responsible for the hospice at the end of the month (*V. Sab.* 44, 135. 4–6). This story indicates that the baskets were sold in the hospice by the monk in charge. However, some monks did their own marketing—for example, Philagrius, who sold his work in the marketplace.[13]

In one of Moschus's stories, we learn of an old monk who sat in his cell weaving baskets and singing psalms at the same time (*Pratum* 160, 3028B–C). While Theognius was at the laura of Calamon, he produced small baskets known as *spourides;* this type of basket was used in the monastery of Theodosius for serving bread.[14] Baskets had many uses in antiquity, as can be seen in mosaics of the time. In harvest scenes, baskets are shown filled with grapes being taken to the winepress—for example, in the mosaics discovered in the monastery of Lady Mary in Beit She'an.[15]

Euthymius learned to twine rope and earned his livelihood thereby while he was at the laura of Pharan (*V. Euth.* 6, 14. 12). The monks of the laura of Gerasimus produced ropes and baskets in their cells. Monks in the Jericho area grew palm trees, from which the raw materials for basketry were obtained. Anthony of Choziba reports that George and his brother Heraclides tended the palm trees in the laura of Calamon. One tree was barren, and Heraclides wanted to cut it down; but George prevented him from doing so, arguing that it might still be possible to obtain palm fronds for basketry from the tree.[16]

A craft less commonly pursued was pottery. It is mentioned only once in the work of Moschus, who relates that a hermit in the Jericho area was well known for making and selling flasks (*Pratum* 163, 3029D). Apparently these were flat flasks to hold drinking water or the holy water taken back home by pilgrims.

Apart from basketry and rope twining, the dominant occupation among the monks of the Judean desert was agriculture. As we will see in chapter 6, most of the cells had small garden plots adjacent to them. After the soil had been prepared and seedlings planted and watered, the monks would still have had a lot of time to weave baskets or twine rope as they prayed and meditated. Moreover, almost every monastery also had agricultural fields, which were worked collectively.[17] The monks' agricultural efforts are depicted in mosaics discovered in various places. As mentioned above, various agricultural motifs embellish the mosaic floors of the churches at Khirbet ed-Deir and Marda; these include

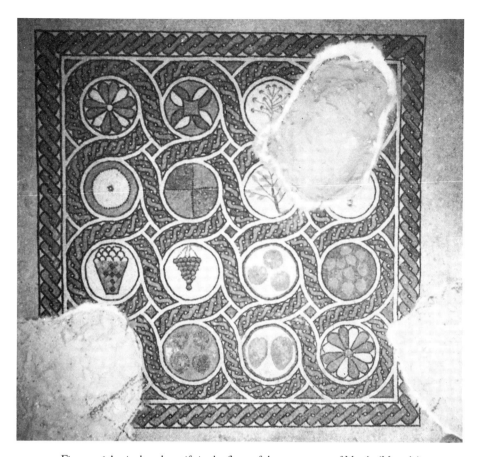

Figure 46 Agricultural motifs in the floor of the monastery of Marda (Masada)

fruits, baskets, and a scythe (fig. 46). It should be noted that these patterns are not peculiar to monasteries but are found in mosaics throughout the country.

The monastery gardens and fields supplied the monks with fruit and vegetables and their products—wine, olive oil, and dried fruits. Though the monks may also have purchased these commodities from outside the monastery, it is likely that their main supply came from their own gardens, at least in the case of more favorably located monasteries.

The independent production of oil and wine, and even their sale in the local market, is attested by the oil presses and winepresses discovered in many monasteries all over Palestine (though rarely in the monasteries of the Judean desert proper). Examples are provided by the monasteries excavated by Corbo at Khirbet Siyar el-Ghanam and Bir el-Qatt, north of Bethlehem.[18] According to Corbo, these monasteries were built like the "rustic villas" typical of the Roman Byzantine period. He maintains that the winepresses in them witness to the conception of the monastery as a self-governing unit engaged in agriculture and the manufacture of commodities. The large dimensions of these winepresses show that they produced more than would have been needed by the monastic community; hence the monks could sell a large part of their yield.

In view of the large number of winepresses and oil presses in the monasteries of Palestine, the relative rarity of such things in the Judean desert monasteries is notable. It can be attributed to the dry climate and rocky topography of the region. Most of the winepresses and oil presses that were found were in monasteries close to the desert fringe—that is, in places permitting the cultivation of vines and olives.

Near the eastern corner of the monastic site of Khirbet Bureikut, about 5 km northeast of Bethlehem, the remains of a small winepress were found. Its gathering vat is preserved almost in its entirety (fig. 47). It is square, 2 × 2 m, and 1.5 m deep, making its capacity approximately 6 m^3.

Figure 47 Plan of the monastic remains at Khirbet Bureikut, with the nearby winepress

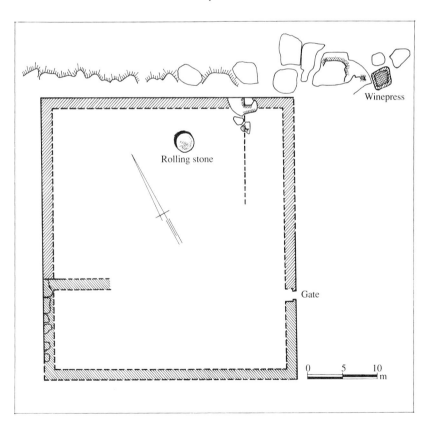

A smaller winepress, probably only for house use, was found in the Nea Laura, on the crest of a hill in the western part of the Judean desert, where climatic conditions are particularly suitable for growing vines. The winepress was situated about 400 m south of the core of the laura. It consists of a threshing floor and a round pit, both carved in the rock (fig. 48). A monk's cell was found about 8 m west of the winepress. It seems likely that the monk living in that cell was responsible for operating the winepress at the time of the grape harvest.

An especially large winepress was found at Khirbet Umm-Rukba, identified as the monastery of Caparbaricha, east of Hebron. It may be assumed that much of the wine produced in the monastery was sold in the nearby markets (in Hebron or in the village of Caparbaricha). This monastery, like the two mentioned previously, is on the western margin of the desert, in a region suitable for growing vines. The winepress is located at the eastern end of the monastery. The threshing floor is now covered with fallen stone and alluvial soil and cannot be examined, but the gathering vat is preserved in its entirety (fig. 49). The vat is square (2 × 2 m), 1.7 m deep, with a volume of 6.8 m³. In a corner of the coarse white mosaic floor is a round indentation, which was presumably for trapping sediment while the grape juice was collected. The walls of the vat,

Figure 48 Winepress in the Nea Laura

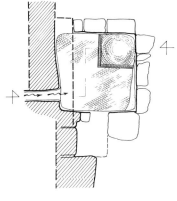

Plan

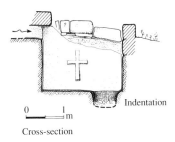

Indentation

0   1 m

Cross-section

Figure 49 Plan and cross-section of
the gathering vat found at the
monastery of Caparbaricha

made of natural rock and hewn stone, were coated with reddish waterproof plaster. A well-made cross is embossed in red in the western wall.

It was not unusual to decorate vats with a cross. In two monasteries in the Jerusalem area, winepresses decorated with crosses have been found: one north of the Old City, the other near the YMCA building in West Jerusalem.[19] These crosses served the same purpose as those found on the walls of water cisterns and reservoirs of churches and monasteries—that is, they signified ownership.

Only 2 km southeast of the monastery of Caparbaricha, at Khirbet el-Quneitira, the remains of an elaborate oil press were found.[20] These remains, found to the west of the monastery's interior courtyard, include two rectangular stone pillars forming the base for a press (fig. 50). The pillars are 1.9 m high and measure 60 × 80 cm. Notches have been carved out along their length to hold the wooden pressing apparatus. The crushing stone and the basin usually stood near the pillars. A fully preserved oil press (except for the wooden parts) was found nearby, at Khirbet el-Qasr (fig. 51). The monks apparently grew the olives in groves near their respective monasteries.[21]

Figure 50 The two pillars of an oil press at Khirbet el-Quneitira

A smaller installation for the production of olive oil was found in excavations of the monastery kitchen at Khirbet ed-Deir, in the southern part of the Judean desert. The olive trees from which the oil was produced probably grew in the plots prepared by the monks on the wide bank of Wadi el-Ghar. The

Figure 51 Oil press at Khirbet el-Qasr

quantity of olive oil produced in this press could not have been large and was probably intended to serve only the needs of the community.

Most of the other Judean desert monasteries did not have land suitable for growing grapes or olives. The monks in those monasteries presumably had to buy their wine and oil in the nearby markets or from neighboring monasteries. It should be remembered that most Judean desert monasteries were of moderate size and housed no more than twenty monks. Thus they were completely different from the vast agricultural and industrial centers typical of Egyptian monasticism, which, besides generating large revenues from their own industries, hired their monks out for work in other places, usually as agricultural laborers. By contrast, "outside work" was almost unknown in the Judean desert, although there is a story of a hermit who helped in the construction of a cistern ordered by the patriarch of Jerusalem in the Jordan region. He did not take up that work as a permanent source of income, however; it was only for the purpose of earning three gold coins to give to another monk in exchange for a book.[22] Besides, he was a wandering hermit, not linked to any community.

CHAPTER FIVE

Architectural Components:
Sacred Elements

THE CHURCH

Since communal worship was regarded as of prime importance in the expression of the Christian faith, the church was an essential component of every monastery. Without a church on the premises, the monks would have had to travel to the nearest Christian settlement for church services. Cyril relates that the monks of the Nea Laura initially "had neither a church nor a chief, but would take Communion on Sundays in the memorial of the holy prophet Amos in Tekoa."[1]

The larger monasteries had more than one church. As already mentioned, the monastery of Theodosius had five churches: a central one, known as "the Great Church," in which the office was said in Greek, and three others, for speakers of Armenian and Bessian and for mentally unbalanced monks. Theodosius's successor, Sophronius, added a fifth church, dedicated to the Virgin Mary. Three churches were installed in the Great Laura. The first was a small chapel in the middle of the ravine. Later, a large cave came to be used as a church, and finally a central church, dedicated to the Virgin Mary, was built opposite it.[2]

Basically, the churches in the monasteries were no different from those commonly found in other settlements. The apses faced east and were usually semicircular, though a number of monastery churches had square apses—for example, the cave churches at Khirbet ed-Deir and Pharan.[3] The apses could be either interior (built inside the perimeter) or exterior (jutting from the eastern wall). Occasionally, the eastern orientation was not strictly observed. The main reason seems to have been topographical constraints.[4] It appears that departure from the norm did not disturb the builders, particularly in the case of monasteries that were relatively isolated.

In general, however, the sanctuary was oriented to the east. It was separated from the nave by a chancel screen. In the center of the sanctuary stood the altar, which was usually made of marble. The main entrance to the church was generally placed at the opposite end, in the western wall or at the western end of one of the long walls, usually the southern one.

Near the church, there were usually several rooms, intended for various ritual purposes. A room almost always found beside the church was the diaconicon, used by the priests and their assistants, the deacons, for storing their priestly garb, various ritual articles, and gifts given to the monastery. In the literature regarding the Judean desert monks, diaconicons are mentioned a number of times. According to Cyril, a spacious cavern adjoining the cave church to the north served as the diaconicon in the Great Laura (*V. Sab.* 18, 102. 4). The diaconicon of the monastery of Euthymius must also have been large—at least, large enough to contain several people—since Euthymius lay there on his deathbed and summoned the elders of the laura to hear his last words (*V. Euth.* 39, 58. 1–2).

Later, after the laura of Euthymius was converted into a coenobium in 482, the diaconicon was composed of two rooms. The inner one was large enough to serve as a dining room when the abbot was entertaining important guests. Cyril's account of a dinner in such a room also mentions the "cabinets" used in the diaconicon to store the treasures of the church.[5]

Table 4 compares the plans of various churches in Judean desert monasteries and indicates the place of the diaconicon in relation to the church (as surmised by the excavators). As we can see, the position of the diaconicon was not fixed; sometimes it was to the south of the church, sometimes to the west, the north, and even the northeast in the case of the monastery of Choziba.

Another element found in some monastery churches is a baptistry. The only explicit reference to a baptismal font appears in Cyril's description of the cave church at the monastery of Theoctistus. Euthymius ordered that "a small pool" be made in a corner of the cave, and then he baptized the Saracens he had converted.[6] It would seem that this was the main function of baptismal fonts in monasteries: for the baptism of visitors, including nomads, who desired it.

It should be remembered that in the fifth and sixth centuries it was still common practice not to baptize babies at birth but to postpone the ceremony until adolescence or even adulthood. Thus it would be natural for unbaptized Christians to make a pilgrimage to a venerated site in order to be baptized there. In some monasteries where such occurrences were frequent, a monk who was also

TABLE 4

Churches of the monastic type in the Judean desert

Name of Monastery	Inner Dimensions of Church (m)	Inner Dimensions of Narthex (m)	Orientation of Entrance	Relative Position of Diaconicon	Type of Apse
Martyrius	6.6 × 25.9	4 × 6.6	North	South	Interior
Marda (Masada)	4.5 × 10	2.2 × 4.5	West	North	Interior
Castellion	5.4 × 15	—	South	South	Exterior
Firminus	7.2 × 16.4	—	South	West	Exterior
El-Qasr	5.1 × 10.3	—	West	South	Interior
Khirbet el-Quneitira	4.7 × 10	—	West	South	Interior
'Ein el-Fawwar	3.3 × 8.8	—	West	South	?
Khirbet et-Tina	4.2 × 11.4	—	South	?	Interior
Choziba	5 × 11.9	—	South	Northeast	Exterior

a priest was charged with the task of performing baptisms. Such was the case at the monastery of Penthucla, near the Jordan River (*Pratum* 3, 2853C). Non-Christian inhabitants of the nearby villages were also converted and baptized by the monks sometimes; Euthymius had many such converts in his coenobium at Caparbaricha (*V. Euth.* 12, 23. 1–3). Remains of baptismal fonts like the one described by Cyril have been found in the cave churches at Khallet Danabiya and Khirbet ed-Deir.

Monastery churches in the Judean desert can be divided into three main types: the so-called monastic type, a chapel consisting of a long, narrow prayer room;[7] the cave church, a natural cave that came to be used as a church; and the basilica. Most monastery churches, both in the Judean desert and beyond, are of the first type, although some churches of the second type are found in the Judean desert, though more rarely in other parts of the country. The third type is hardly ever found in monasteries of the Judean desert.

The Monastic Type

The dimensions of churches of the monastic type vary from monastery to monastery, but they are all long, narrow chambers directed toward a single apse (fig. 52). A good example is the relatively large church of the monastery of Martyrius, which was completed in stages in the sixth century.[8] The main body of the church, including the apse at its eastern end, is 25.9 m long and 6.6 m wide (interior measurements). The narthex, or vestibule, added at a later stage, is 4 m wide and 6.6 m long. The main entrance to the church was placed in the north-

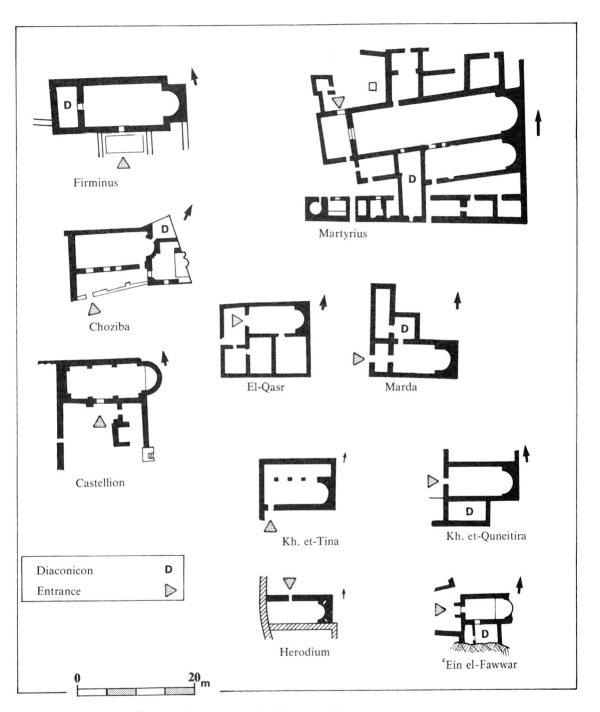

Firminus

Martyrius

Choziba

El-Qasr

Marda

Castellion

Kh. et-Tina

Kh. et-Quneitira

Diaconicon D

Entrance

Herodium

ᶜEin el-Fawwar

0 20 m

Figure 52 Comparative table of churches of the monastic type

ern wall of the narthex, and the northern orientation of the church entrance is apparently due to the position of the monastery refectory. There are three openings in the southern wall of the church. One leads to a room that the excavators assume to be a diaconicon, the other to another chapel. To the south of the latter is a long, narrow room thought to have been a baptistry.

The decision to build the main church without columns is an interesting one; for the builders clearly had the means to construct a basilica, as is clear from the refectory, which has a basilica design. It would seem that the monks preferred the simpler style of building that had become typical of monasteries.[9]

Another church of the monastic type was found in the monastery of Marda. The main body of the church, including its interior (eastern) apse, is 10 m long and about 4.5 m wide (fig. 53). The entrance is on the western side, through a narthex 2.2 m wide and 4.5 m long. (It seems to have been customary for the length of the narthex to equal the width of the main body of the church.) The northwest corner of the church opens into two rooms that are adjacent to each other. The room closer to the church has been identified as a diaconicon.[10]

Figure 53 Church at the monastery of Marda, on Masada (looking east).
Courtesy: Y. Yadin.

In most cases, the southern wall of the church was its facade. This is because the church often occupied the northern side of the monastery courtyard, as in the case of the monastery of Castellion.[11] In this church the opening in the southern wall leads directly to the interior of the church. Another opening in the western wall of the church connects it to a hall to the west of the church, which was probably a refectory.

The church complex of the laura of Firminus is the best preserved of its kind in the Judean desert. The main entrance in the southern wall of the church joins it to a courtyard extending and broadening southward (fig. 54). The church has an external apse, with a window in the center. A similar window has been preserved in the apse of the church at Masada. The church in the laura of Firminus, including the apse, is 16.4 m long and 7.2 m wide (interior measurements). The door in the western wall leads to a room only 3.5 m wide. In Corbo's opinion, this room was used as an atrium; however, I would see it as a diaconicon.[12] East and west of the church were several annexes.

Table 4, which summarizes what is known about churches of the monastic type, shows that there were no general rules controlling the plan of such churches. There is no regularity in the position of the entrance to the church, the position of the diaconicon, or the type of apse. The only feature common to all these churches is the basic structure of the main body of the church, which is long and narrow and terminates in a single apse facing east.

The Cave Church

The many caves found in the Judean desert were utilized by the monks for various purposes, including ritual use. The caves known to have been used as churches are generally found in the center of monasteries and have relatively large, well-lit natural interiors. Stories of several of these caves have come down to us.

The first cave church was created to commemorate Chariton's rescue from robbers. According to his biographer, when Chariton was on his way from Jerusalem to the desert, he was captured by robbers and brought in chains to their cave hideout. He was rescued when a snake dripped its venom into a jug of wine in the cave and the robbers drank the wine and died. "Hence the den of those foul robbers became a holy tabernacle of God, and is today the 'Old Church,' which is in the most saintly laura called Pharan, founded by this great man, Chariton" (*V. Char.* 9, 23. 8–9).

The second cave to have become a church was chosen by Euthymius and Theoctistus for what later became the monastery of Theoctistus on the northern bank of a ravine in the depths of the wilderness of Koutila. According to Cyril, the cave was originally a den of wild animals, "but, reclaimed by the

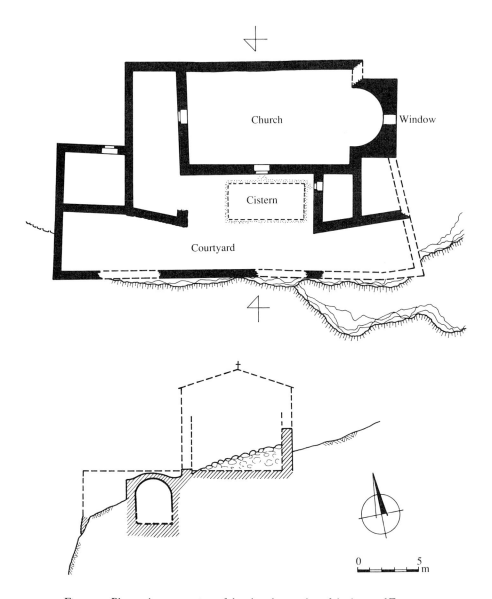

Figure 54 Plan and cross-section of the church complex of the laura of Firminus

hymns and unceasing prayers of the two saintly men, it came to be sanctified as a church of God" (*V. Euth.* 8, 15. 10–22). This was used as a model by Sabas, who spent seventeen years at the monastery of Theoctistus. In the Great Laura, Sabas created the most famous cave church in the Judean desert. According to Cyril, it was "a great and marvelous cave modeled as a church of God. Indeed, on its eastern side there is an apse built by God and in the northern side [Sabas] found a large room arranged like a diaconicon, and an entrance from the south-west, wide and suitably open to receive the illumination of the sun's rays. He decorated and furnished this [cave] with the help of God and decided that the divine service would be held there on Saturdays and Sundays" (*V. Sab.* 18, 102. 1–7). This church, known then as "the God-built [Church]" and more recently as St. Nicholas's Church, remains in use to this day (fig. 55).[13]

The Jordan River region also contains caves that came to be used as churches. One of them, on the eastern bank of the river, was the cave around which the monastery of Sapsas was built (*Pratum* 1, 2853A–B).

Impressive remains of cave churches have been found in the Judean desert. The cave church of the laura of Pharan is a good example. The church is located on the southern cliff of the canyon, 12 m above ground level (fig. 56). Apparently, its cave and three other chambers were hollowed out as early as the Second Temple period.[14] The monks of the laura and its founder, Chariton, thus used previously existing structures.

The monks entered the church via stairs and a vertical shaft, which was

Figure 55 St. Nicholas's church at the Great Laura. Courtesy: J. Patrich.

Figure 56 Cave church of the laura of Pharan

carved into the bedrock (fig. 57). The present stairs were built recently, but their foundations date from the Byzantine period. At the foot of the shaft, a cistern was hollowed out. It was fed by a canal, also carved out of the rock, that drained rainwater from the cliff face. The shaft, 3.5 m high, leads up to a rock ledge 6 m long and 2.3 m wide, with traces of a stone parapet around its outer border. Another flight of stairs ascends to the level of the church.

The entrance to the cave church, in its northeast corner, is large (1 m wide and 1.9 m high); hinge sockets and signs of a locking device can be seen in the threshold. Two windows were carved into the cave wall to admit light and air. The interior of the church is regular in shape, 8.2 m long, 6.2 m wide, and 2 m high. A semicircular prayer niche was carved in the eastern wall, and another, relatively shallow niche was carved to its south. The stone floor opposite the apse contains four sockets for the legs of the altar, surrounding an indentation apparently intended for a reliquary.

East of the church are three smaller chambers, one alongside the other in a northeastward direction. It seems likely that one of them was occupied by the abbot of the monastery, at least in the early days of the laura. The chamber next to the cave is relatively large, 4 m long, 2.3 m wide, and 1.8 m high. The next chamber is smaller, and the third is oblong and more spacious (measuring 2.3 × 3.8 m with a ceiling 1.8 m high). A semicircular niche was carved in the eastern wall of this chamber, possibly serving as a prayer niche. The three chambers are joined by openings of various sizes.

The cave church of the monastery of Theoctistus has been the subject of a number of studies.[15] The cave is located on a steep cliff next to the monastery (fig. 58). It is 9 m above ground level, and the monks ascended to it by means of a tower-like structure and stairways built on the site (today it can be reached only with the aid of climbing equipment). According to Chitty, the cave is irregular in shape. From the slim opening, a narrow vestibule leads to the central, square body of the church, about 15 m per side. The hall is divided by a masonry wall, which is flanked by two large rock piers and lined with stone benches. A prayer niche, 3 m in diameter, was built of masonry and natural rock in the eastern section, thus creating an interior chapel within the cave church. Three meters above the apse are two niches decorated with frescoes. In Chitty's view, these paintings belong to a later period in the history of the monastery.

The northern part of the cave opens into a room, apparently a diaconicon, 3 × 4 m in size. At the other end of the cave, on the edge of the cliff, a cistern was installed; it was apparently fed by drainage canals along the cliff face. In spaces below the cave floor, numerous human bones were found. These spaces, together with a number of alcoves in the rear of the cave, seem to have been

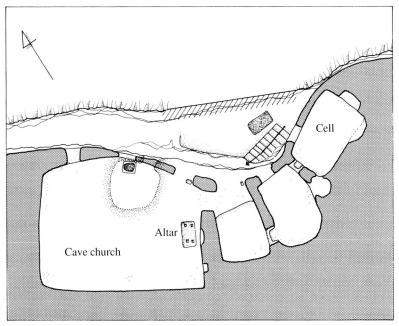

Cell

Altar

Cave church

0   4
        ⌐m

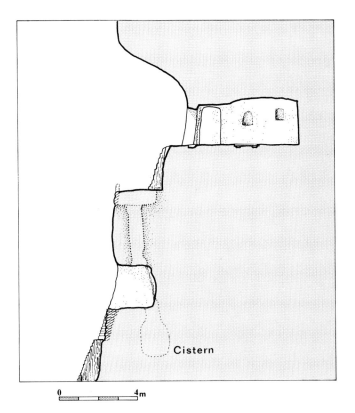

Cistern

0   4m

Figure 57 Plan and cross-section of the cave church
at the laura of Pharan

Figure 58 Cave church at the monastery of Theoctistus

used as burial places for the monks. A similar phenomenon was noted in the cave church at Khallet Danabiya, in the northern part of the Judean desert.[16]

The best-preserved cave church and the one richest in remains was found at Khirbet ed-Deir (fig. 59). A large natural cave, with a wide opening facing south, it is 26 m long, 3–13 m wide, and 3–5 m high. This space houses the main body of the church, a chapel, and three other rooms, easily distinguished because of their good state of preservation (fig. 60).

A facade wall, 1–1.6 m thick, was built at the mouth of the cave, and an opening, 1.2 m wide, was left in the center of the wall (fig. 61). Broken green window panes found next to the wall attest to windows in the facade. These windows, together with the doorway, provided light for the interior of the church. In order to create the regular shape of the main body of the church, which measures 9 × 11 m, its builders carved out sections of the walls and also added masonry where necessary; the walls and ceiling were coated with white plaster. On its eastern side, the sanctuary was partitioned off by means of a marble chancel, the remains of which were found during the excavations. The position of the altar (fig. 62) can be discerned in the center of the sanctuary, and most of its parts were found in a pile in the back room, which was probably a diaconicon. The apse is square, and in its eastern wall are two small niches, which held lamps or sacred objects. A similar arrangement was found in the cave church of the laura of Pharan.

The central part of the church is decorated with a colorful, ornate mosaic floor, surrounded by a frame of square medallions containing agricultural motifs and interwoven with floral designs. Facing the sanctuary is a large Greek inscription, a quote from Psalm 106:4–5: "Remember us, O Lord, with the favor thou hast to thy people; visit us with thy salvation, that we may behold the good of thine elect."[17]

South of the sanctuary, but still within the natural interior of the cave, is a small chapel, with a large prayer niche carved in its eastern wall. A depression carved at the base of the niche, 1 m above floor level, probably held a reliquary.

The importance assigned to the reliquary by the monks is evident from the appearance of the mosaic in front of it. Though the mosaic is not large, it has an elaborate design (fig. 63), in the center of which is a medallion, surrounded by ivy leaves and enclosing a formation of rays whose curved shape creates the illusion of movement. This is a rare pattern in mosaic floors, but familiar from stone lintels, such as those found in the Negev.[18]

Figure 59 Interior of the cave
church at Khirbet ed-Deir

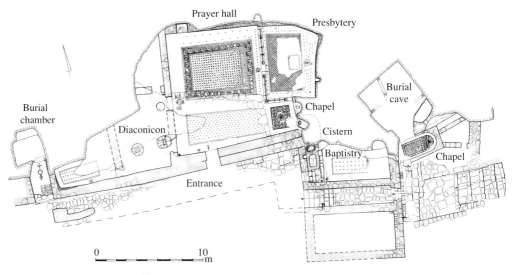

Figure 60 Plan of the cave church at Khirbet ed-Deir

Figure 61 Reconstruction of the cave church at Khirbet ed-Deir

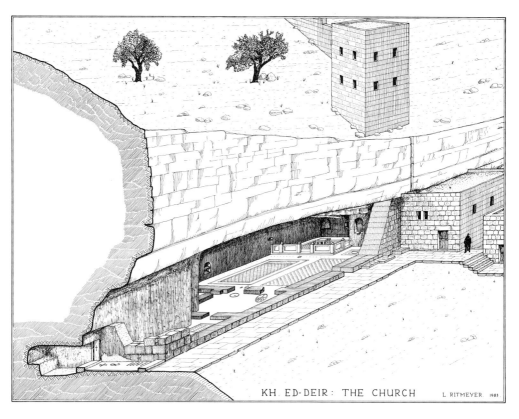

Figure 62 Restored altar from Khirbet ed-Deir

Figure 63 Mosaic floor in front of the reliquary at Khirbet ed-Deir
(looking east)

Various water installations were found in the floor of the church. The opening to a large cistern was carved in the northeastern corner, at the foot of the reliquary niche, and a second opening was found in the nearby baptistry. Near the entrance to the church (inside) is a round indentation designed to hold a pitcher of water, apparently for washing hands. Beside it is the opening to a canal, which drained water used for washing the church floor into the monastery garden; a cross-shaped grating covers the opening.

An opening in the western wall of the main body of the church leads to a medium-size room (4.5 × 6.8 m) with two smaller rooms adjoining it to the north and west. A mosaic floor near the entrance depicts an ornate amphora flanked by baskets of fruit. The mosaic floor in the center of the room has a large medallion (1.3 m in diameter), enclosing three crosses in an arrangement recalling the Crucifixion: a large central cross flanked by two smaller crosses. The three crosses face east, with a slight deviation toward the apse. This is the room in which the above-mentioned altar sections were found and which, judging from its large dimensions, may have been used as a diaconicon.

Two sacred elements were found outside the main body of the church. One of them is a room 2.8 × 3.8 m in size (internal measurements) built adjacent to the wall east of the entrance to the cave. From the threshold, three steps descend to the floor (fig. 64). To the left of the stairs is a small stone, plastered basin, which got its water from the hewn cistern mentioned above. It appears to have been a baptismal font, and the entire room a baptistry. West of the cave church, the tomb of the monastery's founder was discovered (to be discussed later in the chapter).

The features of cave churches in the Judean desert are summarized in table 5.

TABLE 5

Cave churches in Judean desert monasteries

Name of Monastery	Inner Dimensions of Church (m)	Height of Ceiling (m)	Placement of Facade	Shape of Apse	Baptistry	Burial Alcoves
Pharan	6.2 × 8.2	2	North	Square	no	yes
Theoctistus	15 × 15	3–4	South	Round	yes	yes
Great Laura	12.5 × 14.5	?	South	Round	no	no
Khallet Danabiya	9 × 25	3–6	Southeast	Square	yes	yes
Khirbet ed-Deir	10 × 26	3–5	South	Square	yes	yes

Figure 64 Room thought to be the baptistry at Khirbet ed-Deir, with the
baptismal pool in the foreground

The Basilica Type of Church

The basilica type of church—that is, a church whose interior is divided into three aisles by two rows of columns—hardly exists in the monasteries of the Judean desert. This absence is conspicuous in light of the many basilica churches found in nonmonastic settlements in Palestine during the Byzantine period.

To date, only one basilica church has been identified with certainty in the Byzantine monasteries of the Judean desert: St. Peter's Church, east of Jerusalem, a memorial church attached to a monastery.[19] As has already been noted, memorial churches attached to monasteries were usually built in basilica form. This seems natural, since their prime purpose was to serve pilgrims. St. Peter's Church measures 15 × 19 m, including the atrium. It has a mosaic floor (a small part of which was uncovered in a test excavation performed at the site), and there is a round cistern in the center of the atrium.[20] A complete excavation of the church has yet to be made.

In a survey of the monastery of Scholarius, atop Mount Muntar, sections of pillars belonging to the church of the monastery were discovered.[21] Since other types of church lack columns, it seems likely that this monastery had a basilica like the Church of St. Peter; but it is not certain. The similarity, if such there be, may stem from the common history of the two monasteries: the original building on Mount Muntar was the tower built by the empress Eudocia, who also ordered the erection of St. Peter's Church (*V. Euth.* 30, 48. 9–10).

BURIAL PLACES

Written sources provide information about the funerary customs of the Judean desert monks. The most important tomb in a monastery was always that of the monk who founded it.[22]

Euthymius, founder of the monastery named after him, was buried in the underground cave in which he had habitually secluded himself. The cave was converted into an elaborate tomb on the orders of Anastasius, patriarch of Jerusalem. The task of construction was entrusted to the deacon Fidus, who replaced the cave with "a vaulted building, large and splendid," according to Cyril. He relates further that, "in the middle he placed a grave for the saint [Euthymius], and on each side he prepared graves for the abbots, priests, and other holy men of the monastery" (*V. Euth.* 42, 61. 19–22). Euthymius's grave was surrounded by chancel screens and was covered with a tombstone with a silver funnel, customarily used by pilgrims to pour oil into saints' graves. The oil flowed into a container that touched the saint's remains and the oil thereby "sanctified" was then extracted and taken home as a relic. Later, when the laura was converted

into a coenobium, the builders saw to it that the tomb remained in the center of
the complex, where it can be seen intact to this day (fig. 65).

Another example of a founder's dwelling becoming his venerated tomb is
the cave of Theodosius, situated in a central spot in his monastery. An idea
of the esteem in which it was held can be gained from the following account
in the writings of Moschus: "When I [a monk called Christopher] renounced
the world [in the monastery of Theodosius] . . . by nights I went to pray in the
cave where St. Theodosius and other holy fathers lie. And in descending into
the cave, at each step I made a hundred genuflections to God. The steps are
eighteen in number. After I had descended all the steps, I remained there until
they struck the symandron [for the nocturnal prayers]" (*Pratum* 105, 2961D).

The five Syrian hermits who formed the nucleus of the community at
Choziba were also buried in their former dwelling, which was situated at the
center of the monastery (*V. Geor.* 19, 118. 20–119. 1). The cave where Martyrius
once lived was later used as a tomb for the priests of his monastery, but Martyrius was not buried there, since he had left the monastery to become patriarch
of Jerusalem (*V. Euth.* 32, 51. 19–20).

Figure 65 Euthymius's tomb in the monastery named after him

The tomb of Sabas, founder of the Great Laura, is in the courtyard between the two central churches of the laura (fig. 66). He was buried in a crypt especially prepared on the spot where he had seen a pillar of fire marking the site of the "God-built church." His successors were later buried in the same crypt (*V. Sab.* 78, 184. 14–16).

All the founders who remained in their communities were buried in the center of their monasteries. However, Gerasimus appears to have been buried in his monastery's cemetery, about 740 m from the church.[23] The sources indicate that burial practices conformed to hierarchical order. The founder's successors were buried next to him, generally in a special tomb, which was, as noted, a prominent feature of the monastery: a converted cave, a monument, or a crypt. Even Gerasimus's grave may have been marked in a special way. The above-mentioned statement relates the situation just a few days after his death: a tombstone or monument may have been erected later.

Sometimes priests of a monastery and particularly venerated monks were also buried in the founder's sepulcher, as in the monasteries of Euthymius and

Figure 66 Tomb of Sabas in the Great Laura (Deir Mar Saba). Courtesy: J. Patrich

Theodosius; in other monasteries, priests were buried separately, as was probably the case in the monastery of Theoctistus and in the Great Laura.

Maris, Theoctistus's successor, was placed in the sarcophagus that held his predecessor (*V. Sab.* 10, 93. 18–19). Subsequent abbots were also buried in that sarcophagus, judging from the biography of Stephen Sabaites. In the eighth century, when the monastery was in ruins and the tomb almost forgotten, Stephen visited it, entered the burial chamber, and showed his disciple the skeletons of the deceased abbots, identifying each by name (*V. Steph. Sab.* 28, 514–15). This tomb was located at ground level, not in the church, which was already inaccessible without a ladder in Stephen's time.[24] Those buried in the church are identified by an inscription as the "elders and brothers" of the monastery: they probably included the priests of the community.[25]

As for the Great Laura, Sabas's successors were buried in the crypt where he himself lay, and the priests had a crypt of their own. On Sabas's orders, a monk who was not a priest but was renowned for his exceptional asceticism was buried "with the priests," but his body was laid transversely so that it could be recognized and venerated (*V. Sab.* 44, 135. 25–8).

Distinguished monks were sometimes buried in private tombs under the church floor: Moschus mentions a case in the monastery of Coprotha and another in the church of St. Cyricus in Phasael, built by the monks of the monastery of Theodosius.[26]

Ordinary monks were usually buried in simple graves. Moschus tells of an old hermit and his disciple who lived in the Jordan valley. When the old man died, people from a nearby settlement were summoned to dig his grave. His disciple asked them to make the pit larger, and while they dug, he lay down on his mat and died. Then the diggers buried both hermits in the enlarged grave.[27]

Like the founders of monasteries, ordinary hermits were sometimes buried in their own cells or caves. Cyril mentions the burial of a hermit by Sabas, who found him dead in his cave beside the Jordan River and blocked the entrance with stones (*V. Sab.* 24, 108. 23–6). The same was done for a female hermit living in a cave along the path to Sousakim (*V. Cyr.* 19, 234. 18–20). In the community of the Seven Virgins near the Jordan River, seven female recluses lived in cells hewn in the rock within a cave church. When one of them died, her cell was sealed with her body inside, and a new cave was hollowed out for a young girl who was subsequently admitted to the community (*Ant. Plac.* 12, 135).

A similar practice existed in the coenobium of Theodosius, at least in its early period. Theodosius instructed his first disciples to each prepare a *mnemeion*—a monument, as opposed to a trough grave (a built mortar trough)—which he would first use as living quarters (Theod. Petr., *V. Theod.* 8, 21). It is not clear whether this refers to single cells that would in time be transformed into private tombs or to a communal building in which each monk had his alcove, later to become his tomb. Collective burials under the church floor, like the "brothers' tombs" in the monastery of Theoctistus, are also known from the archaeological finds.

It should be remembered that all these manners of burial reflect the burial customs of laymen in Byzantine Palestine, where the dead would be buried in trough graves in cemeteries, in burial vaults or cave tombs, in private tombs under church floors, or in crypts. Like monks, laymen were placed in their graves clothed in their own garments, without shroud or coffin.

The written sources also provide information about the funeral ceremony. If death were not sudden, the dying monk would take his leave from the brothers by giving them each the kiss of peace, and then he would receive Communion.[28] After death, the corpse would be prepared for burial and laid out on a couch in the church. The preparations appear to have been quite simple, as we learn from Cyril's account of the death of Anthimus in the Great Laura. On the night Anthimus died, Sabas "roused the prayer leader and ordered him to sound the signal, and went with incense and candles to the old man's cell. He found nobody there, except the old man himself, lying dead . . . and after having attended to the venerable body, they took it into the church, celebrated the usual service upon it and laid [the remains] in a holy grave" (*V. Sab.* 43, 134. 3–7). Thus, Anthimus's corpse was first prepared for burial, then brought into the church where the funeral service was performed, and later placed in a tomb, seemingly a crypt.

The preparation for burial probably consisted of dressing the deceased in full monk's habit, with his cloak over his tunic and perhaps with a cross. A hermit in the Jordan valley was found buried in his tunic and cape.[29] A female hermit was found dead in a little oasis in Sinai by two monks from the laura of Sapsas in the Jordan valley, one of whom used his own cloak to wrap the corpse before burying it.[30]

The corpse then lay on a "litter" until it was brought into the church.[31] It was stretched out in a west–east direction, with the head in the west as if looking toward the east. This practice is alluded to in the story about George of Choziba. Experimenting with deep meditation, George spread his cloak on the floor, placed a pillow at the western end, and lay upon it without moving for three days: the brothers took him for dead. Subsequently, when he was actually at the point of death, George lay down with his head looking eastward.[32]

Monks were all buried with this orientation (in fact, this was the custom with all Christian burials in the Byzantine period). It seems that secondary burial was not practiced; so the case of Euthymius, whose body was kept in a coffin for three months until his tomb was completed, was exceptional. Another rare exception occurred when the tomb of an unknown ascetic was miraculously discovered, and the monk was then buried with full honors in a place more suited to his sanctity.[33]

Performance of the funeral ceremony did not conclude the relation between the deceased monk and his community. Memorial ceremonies took place in the church on the third, seventh, and fortieth days after his death, as we learn from the testimony of Theodore of Petra, who tells the story of Basilius, the monk who volunteered "to inaugurate" the newly built burial place in the monastery of Theodosius. On Theodosius's orders, the various ceremonies were held while Basilius was still alive. After the memorial service on the fortieth day, Basilius died peacefully; he then miraculously appeared during compline for the next forty days (Theod. Petr., *V. Theod.* 8, 22–3). This story reflects the central role of death in the spiritual life of the monastic community. We know too that deaths were registered in the monastery of Theodosius, since Theodore states that 693 monks had died by the time of Theodosius's death in 529.[34]

Archaeological findings corroborate the written sources. The burial hierarchy of the monks can be seen in the monastery of Choziba. In a survey of the site by Schneider, three burial caves were found, two within the monastery and one outside it.[35] The first was a cave tomb carved in the rock beside the church of the monastery. It is square (4 m per side) and contains three burial troughs next to the walls. The second cave was beneath the Church of St. Stephen; Schneider was not permitted to enter this cave, but one of the monks informed him that the interior was piled high with bones. These two caves were apparently used for the elders of the monastery and for specially selected monks. The third cave was situated outside the monastery, about 100 m east of the entrance gate. This large natural cave is 9 m long and about 7 m wide (fig. 67). Fifteen burial troughs were built in the floor of the cave in two rows: eight graves in the eastern row and seven in the western one (fig. 68). The burial troughs were covered with flat stone slabs. In Schneider's opinion, the monks preferred to build the troughs rather than carve them out of the rock, for practical reasons. The ceiling and walls of the cave were coated with white plaster, decorated with crosses, and inscribed with numerous epitaphs, from the sixth to the tenth centuries. It is supposed that this cave was the burial place of ordinary monks.

The monks of Choziba continue to use the cave to this day, but in a different way. When a monk dies, he is buried in the ground for three years, and the burial place is marked by stones and a simple wooden cross (fig. 69). Then his remains are transferred to a burial trough in the cave, and his skull is added to the group of skulls lying on the floor along the walls. It is not clear when this system came into practice; but judging from the excavations at the monastery of Euthymius, the change took place after the thirteenth century.[36]

Figure 67 Burial cave outside the monastery of Choziba (St. George's
Monastery)

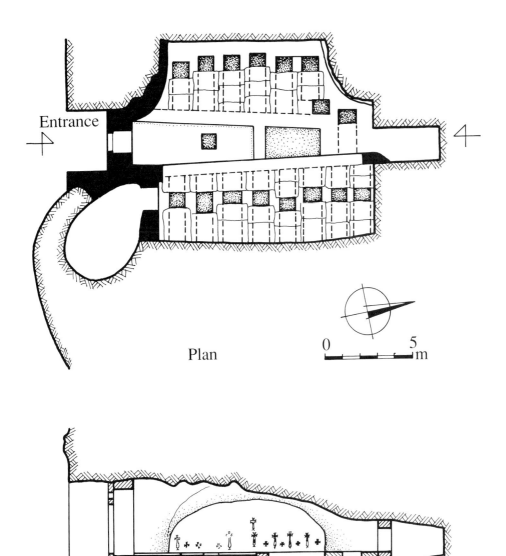

Entrance

Plan

0 ____ 5
‎‎‎‎‎‎‎‎‎‎‎‎m

Cross-section

Figure 68 Plan and cross-section of the burial cave outside the monastery of
Choziba

The importance of the tomb of the founder is clearly evident in the monastery of Euthymius. The tomb of Euthymius was discovered beneath the floor of the funerary chapel in the center of the monastery.[37] Reached via a flight of masonry steps, it is a vaulted structure measuring 4.7 × 5.9 m and 4 m high at its highest point. Along the northern and southern walls are stone benches, and in the center are nine burial troughs. The central trough, which measures only

Figure 69 Present-day graves in the ground at St. George's Monastery (the monastery of Choziba)

0.5 × 1.6 m and is 0.6 m deep (fig. 70), was identified as the tomb of Euthymius, who is known to have been a diminutive man, almost a dwarf (*V. Euth.* 40, 59. 19). Each of the other burial troughs contained many skeletons and several clay lamps that appear to have been brought as offerings.

To the west, another burial chamber was found: an underground, vaulted room 8.5 m long and 4 m high. Its entrance was blocked with stone slabs in secondary use. The Greek word for "tomb" is inscribed on one of them, and another bears the Greek letter *pi,* presumably for "Petros."[38] The bottom of this inner burial chamber consists of two large troughs, divided by a narrow passage. The troughs contain more than a hundred complete skeletons, laid from west to east, corroborating the testimony of the sources. The location of the chamber near the founder's tomb indicates that these are the remains of the monastery priests. If this assumption is correct, then the cemetery for the ordinary monks has not yet been found.

A place of honor was also reserved for elders in the monastery of Martyrius. As noted earlier, its founder, who left soon after the establishment of the monastery to enter the clergy of the Jerusalem Church, was not buried there. The man who transformed the monastery from a hermitage to a great coenobium was Martyrius's successor, Paul, who served as abbot for many years. At a central point in the monastery, in a square room at the entrance to the main church, the excavators discovered Paul's grave inlaid in the mosaic floor.[39] The tombstone, found in situ, consisted of a block of reddish limestone, inscribed with Paul's name and titles. Ten skeletons, apparently those of Paul and his successors, were found in the course of excavating the tomb.

These hierarchical distinctions are also evident in the archaeological and epigraphic remains found in the cave church of the monastery of Theoctistus. The cave contains two burial recesses. Above the more western of the two, a Greek inscription is painted in red on the plastered cave wall.[40] It begins: "This is the burial place for holy fathers and brothers." Apparently this was where both the simple monks (*adelphoi*) and the elders (*pateres*) of the community were buried, whereas the abbots, Theoctistus and his followers, were buried separately, just as Cyril reported.[41]

But the best example can be found at Khirbet ed-Deir. There the recess in

Figure 70 Remains of Euthymius's burial trough

which the founder of the monastery and his successors appear to have been buried is separate from the cave in which, according to an inscription in the floor at the entrance, the bodies of the priests were placed. The burial place of ordinary monks has not yet been found, although the monastery has been completely excavated. It would seem, therefore, that they were buried somewhere outside the monastery.

The founder's burial recess is situated at the center of the monastery, between the refectory and the church complex. It is only 2.8 m long, 2 m wide, and 1.6 m high, with a shelf in its rear. The entrance to the chamber is small and narrow, and locking devices can be seen around it. A cross is engraved on the eastern doorpost (fig. 71).

A perfectly preserved mosaic floor was found in front of the door; it is decorated with two crosses, one of which is a *crux ansata* (a cross with a circle at the top). The mosaic also contains a passage in Greek from 1 Cor. 15:52–3, but

Figure 71 Founder's burial recess at Khirbet ed-Deir

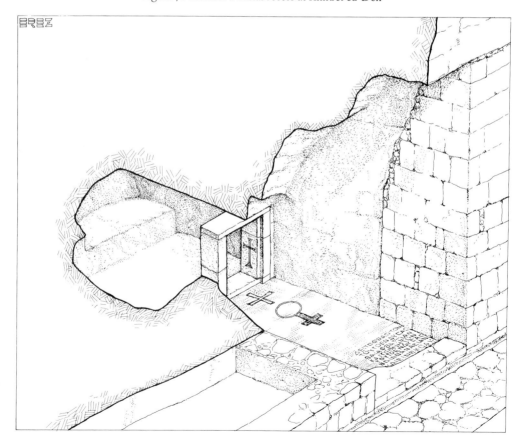

with the order of the verses reversed: "This perishable nature must put on the imperishable, and this mortal nature must put on immortality. For the trumpet will sound, and the dead will be raised."[42] The crosses and the inscription prove without a doubt that the chamber was used for the burial of a key figure in the monastery. Its location at the architectural center of the compound indicates that it was the burial place of the founder, and probably of his successors as well.

The cave tomb of the priests is situated in the cliff east of the cave church. A tiny, funerary chapel (4 × 1.8 meters), has been built in front of the entrance to the cave (fig. 72). The inscription in its mosaic floor invokes the intercession of the priests buried within: "Holy presbyters, intercede for peace for this place and for our souls."[43] The natural cave is square, 5 m to a side, and 2 m high. Its floor contains the remains of the walls of burial troughs, like the burial troughs in the cave near the monastery of Choziba. Judging from the size of the cave, it held about ten graves, one next to the other.

A well-preserved burial cave was found in the monastery of Castellion. It is square, and the ceiling is 2.5 m high. Eight masonry burial troughs were found in it, covered with slabs of polished stone (fig. 73). The plastered walls of the cave are painted with figures, and the accompanying inscriptions identify them as saints and famous monks who were active in the Judean desert.[44]

The monastic remains at El-Qasr include a crypt with a separate entrance from outside the walls of the monastery (fig. 74). The crypt, which lies below a church, is square (4 × 4 m), and its vaulted ceiling is 2.8 m high. There is a small prayer niche in the eastern wall. The separate entrance and the prayer niche seem to suggest that the monks who were buried in this crypt, or at least some of them, were revered figures whose relics attracted people from outside the monastery.[45]

Unlike the coenobia, the lauras of the Judean desert have yielded few burial sites. Two cave tombs were found in the laura of Firminus.[46] One of them, with deep, broad chambers and a small chapel, was found about 1 km east of the laura's core; the other was found among the monks' cells, about 2.5 km east of the core. A fragment of a stone chancel screen found in the cave suggests that it may have had a funerary chapel as well.

A concentration of cave tombs was found on a hill about 1.2 km east of the core of the laura of Pharan.[47] From a survey and test excavations carried out at the site, it was found that the complex included a cistern, reservoirs, and the ruins of a chapel with a colorful mosaic floor. The Byzantine burial caves, numbering in the dozens, were found on the eastern slope of the hill. A typical tomb consisted of a square room carved into the soft chalky rock, surrounded by three vaulted niches, each containing two or three burial troughs. A cross enclosed in a circle was carved on each side of the entrance to one of the tombs.

Figure 72 Funeral chapel at Khirbet ed-Deir

The fact that this large concentration of tombs was situated at the edge of the laura suggests that these were the graves of simple monks of the community of Pharan. The tomb traditionally attributed to the founder of the monastery, Chariton, was beneath the church in the center of the laura.

Figure 73 Burial cave in the monastery of Castellion, with a fresco depicting
famous Judean desert monks. Courtesy: Israel Antiquities Authority.

The examples given above show that burial complexes were often placed
east of the main part of a monastery. This may have been intentional.[48] Since the
winds in the region blow from west to east during most of the year, it seems
reasonable to assume that the location of graveyards to the east of monastic
complexes was due to sanitary considerations. The monks were well aware of
the health hazard posed by decaying corpses. Anthony of Choziba was urged by
his fellow monks to bury his master George (who seemed to be dead) without
delay, "lest he begins to stink and we are in danger in burying him" (*V. Geor.*
36, 135. 12–13).

PRAYER ROOMS

Worship in the coenobia—daily offices and private prayer alike—took
place in the church.[49] There is archaeological evidence of small chapels, such
as the three in the monastery of Martyrius; but they served the whole community, or occasionally only part of it, and therefore cannot be considered private chapels. Indeed, in all the hagiographic literature regarding Judean desert

Figure 74 Entrance to the crypt at El-Qasr (the entrance is outside the monastery)

monasticism, there is no mention of private chapels in coenobia, communal prayer being among the distinguishing features of coenobitic life.

Life in the lauras was completely different, however. The cell-dwellers would recite the daily offices alone in their cells and would meet for communal prayer only on the weekends. Chariton, for example, taught his disciples to say the office in their cells.[50]

A prayer room, or at least a prayer niche, was therefore an essential element of an anchorite's dwelling. Moschus tells of a hermit near the Jordan River who built an altar in his cave (*Pratum* 10, 2860B–C). Other hermits focused their prayers on icons.[51] According to Anthony of Choziba, George had "a small balcony-like cell [the antechamber to his cell] three feet or less in length, where he would perform the divine office and psalmody."[52] Besides noting the modest size of George's prayer room, Anthony mentions special preparations for making the room singled out for prayer more comfortable and well appointed. This small balcony, though roofed, was exposed to the air; it also served as a place for storing odds and ends (*V. Geor.* 13, 109. 8–9).

Such an arrangement was well suited to George, who adhered strictly to the ideals of poverty and self-denial; but the sources indicate that as a rule, recluses invested considerable effort in arranging their prayer rooms. Euthymius, for example, first arranged a corner of the cave church in the monastery of Theoctistus for his private use and then built a chapel on Masada (Marda) with the help of his disciple Domitian. Finally, when he settled in Mishor Adummim, he had the Saracens build him a chapel for private prayer; this was unadorned initially and was decorated only later, when it became the laura's church.[53]

Arrangements for private prayer ranged, then, from a corner set apart, barely distinguishable unless marked with painted crosses or graffiti, to a roughly hewn prayer niche, to more sophisticated built and decorated chapels. The choice depended mainly on the means at the disposal of the individual cell-dwellers. The bare hands of one isolated hermit, with the sole help of the small pick used by hermits to dig wild roots (*V. Euth.* 38, 75. 7), could produce only a modest, rough hollow with a few scratched crosses, as we find in a cave near 'Ein er-Rashash in the northern part of the Judean desert (see ch. 7). A cell-dweller in a laura, on the other hand, had the use of the community's tools and probably some help from his fellow monks or from local peasants.[54] The results of such collaboration may not have reached professional standards but were probably quite adequate.

Sometimes a lauritic community included trained masons or architects, like Sabas's disciples Theodoulus and Gelasius (*V. Sab.* 32, 117. 1–5), who would direct the unskilled monks. In other cases, a monastery actually employed professional builders for its communal structures (*V. Sab.* 82, 187. 9–10). By the same token, a monk who had the necessary means could pay for the erection of his own living quarters, including a well-appointed chapel. In fact, we learn from Cyril that Sabas encouraged his disciples to do just that; indeed, the most elaborate prayer rooms are found in the Great Laura.[55]

The first scholar to identify the archaeological phenomenon of the prayer room was Patrich.[56] Following his detailed survey of the Great Laura, he concluded that each cell had a prayer room or at least a prayer niche.

The basic arrangement was a simple niche hewn out of, or built into, the eastern part of the cell. The best example, and probably one of the earliest, is found in the cave used by Sabas in the eastern side of the laura in his first years at the monastery. (Today, the monks of Mar Saba venerate Sabas's cave and keep an icon of Antony of Egypt, "Father of the Monks," in the prayer niche.) In other cases, Patrich discovered that the original prayer niche grew into a prayer room occupying the entire dwelling, and another living area was built beside it.[57]

One of the most impressive and best-preserved chapels is the one in the cell traditionally believed to have belonged to John Hesychast. This complex, which

Figure 75 Chapel in a cave in the laura of Gerasimus

lies on the eastern side of the ravine, apparently underwent two stages of construction, both during the Byzantine period. In its later, more elaborate form, the chapel was 3.9 × 5 m in size; it was well built, and its walls were covered with red frescoes. The chapel may have been used for Sunday Mass as well as for daily prayer, since we know from the historical sources that John Hesychast was a priest and that he secluded himself in his cell for long periods.[58]

The Great Laura is the only monastery in the Judean desert that has functioned uninterruptedly up to the present time. Since the ravine around the monastery is the private property of the community, the abandoned cells from the Byzantine period have remained in a good state of preservation. The other lauras, as well as the hermitages, are in much poorer condition. Most of the cells, including their prayer niches or prayer rooms, have been damaged by the forces of nature, and only their foundations can be studied.

To date we know of two prayer rooms apart from those of the Great Laura that are relatively intact. The first is the well-built prayer room of Cyriac's hermitage at Sousakim, which will be described in chapter 7. The second was recently discovered near the laura of Gerasimus. In the survey carried out at this laura, four cells and a prayer room were found carved into the southern cliff of Wadi en-Nukheil, which borders the laura to the north.[59] A grove of palm trees grows on the banks of the wadi, hence its name, which means "the Valley of the Small Palm Trees." The monks descended to the cells from the plain above the cliff. The cells and the prayer room are all on one level, about 7 m above the ground. Since the prayer room was meant only for the monks in the four adjoining cells, it was very small, measuring only 2.2 m long, 1.5 m wide, and 2.2 m high. A semicircular prayer niche is carved at the eastern end, with another, smaller niche in the center of it, decorated with a small cross carved into the wall (fig. 75). A small window looks out over the wadi to the north of the prayer room. The effort invested by the workers who carved out the prayer room, the fine finish of the walls, and its careful planning help to date the entire complex to the Byzantine period.

CHAPTER SIX

Architectural Components:
Secular Elements

WATER SYSTEMS

A steady supply of water was essential for the monks' survival in the desert. Water was needed for drinking, irrigation, building, and wetting the palm leaves used in basketry to make them pliable for plaiting. The search for water was the very first consideration in the process of settlement. The veteran wanderers among the monks were skilled not only in the exploitation of obvious sources of water—streams and springs—but also in the art of locating hidden sources and ancient cisterns and of collecting water from natural cavities in the rock. Euthymius, for instance, knew how to find subterranean water in the desert, while Sabas discovered a hidden source by observing the behavior of a wild ass.[1] Both also made use of ancient cisterns on Masada, the cistern known as Heptastomos ("The Seven-Mouthed Cistern"), and cisterns near the laura of Euthymius (*V. Euth.* 51, 75. 1–6). Cyriac had a system for collecting water from the fissures of the rock (*V. Cyr.* 16, 232. 25–9), and Theoctistus and Euthymius probably used the same method when they first settled in the cave that subsequently became the nucleus of the monastery of Theoctistus (*V. Euth.* 8, 15–16).

Drawing and carrying water was among the tasks commonly assigned to new monks. Sabas, Cyriac, and George all carried water as young novices, and their biographers praise the willingness and humility with which they performed this task.[2] It was not only because of their youthful strength and low status in the monastery hierarchy that they were given this back-breaking job. In fact, John Hesychast was assigned the same work when he first came to the

Great Laura, even though by then he was forty and a man of obvious dignity.[3] It is very clear that this task was also an exercise intended to humble the spirit of the new monks and teach them to serve. Though this was undoubtedly necessary, the job could sometimes be performed more efficiently in other ways: the fathers of the laura of Gerasimus, who needed no lessons in humility, had a donkey to do the heavy work of carrying water from the Jordan River (*V. Ger.* 7, 7).

Another task related to the water supply was the building and maintenance of cisterns and drainage canals. Both skilled and unskilled workers were employed in this task. The monks often did the work themselves,[4] but, as we have already seen, in at least one case the building and plastering of a reservoir was done by a hired artisan, Mamas of Bethlehem.

The canals could easily be damaged by violent floods or be blocked by silt. Sabas, foreseeing a storm on one occasion, instructed the monks of the monastery of the Cave (Spelaion) to repair the canals (*V. Sab.* 66, 167. 11–12). If the drainage canals were poorly maintained, the first violent storm would leave the monastery flooded. Since the dampness could undermine the foundations of the monastery walls, the monks would have to sweep away the excess water and carry it in buckets far from the monastery walls, as was the case at the monastery of Theognius.[5]

If too much rain could be dangerous, lack of it could bring about abandonment of a monastery. After a period of drought, the monks of Spelaion asked Sabas's permission to leave the place (*V. Sab.* 66, 167. 6–8). But when the precious liquid was obtainable from other sources, even at a distance from the monastery, transportation on pack animals was arranged. When the monastery of Euthymius could not be dedicated because there was no water for the guests, the beasts of burden of the monastery and of the coenobia of Theoctistus and Martyrius were enlisted for an expedition to the spring of Pharan, about 6 km away.[6] This happened when the monastery was being built and the new reservoir had not yet filled with water; the story clearly illustrates the need to store as much water as possible in order to ensure a water supply in years of drought.

The main water supply for the monasteries of the Judean desert came from rainwater collected in cisterns and reservoirs. Even monasteries located near streams installed central reservoirs to supply most of the community's needs. The installation of a water system preceded the construction of other parts of the complex, as can be seen at the monastery of Martyrius, all of whose courtyards are paved on an incline toward the mouths of the cisterns.[7] Often, however, elements were later added to the original water system to increase its capacity.

Water systems varied according to the topographical situation of each monastery; nevertheless, they all consisted of a series of underground cisterns fed by rainwater through a network of channels. The rainwater was drained from natural slopes and specially built surfaces. In some, lengthwise canals were dug or carved into the slopes of the nearby wadis. An example of such a channel is the lower channel of the monastery at Khirbet ed-Deir, carved in the rock of the wadi, which drains rainwater into a round cistern (fig. 76).

Another kind of installation allowed the collection of rainwater from the roofs, balconies, and paved courtyards of the monastery—which had the advantage of being clean and free from rocks and silt. Ceramic gutters ran along the roofs and walls, carrying water to the underground cisterns. An example of such a system was discovered at the monastic site on the northern bank of Wadi ʿAuja.[8] Under the remains of the mosaic pavement of the courtyard, an elaborate network of clay pipes was found. These pipes probably drained rainwater from the roofs of the buildings surrounding the courtyard into a circular cistern, still intact, in the center of the monastery.

Ceramic pipes, about 12 cm in diameter, were also used to drain water from the roofs of cells built over cisterns at the monastery of Chariton. An example of such a cell has been discovered on the face of the cliff about 70 m south of the core of the monastery (fig. 77). The cistern is preserved to the height of the floor above it. The interior of the cistern was vaulted, and the mouth of a ceramic pipe which could have carried water drained from the roof of the cell was found close to the base of the vault. The pipe itself was probably placed inside the wall, though it is not out of the question that it was an external gutter.

To prevent leakage, builders of cisterns used a standard method of lining the walls, as in one of the two main cisterns at the laura of Heptastomos. The cistern, found 120 m south of the core of the laura, is carved into the rock and is completely preserved, including the ceiling (fig. 78). It is rectangular and measures 7.5 × 2.8 m, and the ceiling is about 5 m high; hence, its estimated capacity is at least 100 m³. The walls of the cistern are lined with three different coatings: the bottom layer consists of dressed building stones, the middle layer of fist-sized pebbles and flat stones, and the outer layer of waterproof cistern plaster. The two inner layers are bonded with grayish mortar, and the mortar for the outer layer has been thickened with crushed pottery, giving it a reddish color. This method of lining the walls are found in most cisterns and reservoirs of Byzantine monasteries in the Judean desert (which thus contrast with the cisterns of the nomadic population, which are characteristically bell-shaped and lined only with a layer of plaster).

A standard element alongside the cisterns was a sedimentary pool (settling tank), which slowed the current temporarily, thereby trapping dirt before it reached the cistern. The more elaborate cisterns developed by the Judean desert

Figure 76 Lower water channel at Khirbet ed-Deir (looking southwest)

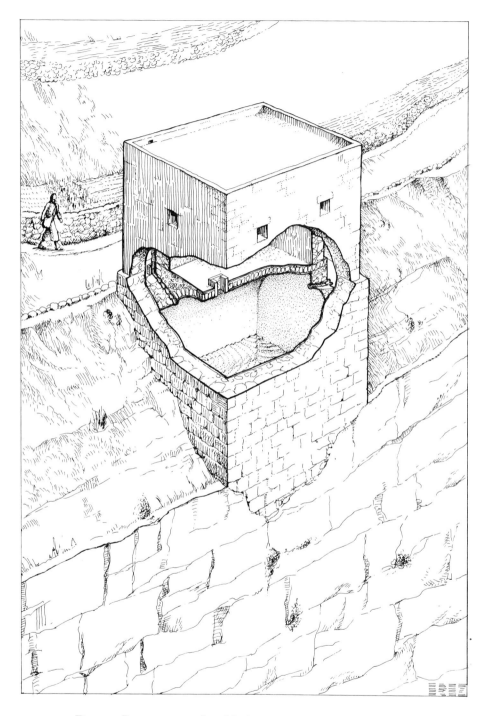

Figure 77 Reconstruction of a cell built over a cistern at the monastery of
Chariton

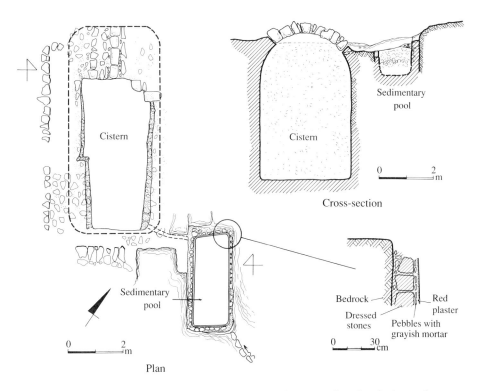

Figure 78 Plan and cross-section of the rectangular cistern found at the laura of
Heptastomos

monks had two sedimentary pools, a larger one to trap stones and coarse silt
and a smaller one in front of the intake opening of the cistern to catch finer par-
ticles from the surface. An example of this arrangement is the cistern preserved
at the center of the monastic remains at Khirbet ed-Deir (fig. 79). It is fed by a
long channel bringing water from the gully next to the monastery. At the end of
the channel is a large, well-preserved sedimentary pool (3 × 1.5 m). The water
overflowed from the large sedimentary pool into a smaller one below it, next to
the cistern (fig. 80).

When the rain was so heavy that the water filled the cisterns and reservoirs
to overflowing, outlets for the excess water were necessary. Such outlets can be
found in all the cisterns and reservoirs of Judean desert monasteries. At Khirbet
ed-Deir, the outlet is visible on the side of the cistern. Beneath the outlet, a
channel was carved into the rock to receive the overflow and to direct it from
the cistern to the garden below the monastery. A similar arrangement is found
in many other monasteries, such as that of Chariton.

The builders of the cisterns and reservoirs of the monasteries showed great
ingenuity both in choosing sites and in building techniques. At Khirbet ed-Deir,

Figure 79 Central cistern at Khirbet ed-Deir

a second large cistern was built in the bedrock foundation of the cave church for the monks living in the tower above the cave. The monks did not hesitate to place the cistern under the tower, even though its mouth marred the fine mosaic in the eastern part of the church.

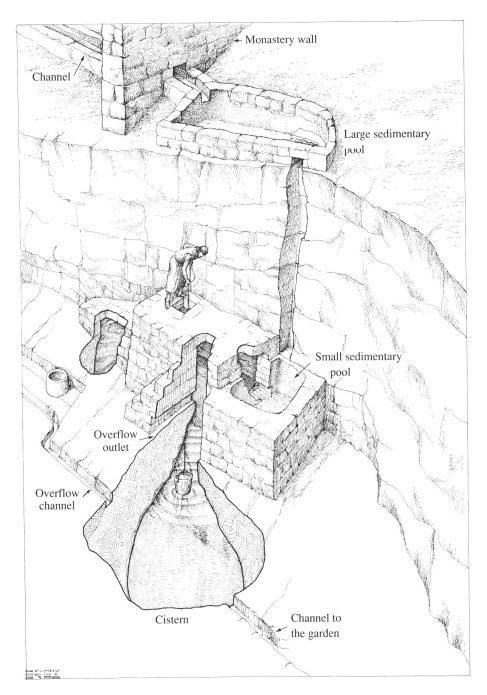

Channel

Monastery wall

Large sedimentary pool

Small sedimentary pool

Overflow outlet

Overflow channel

Cistern

Channel to the garden

Figure 80 Reconstruction of the central cistern at Khirbet ed-Deir

Of course, the greater the capacity of the cistern, the greater the quantity of water available to the occupants of the monastery. On the other hand, the larger the cistern, the harder it was to build a roof over it. Builders could not use wooden beams because of the problem of evaporation, which would rot the wood. In places where the rock strata permitted it, they preferred to use the natural rock as a roof, as in the case of the large reservoir of the Nea Laura (total capacity of at least 370 m³) which was carved out of a soft limestone stratum beneath a hard limestone crust. The rock ceiling of the reservoir, which is more than 2 m thick, has remained intact to this day.

Transverse arches, usually built of conical stones, were frequently employed as supports, and dressed stone beams were laid between the arches to form a ceiling. This technique was used in building the cistern beneath the central courtyard of the monastery at Khirbet el-Quneitira.[9] The interior of this cistern has been preserved in its entirety (fig. 81). The stone beams of the ceiling are supported by three hewn stone arches, whose bases rest on small shelves specially carved in the bedrock for that purpose. The arches, like the walls of the cistern, are coated with waterproof plaster. Above the stone beams of the ceiling is the mosaic pavement of the monastery courtyard. Another example of the use of arches to support a roof is the round cistern of the laura of Heptastomos (fig. 82).

The size and complexity of the water system depended largely on the size of the monastery. In smaller monasteries, one or two cisterns were usually built, generally beneath the courtyard, while in larger monasteries, complex, sophisticated water systems are often found. One of the most impressive examples, in terms of both size and planning, is at the monastery of Martyrius. According to the excavators, this was a well-planned water system designed for maximal storage of rainwater; they estimate that 20,000 m³ of water could have been stored within the monastery.[10] That enormous quantity was collected in two ways: by draining the courtyards and roofs of the buildings using gutters and by draining the ridge west of the monastery using a long canal.

Outside the monastery walls, the canal was dug into the ground, but within the monastery it was an underground masonry channel roofed with stone slabs. Along its path were vertical slits for raising and lowering a wooden plank, thereby affording control over the flow. When one cistern filled up, this barrier could be opened to permit the water to flow on to the second cistern.

The first cistern was just outside the western wall of the monastery. The canal then cut through the foundations of the wall and led directly to a second reservoir, built beneath the courtyard of the living quarters. This reservoir is 22 m long, 14 m wide, and at present 10 m deep; originally, before sediment accumulated in it, it was deeper. The excavators estimate that the capacity of

Figure 81 Interior of the central cistern at Khirbet el-Quneitira

this cistern was once about 3,000 m³. The walls were built of fieldstone and were coated with thick layers of waterproof plaster. The vaulted ceiling was supported by massive stone piers and was equipped with four square openings for drawing water. The canal continued past this cistern and fed another two cisterns close to the church compound. In addition, two huge cisterns were found close to the monastery's northern wall, and a number of other cisterns irrigated the gardens near the monastery.

Sometimes, the reservoirs were adorned with crosses, as at the monastery of Chariton.[11] On the eastern wall of the reservoir, 1.6 m beneath the apex of the vaults, are two embossed crosses, surrounded by medallions 1.3 m in diameter. Both the crosses and the medallions are painted red (see fig. 33 in ch. 2).

A similar cross-and-medallion decoration was found in the Byzantine reservoir beneath the Church of the Holy Sepulchre in Jerusalem, next to a Greek inscription that reads: "The voice of the Lord is upon the waters" (Ps. 29:3). Several crosses and the same quotation in Syriac were found in one of the cisterns of the laura of Firminus.[12] However, the most important parallel for our

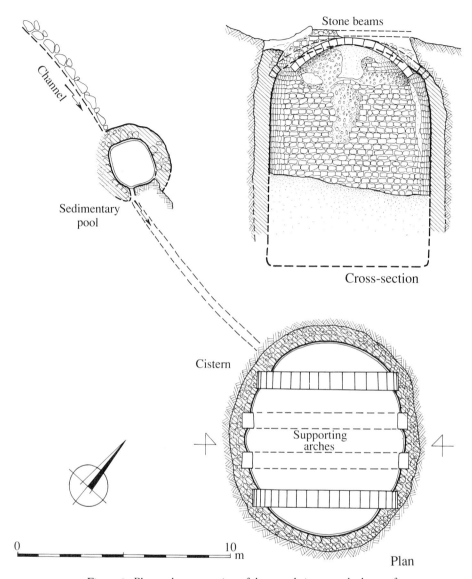

Figure 82 Plan and cross-section of the round cistern at the laura of
Heptastomos

purposes is the cross and inscription discovered in the huge reservoir beneath
the annex of the Nea Church in Jerusalem.[13] In the dedicatory inscription above
the cross, the emperor Justinian is mentioned as having assisted the construction
project.

Some of the more sophisticated water systems were designed for flood control as well as water collection and storage. One such system was found at
Khirbet ed-Deir. The bulk of the monastery's water supply came from the drain-

age of floodwaters flowing through the gully next to the monastery. For that purpose, two channels were built, an upper one (350 m long) to carry water from the gully directly to the central cistern within the monastery and a lower one (220 m long) to carry water from the gully to the round cistern at the outlet of the canyon (see fig. 76). (The local Bedouin continue to use and to maintain this system.)

In addition, a large reservoir was created in a natural pool inside the canyon, which was dammed from one cliff to the other with a massive embankment 14 m long, 1.5 m wide, and 2.5 m high (fig. 83). The rock walls of the pool were carved out to make it wider and were coated with thick layers of waterproof plaster, thereby creating an open reservoir measuring 11 × 15 m, with an average depth of 2 m. The total capacity was therefore about 330 m³.

Besides being an important source of water for irrigation, the reservoir offered two other advantages. First, the dam built across the canyon was a defensive wall against floods, which could threaten the refectory building, whose southwestern corner projected into the canyon. Second, the bottom of the reservoir collected a considerable quantity of fertile alluvial soil, which could be spread in the garden. In this way the soil could be enriched and the crops improved.

This discussion of the water systems of Judean desert monasteries would not be complete without a description of the largest reservoir found in the region, about 800 m from the monastery of Theodosius.[14] The reservoir, known in Arabic as El-Birkeh ("The Pool"), is exceptional both in its dimensions and in the method used to construct it (fig. 84). Judging from the quality of the construction and the use of reddish waterproof plaster, the reservoir dates from the Byzantine period. Between the monastery and the reservoir is a well-worn path, which shows signs of digging and straightening. It would appear that the water was brought to the monastery by pack animals via this path. The builders of the monastery of Theodosius did not dig a reservoir within its confines, apparently because the work might endanger the burial cave in the center of the monastery.

The water of the U-shaped reservoir was intended to supply the needs of the largest monastic community in the Judean desert (as previously noted, as many as 400 monks lived in the monastery of Theodosius), hence its enormous dimensions: 30 m long, 14 m wide, and 8.5 m deep (fig. 85). To make it strong enough to withstand the water pressure, it was built with a broad base, 2.5 m wide, tapering to 1.9 m at the top. The capacity of the reservoir appears to have been about 4,000 m³.

The water was drained from the slope west of the reservoir by means of long canals. The reservoir was too large to permit a stone roof, and it seems that the monks covered it with perishable materials instead. A shelf of uniform-size

Figure 83 Open reservoir at Khirbet ed-Deir created by the dam at the left

Figure 84 Reservoir near the monastery of Theodosius (looking east). The recess in the wall is a prayer niche.

stones, 1.1 m wide, protrudes both inward and outward from the upper edge of the reservoir. A network of ropes may have been fastened by pegs to this shelf, and wicker mats may have been laid on it. This would have been the only way to prevent evaporation of the water, especially during the hot summer days.[15]

While we were investigating this reservoir, we found that the interior of the eastern wall contained a sizable prayer niche (1.6 m in diameter, 2.6 m tall). It was constructed with great care, like prayer niches in churches. Like the crosses decorating other monastery reservoirs in the Judean desert, the niche served as a sign that the reservoir, though distant from the monastery, belonged to that institution.

THE WALLS AND THE GATE-HOUSE

Walls and gate-houses are mentioned several times in the historical sources on the monasticism of the Judean desert, generally in reference to the coenobia.[16] Describing the conversion of the monastery of Euthymius from a laura to

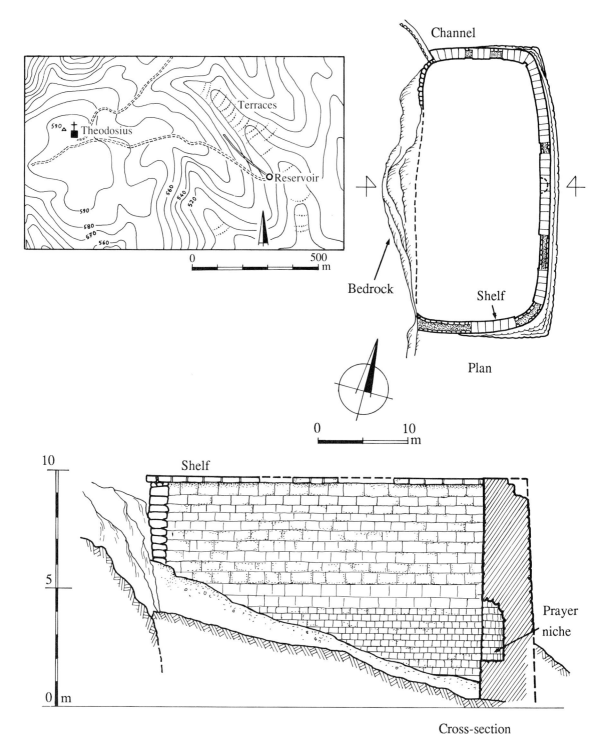

Channel

Bedrock

Shelf

Plan

Terraces

590△ ✝ Theodosius

Reservoir

0   500
                      m

0   10
                m

10

Shelf

5

0 m

Prayer
niche

Cross-section

Figure 85 Location, plan, and cross-section of the reservoir found near the
monastery of Theodosius

a coenobium, Cyril mentions the building of a wall (*V. Euth.* 43, 64. 17). The monastery of Choziba had a double gate, as we learn from Anthony's story of the robbers who entered through the outer gate and reached the "second, inner gate." It also had a side gate, a posternlike entrance used for unloading freight.[17] One of the monks was assigned the post of gatekeeper and lived in a cell near the gate.[18] During the night, the gate was barred, and nobody was permitted to come in or go out, except in special cases (*V. Geor.* 28, 126. 8–9). In the daytime, the bolt or barrier was removed, but the door was rarely left open, and it was the gatekeeper's task to monitor entry. When young George came back half-naked from the stream where he had been sent to draw water, he had to knock at the door, and the gatekeeper admitted him only after he had explained his plight and had received decent clothes (*V. Geor.* 4, 100. 3–6). The gatekeeper was probably also expected to check that monks going out of the monastery, even during the day, had permission from the abbot. (Incidentally, a closed, though unlocked, door was also the rule for hermits living in caves.)[19]

The gate-house and the area in front of the gate had special importance as "social" places: visitors and purveyors would wait there for permission to enter or to unload their goods. The monks would come out to meet female visitors, who were not allowed into the monastery, or to help the drivers unload. Sometimes they simply sat there doing manual work and conversing with each other.[20]

The effort invested in building the walls and the gates of monasteries is very evident at the monastery of Martyrius. The compound is surrounded by a massive stone wall (0.8 m thick) built of hewn stones. The wall has been preserved to a height of 1–2 m, though its original height is estimated to have been 4–5 m.[21] The monastery gates were placed in the eastern wall. The excavators believe that the southernmost gate, which is about 2 m wide, was sealed at some point in the monastery's history. Thus the northern gate, which is 1.8 m wide, remained the main entrance. In front of the gate was an area paved in stone, flanked by benches installed for the convenience of those arriving. The threshold and doorposts of the opening contain slits and hinge sockets for gates, which were apparently made of wood and iron. In addition, a round stone, used to block the gateway for extra security in times of danger, was found in situ.

Several examples from the Judean desert and beyond show that the habit of blocking the entrance with a round stone was not unknown in the monasteries of Byzantine Palestine. Round stones were found, for example, at Khirbet Bureikut and at the Khirbet ed-Deir west of Hebron (not to be confused with the site of the same name in Wadi el-Ghar).[22]

An interior passageway (8.4 × 3.8 m) extends from the threshold of the monastery of Martyrius; the passageway is lined with water troughs for cattle.

South of the passageway—that is, to the left of the entrance—was the gate-keeper's cell (4 × 4.5 m). Just west of the cell was a smaller room, which, in the opinion of the excavators, was where the grooms and servants of visitors to the monastery would rest.[23] At the end of the passageway is a stone bench decorated with an embossed cross. The excavators believe that this bench was for another gatekeeper, who was positioned to prevent animals or strangers from penetrating the living quarters of the monastery. If this assumption is correct, then the monastery of Martyrius had two gates: the outer gate described above and an inner gate in front of the entrance to the church and the interior of the monastery.[24]

The monastery of Theoctistus also has two gates. The monastery is a coenobium of the cliff type, and its external gate-house was built close to the cliff face (see fig. 14). It consists of two long, parallel wings, separated by a passage 2.5 m wide. The gate of the monastery is at the western end of the passageway. The southern wing is long and narrow (3 × 8.6 m), and its walls are built on the edge of the cliff. The northern wing is built against the cliff. It is 8.5 m long and ranges in width from 3 to 6 m (depending on the cliff face behind it). Judging from the thickness of the walls of the gate-house (0.8 m) and the character of its construction, it seems likely that it was two stories high. If so, the second story was probably built over the passageway. Thus, the area of the second floor would have been larger than that of the two wings, and the entrance passage would have been roofed, shaded, and well protected.

The inner gate of the monastery of Theoctistus was installed about 18 m to the east. Between the gates an open courtyard was built. This square, which was bordered on the southern side by the living quarters and on the northern side by a vertical cliff (which contained a large cave), was used as a place for unloading pack animals and other such activities. The bad preservation of the inner gate deprives us of any further details.

A clearer picture can be obtained from a similar gate-house at Khirbet ed-Deir (fig. 86). From the outer entrance, a long passageway (21 × 2.3 m) leads to an area in front of the inner gate.

The gate-house of the present-day monastery of Choziba (St. George's Monastery) is also a two-story structure, with one side leaning against the cliff face (fig. 87). In front of it is a paved courtyard, and beyond it a roofed passageway leads to a large inner courtyard. In the rear of the courtyard stands the inner gate of the monastery. Adjacent to the cliff is a stairway leading up to the residential quarters and various service rooms. The gate-house of this monastery, like the entire monastery, is what can be termed "living archaeology," an extraordinary illustration of what gate-houses of cliff-type coenobia must have looked like during the Byzantine period.

Figure 86 Stairway between the outer and inner gates at Khirbet ed-Deir
(looking west)

The only ancient gate discovered in a laura is the "Byzantine gate" of the laura of Marda, on Masada.[25] The gate is built of recycled hewn stones, and the lintel is arched. It stands at the end of a paved path, opposite the monastery church. According to the excavators, there are signs of partial renovation of the Herodian wall in the Byzantine period. This suggests that the function of the gate and the restored wall was to indicate the boundaries of the laura. But they may also have served to keep the hermits away from the edge of the cliff.

The two present-day gates of the Cells of Choziba, about 2 km from the monastery of Choziba, give an indication of the appearance of the gates of a Byzantine laura (fig. 88). The Cells were resettled by Greek monks toward the end of the nineteenth century. The desire of the monks to preserve the original edifices and the minimal means they used to restore them have safeguarded the Byzantine character of the site. They built both gates of recycled stones, with arches similar to the arched gate on Masada. The function of the two gates is to demarcate the area of the Cells of Choziba.

Figure 87 Present-day gate-house at the monastery of Choziba (St. George's Monastery; looking east, from the inner courtyard)

THE COURTYARD

The courtyard, generally placed in front of the entrance facade of the church, was a regular feature of both lauras and coenobia. It provided a focal point and served as a gathering place before various ceremonies or during the monks' leisure time. It also had an important architectural function, as a source of light and air for the surrounding buildings of the monastery.[26] The Great Laura's "inner courtyard," as Cyril calls it, was built between the two central churches of the laura (*V. Sab.* 82, 187. 17) and is used to this day by both the monks of the laura and visitors.

The courtyard of the monastery of Choziba is mentioned several times in Anthony's work. Situated at the end of a passageway leading to the interior of the monastery, it was a place where the monks would gather and rest and was accordingly equipped with stone benches. When Epiphanius, one of the

Figure 88 Eastern gate of the Cells of Choziba (looking southwest)

monks of Choziba, was a young man, he would test his asceticism by sleeping on one of the benches, apparently facing the grave of the five Syrian saints who constituted the original nucleus of the monastery.[27]

The shape and dimensions of the courtyard varied from monastery to monastery. Typical of large courtyards is the one discovered at the monastery of Martyrius, which was 43 m long and 30 m wide. It was enclosed by the refectory to the north, the living quarters to the south, and the monastery wall to the west. In addition to this central courtyard, the monastery had other, smaller courtyards in its wings. The courtyards of the monastery were paved with polished stone slabs, as was commonly the case in monasteries in the Judean desert. However, the use of mosaics to pave courtyards was not unknown. The interior courtyard at Khirbet el-Quneitira, for example, was paved with mosaics.[28]

In coenobia of the level type, the courtyards are notably regular—for example, the courtyard of the monastery of Castellion, which measures 8 × 17 m. The courtyards of coenobia of the cliff type, by contrast, are characteristically irregular—for example, the courtyard of the monastery of Severianus,[29] which measures 16 × 12 m and is contoured to the edges of the cliff on which the monastery was erected (fig. 89). Its surface is paved with polished stone slabs, beneath which lies the central cistern, a common feature of monastery courtyards. Toward the east, the courtyard remained open to the landscape of the Judean desert (fig. 90).

In lauras, the courtyard in front of the entrance to the church had particular importance. The monks would gather there before and after the weekend prayer services. In the Great Laura, the courtyard was placed between the cave church, to the northwest, and the Church of the Virgin Mary, to the east. It was spacious, and Sabas's tomb was in the center.

The Great Laura has undergone many changes since the Byzantine period. Hence it is difficult to discern the original plan of its various components, including the courtyard. We have good information, however, about the church courtyards of the two lauras that were influenced by the Great Laura. One of these is the Nea Laura, which was established by Sabas himself; the second is the laura founded by Firminus, a disciple of Sabas. On both sites, efforts were made to expand the courtyard in front of the church of the laura.

The church of the Nea Laura stands on a natural stone ledge in the center of the laura (fig. 91). The remains at the site indicate that the builders of the church took care to level and expand the area of the ledge in front of the church, by means of massive retaining walls, totalling about 30 m in length and ranging from 1.2 to 3.1 m in width. A cautious estimate of the size of the courtyard is about 200 m². In that open area, overlooking the impressive landscape of Wadi Jihar, the monks could gather before or after prayers.

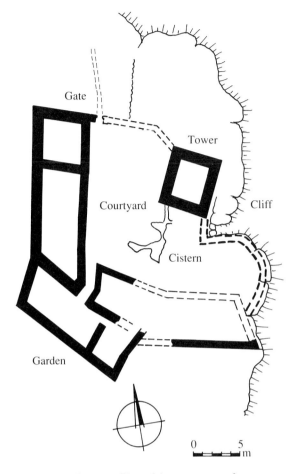

Figure 89 Plan of the monastery of
Severianus, showing the irregular shape
of the courtyard

The remains of the church courtyard at the laura of Firminus are relatively
well preserved. The courtyard is integrated into the complex of the church and
its adjacent rooms. In order to expand the courtyard, a large retaining wall, 31 m
long, 1.2–1.5 m thick, and 2–3 m high, was built along the edge of the cliff. A
large cistern was dug in the center of the courtyard. The total area of the courtyard came to 185 m^2, about 35 percent of the total area of the church compound.
The south side remained open to the splendid landscape of Wadi Suweinit. The
church was built to the north of it, and the various annexes to the east and the
west. This architectural design lent intimacy to the courtyard and provided a
barrier against the cold winter winds.

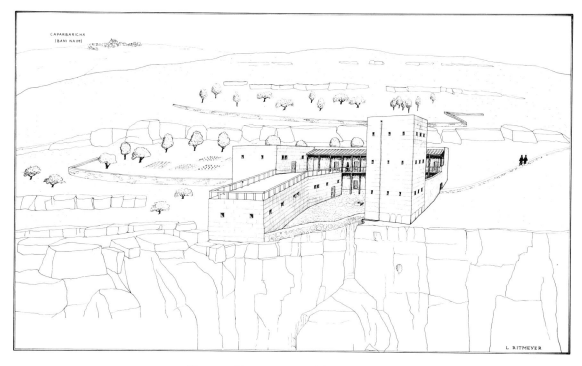

Figure 90 Reconstruction of the monastery of Severianus

Figure 91 Plan and cross-section
of the church complex of the
Nea Laura

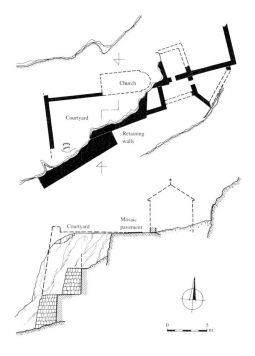

THE TOWER

Towers were a common feature of monasteries in the Judean desert. Their presence is attested in the literary sources as well as in the archaeological findings. They are notable for their simple plan, the thickness of their walls, and their strategic location at the highest point of the monastery or in a place over-looking the entrance gate. Nevertheless, the written sources, as well as the material evidence, indicate that the functions of towers were varied and that their location varied accordingly. Presumably, the structure and dimensions of the towers also varied according to their purpose in the monastic complex.

The sources allude to dwelling towers and to border towers, the latter having the function of defining boundaries of the monastery. There is no ex-plicit mention, however, of what must have been the most important reason for building towers—namely, defense—although Cyril remarks on the "strength" of the tower built at the center of the monastery of Euthymius (*V. Euth.* 43, 64. 20). But it is well known that monks were exposed to attacks by bands of Sara-cens or prowling brigands, especially in times of war and political unrest, and that they required military protection or protected themselves by gathering at such times in monasteries that were not too isolated and were better defended.[30]

It seems a fair inference, therefore, that the towers, whose remains can be observed in many monasteries in the Judean desert, served as a refuge. It is not clear, however, whether this use developed in response to circumstances, as an extension and adaptation of the dwelling tower, or whether the structure of the towers was in fact influenced by military architecture.[31] Nevertheless, there is no evidence to support the proposition that desert monasteries in the Byzan-tine period played a role in the defense of the border area against attacks by nomads.[32]

One of the first towers mentioned in the sources is that built by the empress Eudocia on the highest peak in the Judean desert as the venue for her meeting with Euthymius. It was later inhabited by successive groups of two or three monks and in Sabas's time was used as the core of the monastery of Scholarius.[33] The monastery of Theognius was apparently erected around a small tower, which was inhabited by its founder and his first disciples (Paul. El., *V. Theog.* 9, 88. 8). In these cases, then, the tower was the embryo of the monastery.

An example of such growth, starting with a tower, can be seen at Khirbet ed-Deir. The upper tower is situated at the top of the hill, east of the block of buildings that were used as the living quarters. It is nearly square, measuring 5.5 × 6 m, with walls that are 1.1 m thick, made of carefully dressed hewn stones and preserved to a height of about 0.8 m. The orientation of the walls is different from that of the monastery adjacent to it. There is also a "seam" (a separation between two walls), indicating a chronological gap between the building of the tower and that of the monastery complex. It appears that the tower was built first and that the other parts of the monastery, including another tower in a lower level, were added at a later stage.

The lower tower at Khirbet ed-Deir stands at the edge of the cliff, above the cave church and overlooking the entrance gate. Unlike the upper tower, it was built during the main phase of construction of the monastery. It is nearly square, measuring 4.9 × 5.1 m, and its walls are about 1 m thick. The walls have been preserved to a height of 2.5 m, but it seems likely that they were originally at least twice that height. According to the proposed reconstruction, it would seem that the tower had at least two stories (fig. 92). The builders of the tower dug a cistern beneath the floor of the church and cut a shaft through the ceiling of the church and the floor of the tower. In that way, monks dwelling in the tower could draw water directly from the cistern. The placement of the tower and its relation to the cave church are highly reminiscent of the description of the tower in which Sabas lived in the Great Laura (see below), and it is possible

Figure 92 Reconstruction (cross-section) of the lower tower at Khirbet ed-Deir (looking east)

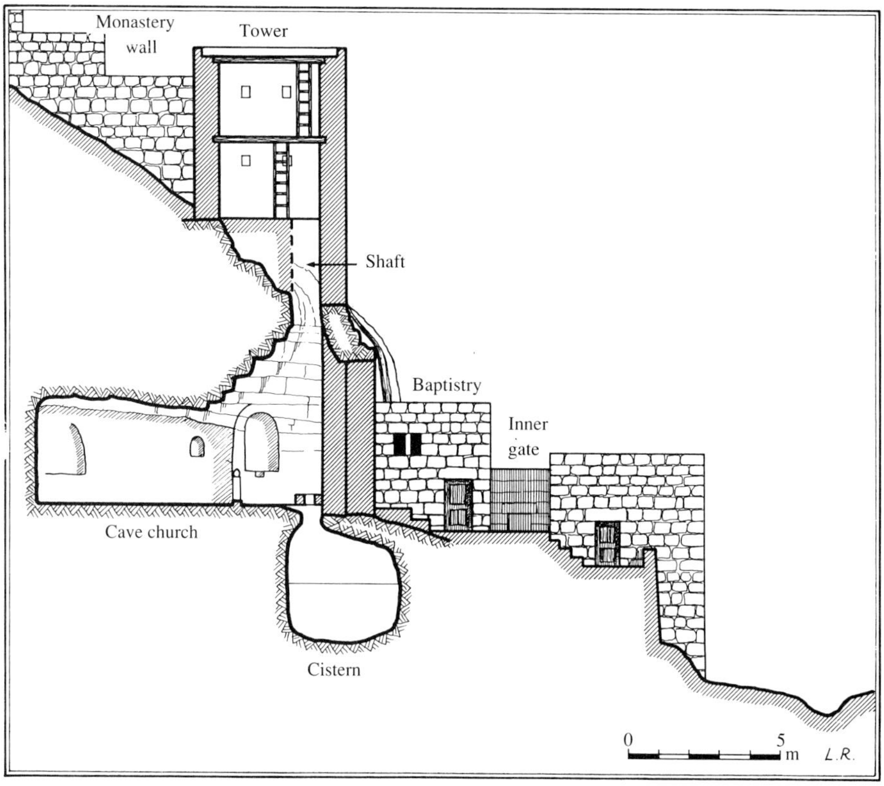

that this tower served as the dwelling place of the abbots of the monastery at Khirbet ed-Deir.

At the center of the Great Laura, above the cave church, Sabas built a tower that functioned as his cell (*V. Sab.* 18, 102. 25). But the foremost example of the adaptation of a tower as a dwelling unit to the lauritic way of life is known only from the sources. Moschus notes that the laura of the Towers owed its name to the fact that its cells were towerlike.[34] These cells may have been two or even three stories high, in contrast to the simpler cells in other lauras, which had only a single story.

As already mentioned, another function of the tower in a monastery was to demarcate its boundaries. According to Cyril, the construction of the Great Laura began with the erection of a tower on a high hill at the northern extremity of the ravine, in order to establish the monks' claim to the area within (*V. Sab.* 16, 100. 8). The remains of that tower were indeed found at the northern end of the canyon.[35] However, their poor state of preservation prevents any reconstruction of its plan.

We do have detailed information about the tower at the laura of Firminus, however. That structure stands at the western end of the monastery, and its purpose was to mark the boundary of the land belonging to the laura.[36] Great skill and care went into the construction of the tower, and well-dressed hewn stones were used. The building is nearly square, measuring 8.6 × 9.4 m, with walls that are 0.8 m thick (fig. 93). The entrance, facing south, is 1.1 m wide and has indentations indicating that it held a wooden door. The tower is divided into four rooms, two on the east side and two on the west, and, judging from the quality of the construction, it was at least two stories high. There is a cistern nearby, which was apparently used by the monk who lived in the tower during the Byzantine period. Owing to its location at the beginning of the canyon section of Wadi Suweinit, the tower is particularly prominent. It marks the beginning of the path leading to the center of the laura. These characteristics are also features of Sabas's tower.

According to Cyril's description of the monastery of Euthymius, there was one tower inside the monastery and another outside it (*V. Euth.* 43, 65. 3). Remains of the external tower were found about 180 m to the northwest, at a site called Qasr el-Khan.[37] It seems likely that in this case as well, the function of the tower was to mark the boundary of the monastery and its holdings. This theory is supported by Cyril's report that Paul, abbot of the monastery of Theoctistus, fenced in his monastery's lands after they were separated from those of the monastery of Euthymius and built a tower overlooking them (*V. Cyr.* 7, 226. 14).

The main function of the tower, however, was probably as a place of refuge for the monks.[38] As we have already seen, in writing about the conversion of the

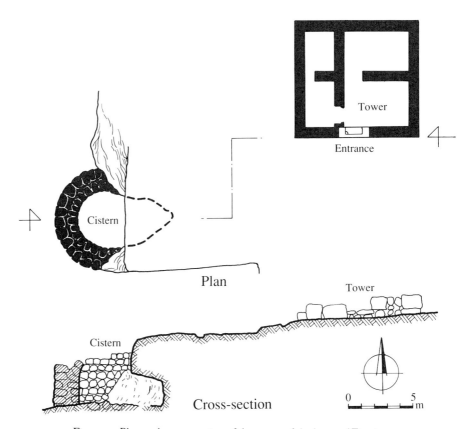

Figure 93 Plan and cross-section of the tower of the laura of Firminus

laura of Euthymius to a coenobium, Cyril emphasizes the strength and beauty of its tower and gives an indication of its importance in the architecture of the monastery (*V. Euth.* 43, 64. 19–20). In excavations that I conducted in the northern wing of the monastery, a towerlike structure was exposed. This structure was rebuilt in the early Muslim period, but its foundations appear to date back to the Byzantine period.

One of the common characteristics of monastery towers is their position next to the entrance gate, as can be seen in figure 94, which is a comparative chart of towers. (See also table 6.) The presence of a tower and its location near the gate reflect the influence of military planning on the design of monasteries.[39] This influence was purely architectural, however, and did not extend to functional matters, since monks never bore arms and were not permitted to defend their monasteries by force. One example is the tower of Khirbet el-Quneitira. The tower, whose external dimensions are 16.2 × 18 m, was placed at a point that afforded a commanding view of the two gates of the monastery (see fig. 24

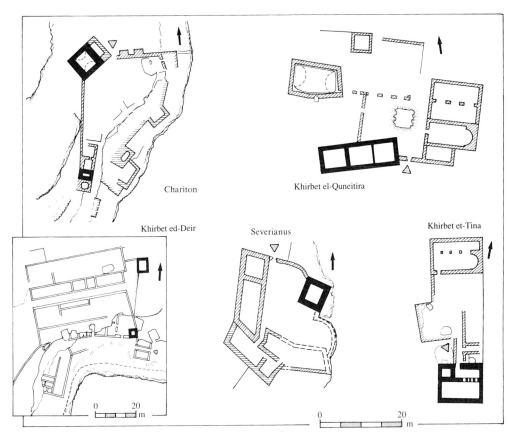

Figure 94 Comparative chart of locations of towers in Judean desert
monasteries

in ch. 1). Its interior is divided into a central hall and a room adjoining it to
the west; judging from the quantity of fallen stones around the tower, it was
probably two or three stories high.

A tower with a unique feature was found at Khirbet et-Tina. The wall dividing the two rooms that make up the interior of the tower contains four interior
windows, 0.6 m wide and 0.7 m high. This architectural element is known in
various places in Syria and Palestine as a provision for feeding troughs for animals (so that they could eat from both sides). Thus, one of the functions of the
ground floor of this tower may have been to house animals. In addition, a cistern
was discovered within the foundations of the tower. It measures 2.5 × 2.5 m (its
depth being unknown because the bottom is full of debris). Judging from the
thickness of the tower's wall (1 m) and its construction of large hewn stones,
the tower was three stories high.

TABLE 6
Towers in Judean desert monasteries

Name of Monastery	Outer Dimensions (m)	Thickness of walls (m)	Interior Division	Cistern	Location Near Gate	Boundary Function	Comments
Khirbet ed-Deir							
upper tower	5.5 × 6	1.1	no	no	no	yes	
lower tower	4.9 × 5.1	1	no	yes	yes	no	Passage to cave church below
Firminus	8.6 ×9.4	0.8	yes	yes	no	yes	
Euthymius	10.5 × 10.5	1.1	yes	no	yes	no	Early Muslim period
Khirbet el-Quneitira	16.2 ×18	1	yes	no	yes	no	
Khirbet et-Tina	9.8 × 11.4	1	yes	yes	yes	no	Stable on ground floor
Severianus	5.8 ×6.4	0.9	no	yes	yes	no	
Chariton							
northern tower	11.4 × 11.4	1.2	yes	yes	yes	yes	Early Muslim
southern tower	4.4 × 6	2	no	yes	yes	no	period. Remains of a chapel in the northern tower

THE CELLS

In discussing the cells in Judean desert monasteries, a clear distinction must be made between lauras and coenobia. In contrast to the plentiful details available on the cells of lauras, we have little information about the cells of coenobia. One reason for this lack of knowledge is the fact that in the large coenobia, such as the monastery of Martyrius, the cells were built on the second floor, of which nothing remains. The existence of second-floor living quarters is attested by the stairways found on the site. In some of the smaller monasteries, such as the monastery of Gabriel, the second story was also used for the monks' living quarters. One of Moschus's stories mentions a monk who could see what was happening inside the church from his window.[40] His cell was probably situated at the height of the church windows, which were generally on the second floor (though it is possible that the interior of the church was visible through the doorway or a lower row of windows).

To date, the remains of cells have been found in only two coenobia, Khirbet et-Tina and Khirbet ed-Deir. Those found at Khirbet et-Tina were part of the wing used for living quarters,[41] which encloses the monastery courtyard to the

east. A small excavation carried out at its southern end, next to the tower, revealed two cells, whose entrances face the courtyard (fig. 95). The southernmost
cell is well preserved. It is 3.3 m long and only 2.2 m wide (interior dimensions);
hence the area in which the monk lived was 7.2 m^2 (like the smallest cells of the
lauras). On the basis of these measurements (and assuming that their dimensions were more or less uniform), another six cells can be reconstructed in the
living quarters of the monastery of Khirbet et-Tina (fig. 96). Assuming that
the residential wing was two stories high, this would mean that the monastic
community probably numbered not more than twenty monks.

Since the upper story of the monastery at Khirbet et-Tina is not preserved,
it is not clear whether the monks lived in common dormitories (as required by
Justinian's code for monastic life) or in separate cells. But the two arrangements
seem to have coexisted, at least in the coenobia of the Judean desert.

The cell found at Khirbet ed-Deir was in the corner of a stable and was
probably inhabited by the monk in charge of the stable; its modest dimensions
(2 × 3.5 m) reflect the monks' simple life. Nevertheless, the ordinary monks of
the community at Khirbet ed-Deir lived in dormitories in the upper parts of the
monastery (which are badly preserved).

The laura cells pose no such enigma, thanks to an ample supply of archaeological and historical evidence. Usually a cell was occupied by a single monk.[42]
And even where we have evidence of two or more monks living in the same
space, like the brothers Zannos and Benjamin at the Great Laura or George of
Choziba and his brother Heraclides, who lived together in the "Old Church"

Figure 95 Plan of Khirbet et-Tina

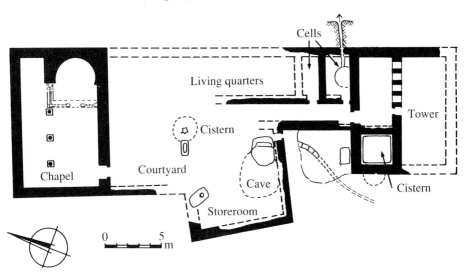

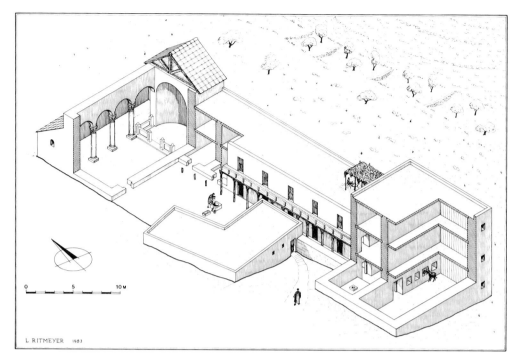

0   5   10 M

L. RITMEYER 1983

Figure 96 Reconstruction of Khirbet et-Tina

of the laura of Calamon, it seems that they lived next door to one another in dwelling complexes with more than one room.[43]

The cell belonged to the laura or to the community in the case of the coenobium but was given to the monk for his lifetime. In the collection of laws of the Great Laura attributed to Sabas, it is stated explicitly that a monk has no right to bequeath his cell to another monk.[44] After a monk's death, his personal effects were transferred to the service building of the monastery, as Moschus mentions and his cell was cleared for another occupant.[45]

The monks' cells in the lauras of the Judean desert are different from each other in detail but similar in overall plan and in the features added to them, such as a cistern and a garden plot (fig. 97). Most of the cells were small, their internal area usually about 23 m². They generally had low ceilings, as in the case of Theognius's cell, of which his biographer writes: "Very small is the cell and it is so low, that when you enter it, if you do not take care, you will knock your head against the ceiling" (Paul. El., *V. Theog.* 10, 89. 7–10). Euthymius ordered that the cells of his laura at Mishor Adummim be built to modest and uncomfortable proportions.[46] Martyrius and Elias left the laura because their cells were too small. They probably did not leave for reasons of discomfort but

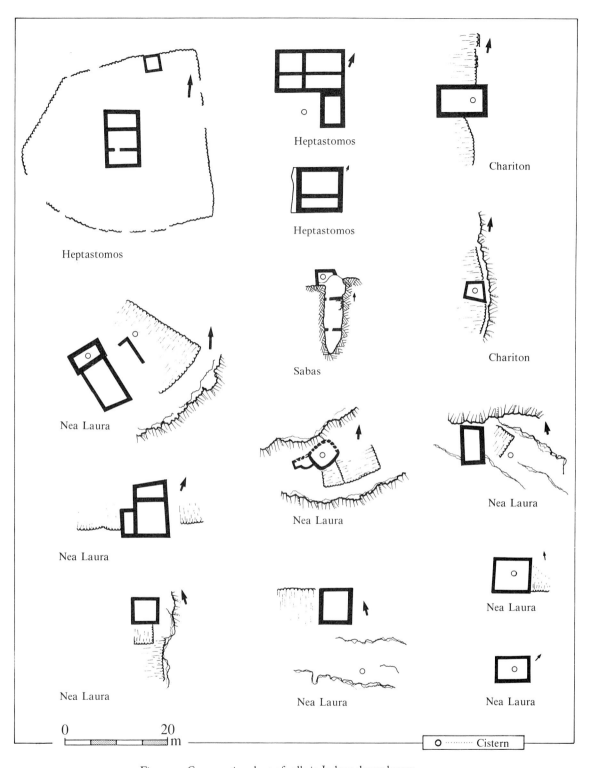

Heptastomos

Heptastomos

Heptastomos

Chariton

Chariton

Sabas

Nea Laura

Nea Laura

Nea Laura

Nea Laura

Nea Laura

Nea Laura

Nea Laura

Nea Laura

Nea Laura

0   20
                m

○ ········· Cistern

Figure 97 Comparative chart of cells in Judean desert lauras

rather because they conceived of the monk's cell as a place suitable for receiving visitors, as was the custom in the monasteries they knew in Egypt. Sabas, on the other hand, permitted monks with private means to build their own cells to their own specifications (*V. Sab.* 28, 113. 22). This might explain, to some extent, the exceptional dimensions and high quality of the relatively elaborate dwelling complexes surveyed at the Great Laura.

Archaeological research has found that the average distance from one lauritic cell to the next was about 35 m. But if remote cells are not taken into account, it emerges that the density was much greater. Sometimes the cells' garden plots even adjoined each other, as at the monastery of Chariton. Sometimes separation between cells was achieved not by distance but by using the steep slopes and the natural terraces of the cliffs, as in the Great Laura and the Nea Laura. In lauras of the level type, like the laura of Heptastomos, the cells were sometimes enclosed by a low fence marking the borders of each plot.

The monks of the Judean desert sometimes used caves and natural depressions in the rocks as lauritic cells. Such a cave dwelling was surveyed in the Great Laura. According to local tradition, the cave, which lies on the eastern bank of the Kidron valley, was Sabas's hermitage during his first years at the site.[47] It is 6 m long, 3.2 m wide, and an average of 2.5 m high. A small prayer niche is hewn in its eastern wall. Access to the cave is through a vertical shaft about 6 m above ground level. According to Cyril, Sabas used a rope to facilitate climbing (*V. Sab.* 15, 98. 17–18).

In the Jordan valley, much use was made of natural caves formed by the soft Lissan marl formation. Moschus refers to these as "the caves of the holy Jordan" (*Pratum* 10, 2860B). He tells of a monk living in a cave in the laura of Calamon who heard knocking at the door of his cave. When the monk looked through the window, he saw that the visitor was none other than a lion.[48] We learn from this story that the natural cave had been altered, and that windows had been carved out and a door inserted in the opening.

The cell-dwellers of the laura of Gerasimus were also known as "the Cave-Dwellers" (*V. Ger.* 7. 8); so at least some of the hermits of this laura apparently lived in caves and not in built cells. Their dwellings had doors, which they were instructed never to lock.

There were two types of caves in the Jordan valley: natural, almost untouched caves, used for seclusion, and artificial caves, carved out of the rock by the monks. A cave discovered at the laura of Calamon is an example of the first type (fig. 98). It is irregular in shape and large enough for only one occupant. Like Sabas's cave, it is the simplest type of dwelling, typical of the first stage of settlement in the laura.

A compound of four artificial caves was discovered in the laura of Gerasi-

Figure 98 Cave dwelling in the laura of Calamon (looking north)

mus.[49] These caves were carved in the southern cliff of Wadi en-Nukheil, which borders the laura to the north (fig. 99). The caves, as well as a small chapel carved out of the rock beside them, are all on the same level, about 7 m above the ground. The monks would climb down to the complex from the plain atop the cliff. In order to ease their descent, they built a retaining wall and two ledges, the western ledge 9 m long and the eastern one 8 m long, with a carved corridor connecting the two ledges (fig. 100). The remains of the wall can still be seen at the site.

The entrance to the first (and westernmost) cell, like the entrances to the other cells, requires a 90° turn, apparently to ensure privacy. The cell, 2.5 m long, 1.2 m wide, and 1.8 m high, has three small niches in its western wall.

The other three cells are on the eastern ledge. The second is irregular in shape, with a length of 4.3 m and a width of about 1 m. At the opening of the cell a cistern has been carved into the rock and lined with plaster. The cistern was fed by a canal bringing rainwater from the cliff. The third cell is rounded at the edges, 2.1 m long, 1.5 m wide, and reaches a height of 1.8 m. Its northern

Figure 99 Cave cells carved in a cliff at the laura of Gerasimus (looking south)

Figure 100 Corridor connecting the four cells found carved in the cliff at the
laura of Gerasimus (looking east)

wall has a small window overlooking the wadi (fig. 101). The fourth cell, at the eastern end of the complex, is 6 m long, and its ceiling is cracking.

Often masonry cells were built in front of caves. Cyril tells of Sabas allotting "a small cell and cave" to the monks when they joined the Great Laura.[50] From Cyril's writings, we know that John Hesychast's cell in the Great Laura was also in front of a cave in the cliff. It was covered by a small roof and had a window through which the other monks could speak with him and hand him his food (*V. John Hes.* 25, 220).

Several examples of cells in front of caves were surveyed in the Great Laura. One of the best preserved is the cell that, according to local tradition, was inhabited by Xenophon, who entered monastic life, together with his sons Arcadius and John, in the fifth century; cells said to have been his sons' are nearby.[51] Situated on the western bank of the Kidron valley, the cell is built on a natural shelf 35 m long and 3.5 m wide which protrudes from the middle of a steep cliff at a point about 20 m above ground level. Access is possible only via a rope ladder. The dwelling complex consists of a cave, a room that has been fabricated, a courtyard, a cistern, and a small garden plot (fig. 102). The cave is 3.25 m

Figure 101 Window in the third cell
of the complex found at
the laura of Gerasimus

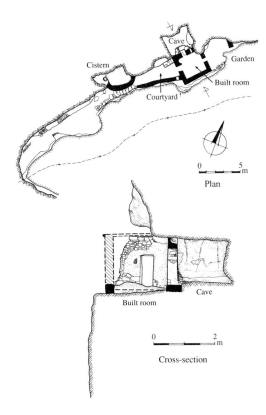

Figure 102 Plan and cross-section of
"Xenophon's cell" at the
Great Laura

long, 2.25 m wide, and 2.25 m high. Its opening is blocked by a nearly intact
wall, with an arched door and a small rectangular window. Inside the cave, to
the left of the entrance, is a low bench, built of stones and mortar, and to the
right are the remains of a wider platform, which was probably used as a bed.
The room in front of the cave is small (2.5 × 2.75 m). Its ceiling, which is no
more than 1.8 m high, is made of wooden beams, and its floors and walls, like
those of the cave, are plastered. A rectangular opening leads south to the courtyard, a narrow space 5.5 m long and 2.2 m wide. The courtyard, enclosed by a
built parapet, contains a bench carved in the cliff and a small cistern. The small
garden plot is located east of the cell.

A similar cell–cave combination can be found among the Cells of Choziba.[52]
The complex includes a cave, a room, and a small garden plot measuring about
30 m² (fig. 103).

But caves were not the most common form of dwelling in the lauras of the
Judean desert. Most of the cells were built of masonry and stood on their own,

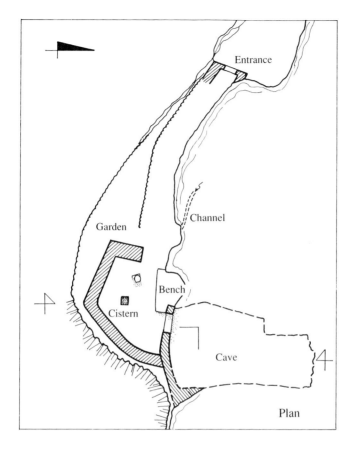

Entrance

Channel

Garden

Bench

Cistern

Cave

Plan

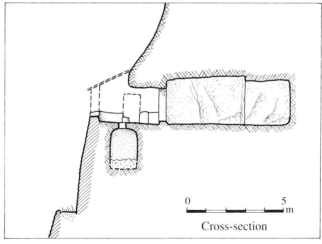

0   5
                m

Cross-section

Figure 103 Plan and cross-section of one of the
Cells of Choziba

without benefit of a cave or any other natural rock cover. On the Jericho plain,
cells were built of light materials and were roofed with wood, reeds, and mud.[53]
The above-mentioned cells of the laura of the Towers were apparently more
than one story tall and may therefore have been of a more solid construction.

More than forty well-preserved cells were found and surveyed in the Nea
Laura.[54] Most of them were equipped with water cisterns, which were dug beneath them, and small gardening plots.

Since the Nea Laura stands on cliffs that contain no caves, all its cells were
built without the aid of natural enclosures. Most are simple square or rectangular structures, but there were also larger, more elaborate cells—for example, a
three-room dwelling on the western slope of the laura (fig. 104). This cell consists of a square central room measuring 7.3 m per side (exterior measurements)
and two smaller adjacent rooms to the north and the west measuring approximately 2.5 × 5.5 m. It is flanked by garden terraces 15 m long. The area of the
garden was at least 40 m².

The practice of dividing a cell into two or three rooms is known from the
sources. For example, when Euthymius was angry, he is said to have shut himself off in the "inner cell"; and George of Choziba is known to have prayed in an
outer room, which he reached via a corridor from the interior part of the cell.[55]

In a survey of the Great Laura, about forty-five cells were documented.[56]
They included the usual simple cells consisting only of a cave or a combination
of a cave and a built cell and also some more imposing dwellings: cave–cell units
built on massive foundations, thereby allowing the cell to be unusually large.

Figure 104 Plan of a three-room cell in the Nea Laura

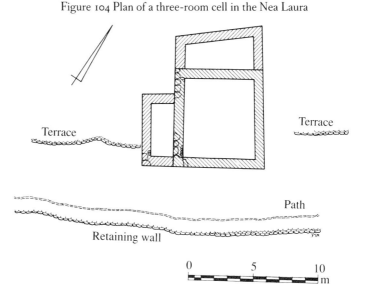

0   5   10
                          m

An example of such a cell is the one said to have been inhabited by Arcadius, son of Xenophon, which lies about 200 m southeast of Mar Saba. It is reached via a stairway to the east. The foundations of the cell are about 11 m high. It is rectangular, 8.2 m long and 4 m wide, and its walls have been preserved to a height of 10 m (fig. 105). A cistern with a capacity of about 20 m³ was installed below it. The walls of this room are 2 m thick, creating an interior space of about 18 m², and the ceiling is about 3 m high. The floor is of white mosaic.[57] The interior of the cave (13.5 × 5 m) is divided by two walls into three chambers: a living area, a prayer room, and a storeroom. The living area is almost square (3.5 × 4 m). Its floor is made of mosaic, and its walls and ceiling are coated with a thick layer of white plaster. A masonry bench attached to its eastern wall probably served as a bed. The prayer room occupied the inner section, which was larger (4 × 5 m), and the storeroom took up the remainder of the cave. Another cistern, with a capacity of about 5 m³, was installed beneath the floor of the storeroom.

Arcadius's cell illustrates the unusual size and quality of construction of the cells of the Great Laura. There are a number of possible explanations for this. First, some of the cells of the Great Laura may have been enlarged after the Arab conquests, so that their remains reflect later periods. Second, the monks of the Great Laura may have had private means not available to monks of other lauras. As mentioned before, Sabas encouraged his disciples to build their cells in the Great Laura at their own expense, and the quality of construction can probably be credited to professional builders and masons.

In addition to single-occupant cells, the Great Laura had complexes intended to house groups of monks. These complexes were even more elaborate and included a variety of architectural features. Some consisted of clusters of caves, with masonry rooms built on the rock shelf in front of them. Some were erected on gentle slopes, and others were built at several levels flush against the cliff face. These complexes probably housed groups of monks who had something in common over and above their commitment to monastic life—for example, an old monk and his disciples, blood brothers, or men of the same ethnic origin.[58] Each of the complexes was equipped with a water storage system; many had a small chapel, and they were all linked by paths and steps carved into the rock. Judging from the archaeological evidence, the builders of the complexes strove for separation and isolation: the cliffs they chose were usually difficult to climb, and stone fences were erected around some of the complexes.

The above descriptions of cells and dwelling complexes point to several components found in most of the cells. One such component was a cistern, to provide water for both drinking and irrigation. In many cases, the cistern was installed beneath the floor of the cell; but sometimes it was built near the cell, close to the garden plot, another common feature. The vegetable garden both

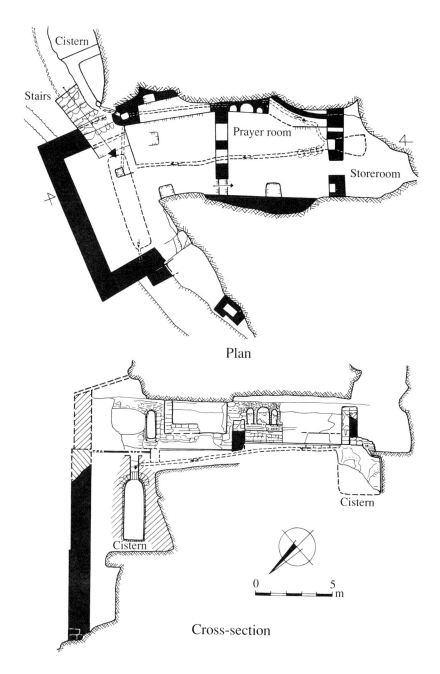

Figure 105 Plan and cross-section of Arcadius's cell in the Great Laura
(looking east)

enriched the monk's diet and satisfied the requirement for manual work found in monastic regulations. The size of the garden plot varied from 25 to 50 m². In some cases, mostly in lauras of the level type, the agricultural area was protected by a low fence made of fieldstones. But in lauras of the cliff type, the plot was usually laid out on a terrace built on the steep slope near the cell.

The doors and windows of the monks' dwellings were arranged with care, both in masonry-built cells and in caves, to ensure air and light while guarding privacy and allowing some degree of protection from strangers and animals. The sources indicate that the mouth of a hermit's cave was rarely left open and usually had a door of some sort. Many stories of anchorites begin with a visitor or a fellow hermit approaching a cave and knocking at the door with a pebble; once we are even told that this behavior was standard desert etiquette.[59]

Sockets for door hinges have been discovered in several hermit caves—for example, the hermitage near 'Ein er-Rashash in the northern part of the Judean desert. In caves where no such sockets have been found, it may be assumed that a movable partition or even a hanging mat answered the hermit's need to keep out uninvited guests.[60] Even the Senator's daughter, who lived in complete isolation for eighteen years, blocked the mouth of her cave with a screen of branches and dry shrubs (*De syn.* 2, 307. 6–8).

Cells in organized lauras, on the other hand, appear always to have had doors. In the laura of Gerasimus, the monks were forbidden to lock their doors (*V. Ger.* 4, 4), which shows that doors existed and were probably closed as a rule, though not locked. The entrances to rock-carved cells are small, and visitors had to bend down to enter. The same is true of the well-preserved main entrance of Xenophon's cell in the Great Laura, which is only 1.6 m high and 0.6 m wide.

The custom of keeping the door closed increased the need for windows to give air and light. Openings for windows were left in masonry walls or were carved out of the rock, whenever possible. They were generally small, as a protection against both the elements and wild animals. Windows found in the Great Laura and the laura of Gerasimus have an average size of about 20 × 40 cm. Sometimes the windows were equipped with a wooden shutter, as in John Hesychast's cell in the Great Laura.[61] A carved window in the laura of Gerasimus has a hewn socket on its inside edge, possibly intended to fit a wooden shutter or a mat stretched on a frame.

The interior of the cell was simple and included only the barest necessities. The floor was built solidly to prevent dampness. In some cases, a plain white mosaic floor was installed. In most cells, as in those of the laura near 'Ein el-Fawwar, floors made of stone slabs have been found. White plaster was used to coat the floor, the walls, and, in the case of a cave cell, the ceiling as well. The ceilings of built cells were made of wooden beams and branches, covered with mortar. The remains of ceiling beams have been found in "Xenophon's cell" in the Great Laura.

A usual feature of a cell was a bench, made of stones and mortar and usually attached to one of the walls. Sometimes a second bench was found in the front courtyard. In some cells, remains of a stone couch have been discovered, though most items of furniture were made of a light material that disintegrated over the centuries. A hole was found cut through a protrusion in the ceiling of a cell in the laura of Firminus. It probably served as the fixture for a rope that held the hermit in a sitting position while he slept, a practice mentioned in the sources. Occasionally an indentation for a jar of water can be found in the floor, as at the hermitage near 'Ein er-Rashash. Small recesses for oil lamps have also been found.

Prayer niches were found in many cells in the Great Laura, and it may be assumed that each cell had its own prayer room.

These features indicate that each cell in the lauras of the Judean desert functioned as a separate unit, like a monastery within a monastery. Life in such a "microcosm" was considered the highest form of monastic life by monks of the Judean desert and beyond.

THE REFECTORY AND THE KITCHEN

The written sources mention refectories only in coenobia, and the archaeological finds do not indicate their existence in lauras. Indeed, one of the expressions of the communal life of coenobites was the common meal in which most of the residents of the monastery would partake at least once a day. In Cyril's description of the conversion of the laura of Euthymius to a coenobium, the refectory is listed, together with the wall, the tower, and a new church, as part of the construction project (*V. Euth.* 34, 64. 18). The monastery, it seems, had no refectory when it was a laura, although the cell-dwellers had meals in common. Special feasts were celebrated in the lauras, and a common meal after Mass on Sundays appears to have been customary.[62] We do not know where the meal was served, however. It may have been in the diaconicon, in the church itself, or in the adjacent courtyard—a venue that was suitable all year round in the desert. Since the fare would have been very simple, there would have been no need for tables. It is possible, too, that the largest lauras had a common room, which could also have been used for dining, although none is mentioned in the sources.

No kitchen is mentioned in connection with the lauras themselves. However, there was a kitchen in the hospice of the Great Laura, apparently for the use of guests and construction workers,[63] and this kitchen may have served the monks on weekends. Moreover, some simple cooking could have been done in the bakery or in a service room (a storeroom, for example). By the same token, the hospice dining room may have been used by the monks occasionally. In other words, in the absence of a proper refectory, various alternatives may have been utilized in accordance with the needs and possibilities of each laura.

In the coenobia, in which communal prayer and communal meals constituted the heart of the life, the refectory generally stood near the church building. Since the only times the community came together were for prayer and meals, these would have been the only times when the monks would have had a chance to talk to all and sundry! It is natural, too, that visitors would be invited to participate in both aspects of communal life: eating and praying. After prayers in the church, the monks would walk across to the refectory to dine together. Several times in the sources, the church and the refectory are mentioned together. For example, Euthymius instructs the monks of the monastery of Theoctistus that they must refrain from superfluous conversation in the church and the refectory. Anthony notes that the cell-dwellers would come to the monastery of Choziba to take part in "the prayer ceremony . . . and eat with the fathers of the monastery."[64] Consequently, it would seem that one of the basic elements in planning a coenobium was to allow convenient passage from the church to the refectory. This phenomenon is found in monasteries both within the Judean desert and outside it.[65]

The most impressive refectory compound found so far in the Judean desert, as regards both preservation and the richness of finds, is that of the monastery of Martyrius (see table 7).[66] This compound dates to the monastery's most prosperous period, the second half of the sixth century. The refectory and its various components stand in the northwest corner of the monastery and are linked to the main church by a paved corridor, the roof of which was supported by a colonnade. The two principal components are the dining room and the kitchen, which is adjacent to it (fig. 106). The dining room, rectangular in shape, is quite

TABLE 7

Refectories in Judean desert monasteries

Name of Monastery	Dimensions (m)	Entrance	Stories	Dimensions of Kitchen (m)	Location of Kitchen vis-à-vis Refectory
Martyrius	12 × 26.5	East	2	6 × 21	Adjacent
Khirbet ed-Deir	6.3 × 27.5	West	2	6.3 × 27.5	Beneath
Khirbet Makhrum	6.5 × 22	North	2	6.5 × 22	Beneath

Figure 106 Refectory at the monastery of Martyrius (looking east)

large—26.5 m long and 12 m wide. The interior is divided into three longitudinal sections by two rows of columns, as in churches of the basilica type. A long, narrow corridor (11 × 4 m) leads from the entrance, which is in the eastern wall. The corridor is a direct extension of the colonnaded portico connecting the church and the refectory. It has a stone bench along its walls, built for the convenience of monks waiting for their meals or resting after eating. Although the excavators believe that the corridor served as an additional dining room, its narrow dimensions and wide opening to the courtyard suggest that it was merely a passageway and a waiting area.

The dining room has a colorful mosaic floor, and its walls are lined with stone benches. The benches are coated with the reddish plaster used for the cisterns, as opposed to the white plaster used on the walls. The excavators believe that this was to prevent the monks' dark-colored garments from being stained by white plaster. The walls were decorated with Greek inscriptions painted in red. Fragments of glass panes found during the excavation suggest that there may have been windows in the upper parts of the walls.

The mosaic floor of the refectory reflects the room's architectural plan: there is a central pattern in the nave and two side patterns in the aisles. The central pattern consists of interwoven circles and crosses, whereas the side patterns depict flowers on a white background. The designs in the spaces between one column and the next are particularly beautiful and rich in hue. These spaces were probably left free of furniture.

The floor at the entrance contains a dedicatory inscription in Greek, commemorating the completion of construction of the monastery in the time of Abbot Genesius. The orientation of this inscription is to the east, which means that it was meant to be read not upon entering, but when the monks were sitting or standing in the room and looking east. This suggests that meals were accompanied by grace, which was recited toward the east.

The ceiling of the refectory was supported by wooden beams resting on the two rows of columns, which were connected to each other by arches. In each row were seven stone columns with decorated capitals. (Four capitals and a single fragment of a column were found in the excavations; all the rest were plundered in antiquity.)

The refectory building was two stories high, but the floor of the second story, made of wooden beams, did not cover the entire space, and the central area of the first story, between the columns, was open up to the roof. This architectural plan, common in basilica construction, allowed most of the available light to reach the central part of the room. Judging from the hundreds of nails of various sizes found during the excavation, it seems that the gabled tile roof of the hall was supported by a wooden scaffold. The bottom section of the stairway to the upper story was found near the main entrance (fig. 107).

The refectory of the monastery of Martyrius was, then, a huge, well-lit hall accommodating a large number of diners. In addition to the 320 m² of space on the ground floor was an extra 200 m² on the upper floor. Moreover, the excavators suppose that monks also dined on the upper story of the kitchen, which had an area of about 120 m². Thus the overall area for tables came to about 640 m². Though it is difficult to calculate the number of monks that could be accommodated in such a space, because we have no precise information regarding the number of tables and the number of monks per table, it is probable that in a refectory of this type, hundreds could be served.

The kitchen was built close to the southern wall of the refectory. Its function is attested by the cooking facilities and the various storage vessels found in it. The room was 21 m long and 6 m wide (interior dimensions), similar in size to kitchens found in other monasteries. The kitchen was entered directly from the courtyard through two doorways, and a wide service window in its northwestern corner, with a sill about 1.2 m above the floor, allowed food trays to be passed from the kitchen through to the refectory. The floor of the kitchen was made of white mosaic, decorated in the center with an amphora pattern from which vines ascend and form eight medallions. The ceiling was supported by seven stone arches traversing the width of the room.

Figure 107 Stairway to the upper story of the refectory at the monastery of
Martyrius

During the excavations, parts of the mosaic of the second story were found
on the floor, as was a stone threshold from the upper floor. The mosaic of the
second story had a black and red geometric pattern set against a white background. The discovery of the stone threshold attests to the division of the upper
story into at least two rooms. The excavation also yielded an assortment of
ceramic dishes, storage and cooking vessels, and other pottery items that had
been stored on the upper floor. This is why the excavators surmise that the
upper story was actually part of the refectory.

The refectory complex found at Khirbet ed-Deir illustrates the ability of
Byzantine builders to find optimal architectural solutions to the problems of
building in an area of steep cliffs. The refectory was built as a two-story structure in the narrow space available, thereby creating a functional division between the dining room (above) and the kitchen (below) (fig. 108). A similar
solution was adopted by the builders of the monastery of Theognius, which,
like the one at Khirbet ed-Deir, was of the cliff type.[67] But the arrangement at
Khirbet ed-Deir had the advantage that, between the dining room and cliff face,
a courtyard was created, where the monks could gather before and after communal meals. This courtyard was shaded by vegetation, probably vines hanging

Figure 108 Refectory complex at Khirbet ed-Deir (looking south)

from a pergola. The existence of a pergola is attested by the remains of rectangular niches carved horizontally at regular intervals along the cliff face at the
western edge of the courtyard. It is assumed that each niche contained a wooden
beam that was part of a trellis construction designed to support a vine or some
other climbing plant.

THE HOSPICE

Hospitality was one of the virtues cherished by the monks: it was often
recommended by monastic leaders in the rules dictated to their disciples. On
their deathbeds, Chariton and Euthymius told their monks not to turn away any
visitor or let him leave empty-handed.[68] Cyriac is represented as always serving
his guests himself, even in extreme old age (*V. Cyr.* 21, 235. 11–12). Sabas received and fed hungry Saracens, and Theodosius refused to limit the quantity
of bread to be given to guests, even when there was a shortage.[69] We find no
clear distinction between hospitality and charity in Byzantine sources, and feeding the poor was considered but one aspect of the virtue of openhandedness.
Thus it may be assumed that even small monasteries and hermitages made some
arrangement for overnight guests. Such accommodation was very simple, however—an empty cell or a service room—and so cannot be recognized as guest
accommodation on monastic sites. For example, when Cyril of Scythopolis and
John, Cyriac's disciple, spent a night at Cyriac's hermitage in Sousakim (*V. Cyr.*
16, 232), they probably slept on the ground in the antechamber of their master's
cave (Cyriac probably slept in the inner room).

When a noblewoman and her attendants stayed at the monastery of
Choziba, she spent the night in the diaconicon for lack of a better alternative.[70]
The anonymous compiler of *The Sayings of the Desert Fathers* tells of a monk who
stayed as a guest in a laura on Mount Sinai and was given an empty cell and
a book to read.[71] We also learn from this story that being a guest included the
duty of taking part in the daily chores, and that the above-mentioned monk,
who declined to work, was not invited to partake of the daily meal.[72]

In small and medium-sized coenobia, guests may have stayed outside the
monastery gate in caves or shelters made of light materials. Traces of a camp-
site for visitors can be seen near the monastery of Theoctistus.[73] These include
a bench, a cistern, and several holes in the cliff for hitching up pack animals.
Several inscriptions found on the rock above the bench include women's names,
which indicates that women, who were not allowed inside the monastery, were
accommodated there. Male visitors, on the other hand, were probably accommodated in a small hospice inside this monastery; and the same applies to other
coenobia, such as Khirbet ed-Deir. The location for such a hospice may have

been the second floor of the gate-houses found in both monasteries; but we have no evidence to support this assumption.

Only in relation to the larger monasteries in the Judean desert are hospices explicitly mentioned in the sources. A hospice was built in the Great Laura, and a monk was put in charge of it. The hospice was placed next to the core of the laura, as we see from the story of Jacob, the monk in charge, who threw some leftover vegetables out of the window into the Kidron valley. Sabas witnessed this act from his tower above the cave church, gathered up the vegetables, let them dry in the sun, and later served them to Jacob (*V. Sab.* 40, 130–1). Thus the hospice was sufficiently close to Sabas's tower in the core of the laura for Sabas to see Jacob throwing out the vegetables. In fact, it is thought to have been atop the hill to the south of the present monastery. Ruins found there accord, in their size and position opposite the core buildings, with the historical data presented above.[74]

A hospice building has actually been discovered at only one site in the Judean desert: the monastery of Martyrius.[75] The hospice, erected in the mid-sixth century at the height of the monastery's prosperity, is situated outside the wall of the monastery, near its northeastern corner. The building forms a trapezoid that widens from east to west. It ranges in length from 33 to 43 m and in width from 22 m in the east to 27 m in the west. One section housed living quarters and a church, the other section the stable. The facade of the hospice, facing southeast to the square in front of the monastery gate, contains four entrances: three leading to the living quarters and one, at the western end, to the stables.

The living quarters consisted of a series of bedrooms and dormitories. The dormitories were generally narrow and long, ranging in length from 8 to 12 m, with an average width of 3.2 m. The overall area of the living quarters is about 320 m². This area, in the opinion of the excavators, could accommodate sixty or seventy people.

The stable is completely separate from the living quarters—yet another sign of the monks' concern for hygiene and order. Its wide entrance (3.2 m) faces south, toward the gate area. Inside, it is arranged around two courtyards: one in the front and one in the rear. The front courtyard has two rows of stalls adjacent to its walls. The inner courtyard is poorly preserved. To the east there is a large hall (3.6 × 18 m) with one row of stalls adjacent to its western wall (fig. 109).

The Byzantine hospice of the monastery of Martyrius is one of the few discovered in Palestine. The dimensions, complex design, and quality of construction of this hospice indicate its importance to the monks.

There seems to have been a tendency to keep the hospice and the monastery separate, in order to prevent disturbance of the monks' daily routine. This also

Figure 109 Stable of the hospice at the monastery of Martyrius. The long row of
vertical flat stones on the left borders a trough.

seems to have been the case in monasteries far away from the Judean desert. In
the monastery of Alahan, in southern Anatolia, for example, the hospice stood
near the entrance gate, and a large church of basilica type was built beside it
for visitors. The church and the refectory that served the monastic community,
on the other hand, were placed in the eastern part of the monastery.[76] Unfor-
tunately, the available data do not allow us to prove or disprove this inference
with regard to the monasteries of the Judean desert.

The literary sources tell us that, with the exception of the monastery of
Choziba, female visitors were always accommodated outside the walls of the
monasteries; this seems to imply that male visitors were normally accommodated inside the monastery.[77] At the monastery of Euthymius, the visitor who
stole the silver funnel apparently spent the night inside and left the monastery
before dawn, when the gate was opened to let the pack animals out (*V. Euth.* 59,
81–2). The monastery of Theodosius had three hospices, which also functioned
as hospitals, and many monks were employed there as physicians, orderlies, and

apothecaries. These were full-time jobs, often requiring night duty, and it seems unlikely that the monks so employed would have served outside the monastery walls. So it seems that the location of the hospice could vary, according to its main aim—whether to house visitors or care for the needy and the sick—and perhaps depending on whether a building had been planned especially for this purpose or whether a group of rooms in the monastery had been simply set aside to accommodate guests.

Lodgings in the hospice were offered free of charge, and the needy even received a parting gift of money or food.[78] Caring for guests demanded a great deal of work, which sometimes continued late into the night (*V. Geor.* 57, 356); a major part of the work was baking bread, cooking, and serving meals. Since a lot of cooking was done in the hospice, its kitchen was often used by the monks and the employees of the monastery as well. The monk in charge of the hospice of the Great Laura would cook for the monks who went out to gather edible plants in the desert and for the builders of the Small Coenobium.[79] Since there were always many people at the hospice, it also functioned as an outlet for the sale of the baskets produced by the monks; the raw materials used in basketry were stored there as well (*V. Sab.* 44, 135. 4–6).

Another important function of the hospice, to care for the sick and the disabled elderly, has already been mentioned. The monastery of Theodosius specialized in such care, but there is no doubt that other monasteries also did this kind of charity work, either in infirmaries or in the hospice itself.[80]

In addition to the hospice at the monastery, some of the large monasteries in the Judean desert operated other hospices in the nearby cities of Jerusalem and Jericho.[81] The monasteries of Euthymius and Theoctistus shared a hospice in the vicinity of David's tower in Jerusalem; this hospice had previously belonged to the monastery of Chariton (*V. Cyr.* 7, 226. 15–20). In the same area, Sabas purchased cells and created three hospices: two belonging to the Great Laura and one to the monastery of Castellion. Sabas also purchased a hospice with gardens and a water supply in Jericho. In this town, which was an important way station for pilgrims en route to the Jordan River, there was also a hospice operated by the monastery of Euthymius and another run by the monastery of Theodosius.[82] The hospices in the cities served as the monasteries' representatives in town.

Cyril mentions a workroom that was part of one of the Great Laura's hospices in Jerusalem (*V. Sab.* 86, 194. 11); it may be assumed that some of the tools that were needed for use in the Great Laura were manufactured in the hospice. The hospices in the cities also served as places for recruiting new monks. Cyril himself first stayed in the hospice of the monastery of Euthymius in Jericho before joining the community (*V. John Hes.* 20, 217). Thus the hospice played a vital role in monastic life, whether it was within the monastery, beside it, or in a nearby city.

THE GARDEN

The garden was one of the standard features of both the coenobium and the laura. It was situated in the center of the monastery or next to it, and the vegetables and fruits it yielded enriched the monks' diet. According to Cyril, the garden of the monastery of Euthymius contained a reservoir with two spouts; this reservoir was identified 60 m east of the monastery. The plot was the nucleus of a larger garden that was developed in the area south of the monastery. A survey revealed that the cultivated land of the monastery of Euthymius covered an area of at least 2,500 m². The agricultural terraces and the garden plots were irrigated by three reservoirs: the one mentioned above, another cistern nearby, and a large reservoir near the monastery, which Cyril mentions.[83]

Another garden described in detail in the sources is the garden of the monastery of Choziba, which apparently lay at the foot of the monastery on a terraced area between the monastery and the streambed. It seems that its area was enlarged by the addition of plots prepared by the monks. When George arrived at the monastery, he was appointed assistant to the gardener of the "new garden."[84]

Moschus mentions the garden of the laura of Marda (Masada), which was far away from the laura (6 Roman miles, or 8.9 km) on a separate plot protected by a fence. The monk in charge of the garden lived in it, and when the monks wanted fresh vegetables, they sent a donkey, which found its way to the garden without any help.[85] Small garden plots also existed in the hermitages of the Judean desert. Cyril mentions the presence of such a plot at Cyriac's hermitage in Sousakim (*V. Cyr.* 16, 232). It is worth mentioning that garden plots were typical of Byzantine monasteries throughout the empire.[86]

The remains of several other monastery gardens in the Judean desert have been studied. An impressive cluster of garden plots, totaling more than 18,000 m², was found in the lower part of the monastery of Chariton. On the edge of a high cliff were two main plots, which were shared by the whole community. The larger of the two had an area of about 3,000 m². Along the length of the plot, a long solid terrace wall was built (fig. 110). This wall, which was about 30 m long and 2.3 m high, had a dual function: to help level the area of the garden and to protect the garden from the floodwaters of the stream. The other large plot lay south of the streambed, on the same raised level, and covered about 600 m². All the plots were irrigated by the monastery's efficient water supply system.

Figure 110 Terrace wall along a garden plot at the monastery of Chariton
(looking northwest)

An example of a garden within the confines of a monastery was found at
Khirbet ed-Deir. The garden was about 150 m long and ranged in width from 10
to 20 m. Its total area thus came to about 2,200 m² (fig. 111). At the wide end
of the garden, the monks built a large, L-shaped terrace wall, about 1.5 m high.
The shorter section, 8 m long and 2 m thick, was used as a dam to divert the
winter floodwaters. The other section was 23 m long. The soil was brought by
the monks from the broad bed of Wadi el-Ghar and the bottom of a reservoir
built in the garden.

The monks also erected stepped agricultural terraces on both sides of the
streambed. One terrace is 32 m long. But it seems that the main cultivated areas
of the monastery were situated in the bed of Wadi el-Ghar (fig. 112). The section
of the stream bordering the hill on which the monastery was built is quite level
and covers 26,000 m². Stone walls built by the monks divide it into three large
fields, and another stone wall bounds the plots to the west. It seems likely that
the large agricultural fields in the bed of Wadi el-Ghar formed an olive grove.

All told, the agricultural holdings discovered in and around the monastic remains at Khirbet ed-Deir cover 33,000 m². This area was used by the monks for

Figure 111 Sketch plan of the garden plots at Khirbet ed-Deir

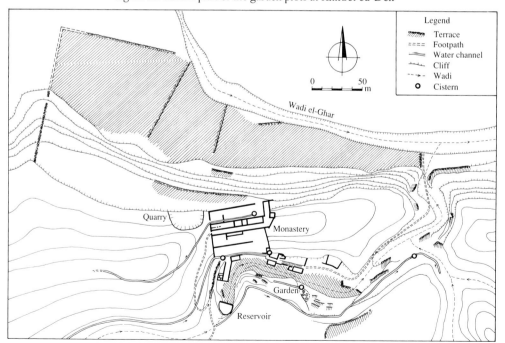

Figure 112 Cultivated areas and garden plots at Khirbet ed-Deir in the bed of Wadi el-Ghar (looking west). In the foreground is the mosaic floor of the monastery.

intensive cultivation of vegetables and seasonal fruits. As already noted, home-grown agricultural produce was an important component of the monks' diet. The monastery at Khirbet ed-Deir was a medium-sized complex intended for forty or fifty monks, which means that it had 660 m² of cultivated land per monk. These large holdings demonstrate the major role of agriculture in monastic life, especially in the coenobia.

The well-preserved remains of the garden terraces at Khirbet ed-Deir gave the team of excavators, which I directed, the opportunity to experiment with a small garden plot inside the ancient monastery. We chose an area of about 60 m² in the monastery ravine; the soil, 1 m thick, was laid out by the monks. A channel carved by the monks to the south of the garden plot supplied rainwater in winter. We planted olive trees, fig trees, pomegranate trees, and grapevines, and entrusted the care of this mini-plantation to a Bedouin family nearby. The saplings took root and are now thriving, proving that even with only minimal care, these species grow successfully in the desert. It may be assumed that the monks gave intensive care to each tree, and thus created an artificial oasis around their monastery.

One interesting discovery relating to this aspect of monastic life was the "vineyard" found in the Nea Laura. It was on the northern slope of the laura, about 300 m northwest of the core. The plot was surrounded by a stone fence, of which many parts are well preserved. The fence encloses an area 55 m long from east to west and between 40 and 50 m wide from south to north, making the total area about 2,500 m². Near the eastern part of the fence is a large reservoir (with exterior dimensions of about 6 × 12 m) beside a small cell, which was apparently the dwelling of the monk responsible for the garden. There is another cistern in the foundations of the cell. The interior of the garden is rocky, but, judging from the many piles of stones, the monks created stepped agricultural terraces there. By this means, it was possible to create pockets of soil suitable for growing various plants, mainly grapevines. The altitude of the garden, 750 m above sea level, assured the low temperatures needed for growing vines, and to this day the area is an ideal place for growing them. Thus it would seem likely that the monks used this plot as a vineyard.

The garden was not always adjacent to the monastery building. From written sources we learn that the monastery of Theoctistus had agricultural holdings about 5 km to the west, in the plain near the monastery of Euthymius. According to Cyril, the two monasteries initially worked the plots in common. After they severed relations with each other in 485, the fields were separated by stone walls, and watchtowers were built nearby (*V. Cyr.* 7, 226. 13–17).

This information may explain a phenomenon found occasionally in the Judean desert: the presence of a farmhouse a short distance from a monastery. Remains of such a farmhouse were discovered 250 m east of the monastery of El-Qasr. An olive press and winepresses indicate the agricultural function of the building. The farmhouse is rectangular, with external dimensions of 12 × 21 m, and has two wings built on either side of a broad courtyard (fig. 113). A cistern was dug in the center of the courtyard. The western wing houses three residential rooms, while the southern wing consists of a single hall measuring 5.3 × 6.2 m. The potsherds collected in the area are from the Byzantine period, and a paved path leads from the monastery to the farmhouse. It seems reasonable to suppose that the monastery and the farmhouse were connected. If that is the case, it would seem that the farmhouse was used by the monks to process agricultural produce. Nevertheless, we cannot rule out the possibility that the farmhouse belonged to a private individual with no connection to the monastery.

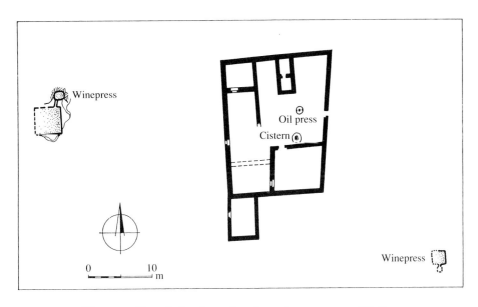

Figure 113 Plan of a farmhouse found near the monastery of El-Qasr

THE FOOTPATH

Between the various monasteries and between the monasteries and the settlements on the edges of the desert, the monks created an extensive network of footpaths, which changed the face of the desert during the Byzantine period. These paths connected the desert with the inhabited areas near them. They should, in fact, be viewed as an integral part of the plan of the monasteries. This is true of both coenobia and lauras. For both, these pathways were direct extensions of the main passageways within the monastery. Archaeological study of the remains of these footpaths has enabled us to draw a relatively precise map of their routes (map 5). This map demonstrates the aptness of the title of Chitty's book *The Desert a City*.

The paths were meant to serve two main groups of people: the monks who lived permanently in the monasteries and visitors and pilgrims. Since most of the monks in the Judean desert were not natives, they did not know their way around the desert, at least on arrival. The sources tell us that Sabas needed a guide on his first visit to the Judean desert in order to go from Jerusalem to the laura of Euthymius (*V. Sab.* 7, 91. 3–4). Cyril needed a guide when traveling from the monastery of Chariton to the place where Cyriac had secluded himself.[87] "The strangeness of the land and ignorance of the local language" were among the arguments used by the monk Auxentius in refusing to accept the post of mule-driver at the monastery of Euthymius (*V. Euth.* 18, 281. 25–6).

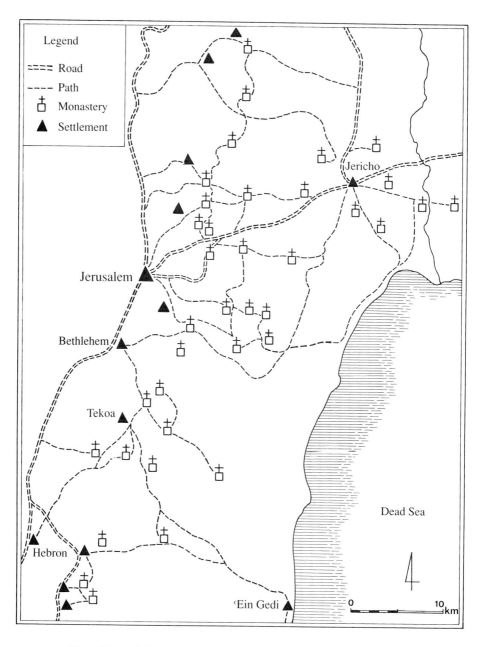

Map 5 Footpaths between the monasteries and the main settlements of the
Judean desert

Moreover, the desert paths were often dangerous: the sources report many accidents caused by strong winds or difficult terrain.[88] Therefore, the monks invested considerable effort in laying trails, and even built retaining walls to make the trails broader and more solid. Cyril refers several times to the "road" from Jerusalem to the Great Laura along the course of the Kidron valley. Near that road was the Heptastomos cistern, as we learn from the story of the founding of the laura of Heptastomos by the monk Jacob. Sabas ordered the monks of the Small Coenobium attached to the Great Laura to plant trees along this road and take care of them. This indicates the great importance the monks attached to maintaining and developing the road to their monastery. To this day, this path is the most convenient way of reaching Mar Saba by foot from Jerusalem. Several sections of the Byzantine retaining walls have been preserved along it, and the cistern called Heptastomos was identified near the path, 3.5 km west of Mar Saba.[89] It seems likely that the water stored in the cistern was meant to quench the thirst of those traveling to and from the Great Laura, since, according to Sabas, the cistern belonged to the Great Laura (*V. Sab.* 39, 129. 16).

The trails of the monastery and Cells of Choziba have received particularly detailed study. Two main paths led to the monastery (fig. 114). One linked the

Figure 114 Plan and cross-section of the Cells of Choziba

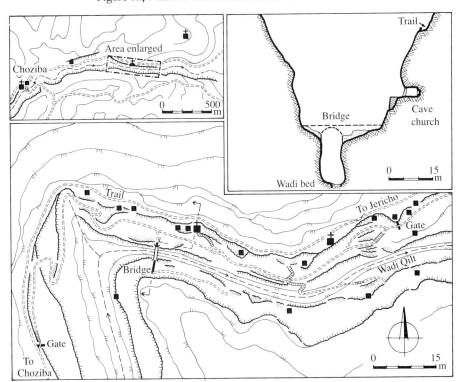

monastery with the main road descending from Jerusalem to Jericho and served the many pilgrims who came to the monastery. Anthony tells of a noblewoman from Byzantium who wanted to visit the monastery. En route from Jericho to Jerusalem, she ordered her escort to take her "to the monastery on the right side below the stream" (*Miracula* 1, 361. 10–11). Her escort claimed that the sedan chair in which she was being carried could not go down the steep trail. That trail is used to this day, plunging to the streambed, crossing it via a bridge, and ascending northward to the cliff on which the monastery stands. (The modern path was paved by laborers employed by the monastery.)

The present bridge was built when the monastery was reestablished in the late nineteenth century, but there was a bridge in Byzantine times as well. Further on in Anthony's account, he mentions "the bridge opposite the monastery" (*Miracula* 4, 365. 6). The bridge was necessary for crossing the stream, and although the remains of the original bridge were demolished at the time the new bridge was built, there can be no doubt of its existence.

The fact that Anthony refers to a specific bridge, the one "opposite the

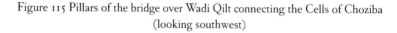

Figure 115 Pillars of the bridge over Wadi Qilt connecting the Cells of Choziba
(looking southwest)

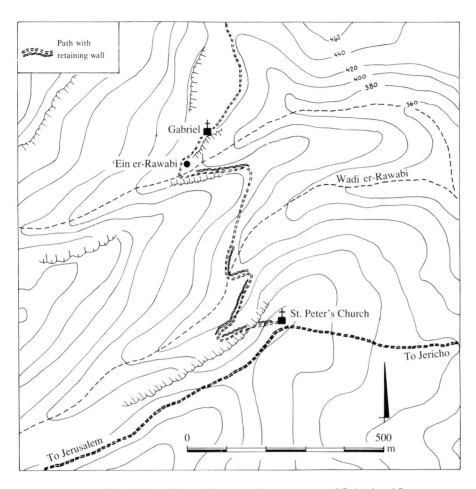

Map 6 Sketch plan of the trail between the monasteries of Gabriel and St.
Peter's Church (looking southwest)

monastery," suggests that there was another bridge. Indeed, in a survey we conducted at the Cells of Choziba, we found traces of such a structure, at the point
where the distance between the two cliff walls is at its smallest, about 8 m. Two
pillars, one on each side of the stream, have remained from this bridge (fig. 115).
They are about 1 m thick and have been preserved to a height of 3 m. It seems
likely that the bridge was built in the form of an arch; but we cannot rule out
the possibility that it was built of wooden beams laid on the two pillars.

The second path leads to the monastery from the direction of the Jericho
oasis, without crossing the stream. Many sections of retaining walls from the
Byzantine period have been found along its length. This appears to have been
the path taken by the monk Zenon, who was sent to Jericho to bring eucharistic

Figure 116 Trail to the monastery of Theoctistus (looking west)

bread back to the monastery of Choziba.[90] The Cells of Choziba are situated on the cliff below the trail. The path forks, and one section descends directly to the cells. Anthony notes that George would walk along the "path" on his way from the monastery to his cell. He also tells of a monk who was making his way along "the path of the cells" and, upon reaching a steep section, found himself face to face with a leopard.[91]

Surveys carried out in the Judean desert have uncovered many sections of paths that were laid by the monks of the Byzantine period. One of the most complete and best instances of a trail between two monasteries is the path between the monastery of Gabriel and the monastery beside St. Peter's Church (map 6). The distance between these two monasteries is only 500 m. Because of the difficult topography, however, the trail between them is considerably longer, coming to 1,100 m. The trail crosses two steep streambeds: that of Wadi Rawabi near the monastery of Gabriel and another one further south. In laying this path, the main effort was concentrated on the spots where it crosses the streambeds. The retaining wall is solidly built and in some places is preserved to a height of more than 2 m.

Sometimes it was difficult to follow these serpentine paths, particularly in the case of the monastery of Theoctistus (fig. 116). To mark the exact point

Map 7 Trail to the monastery of Theoctistus

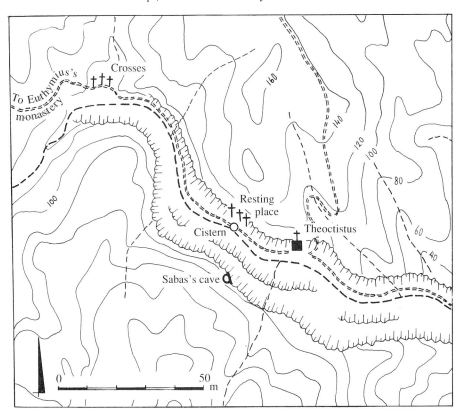

where the path entered the canyon in which the monastery stands, a group of crosses, visible from a distance, was carved into the rock beside the path (map 7). From this point on, the path became a paved road, fortified by retaining walls. Closer to the monastery, another group of crosses was found, together with a bench, a cistern, and a number of inscriptions.[92] These crosses apparently marked the site of a rest area for visitors to the monastery.

CHAPTER SEVEN

Hermits and
Their Way of Life

A description of monasticism in the Judean desert would not be complete without a chapter on the way of life of the hermits who lived there. There were numerous hermits in the Judean desert, judging by their frequent mention in the hagiographic literature. Some of them lived in the wilderness for long periods. Moschus tells of a hermit named George who secluded himself in the mountains for thirty-five years, until the day of his death (*Pratum* 91, 2948–9). Several stories are told of hermits who were unknown and went unrecognized until their discovery, sometimes after their death.[1]

In most cases, though, the hermits appear to have maintained ties with a mother monastery while residing in the desert. An excellent example is Cyriac, who secluded himself at Sousakim for almost fifteen years and throughout that time was affiliated with the monastery of Chariton. One of Moschus's stories concerns a monk from the monastery of Theodosius who spent a long period in seclusion on the eastern shore of the Dead Sea and then returned to his monastery. John Hesychast secluded himself in the desert of Rouba for six years but retained his cell in the Great Laura. He maintained contact with the laura during this time, and when the security situation deteriorated, the monks called him back to the monastery.[2]

The means by which contact was maintained are not always stated. In the case of Cyriac, it was his disciple John who went back and forth between the monastery of Chariton and the hermitage at Sousakim, providing the old man with bread, news, and occasional visitors, including Cyril himself (*V. Cyr.* 15, 232. 4–5). In the eighth century, when security conditions in the desert became very bad, hermits did not stop living in the wilderness, but a system was developed to keep them in constant touch with the mother monastery and to provide them with food—an essential arrangement since famished Saracens would rob them of their provisions.

A monk from the mother monastery would visit the hermits regularly and bring them food and other necessities. The Great Laura observed this practice, and though it is not mentioned in the sixth-century sources, it is referred to in later sources as a tradition handed down from earlier times.[3] Thus it is possible that this arrangement already existed when Judean desert monasticism was at its height. Ongoing contact was necessary not only to provide food and a measure of security, but also for the mental well-being of the hermits. Indeed, hermits who became unbalanced were sometimes gathered in and taken care of at the monastery of Theodosius.[4]

In addition to hermits who lived permanently in the desert were many monks who went down "to the depths of the desert" for Lent. As far as we know, it was Euthymius who brought this custom to the Judean desert, from his birth-place in Asia Minor.[5] During Lent, the monks would wander vast distances.[6] On several occasions, Sabas reached the desert of Zoar, south of the Dead Sea, and on one such occasion he went out to a desert island in the southern Dead Sea and had much difficulty extricating himself from the swampy banks. His skin and beard were severely burned by sulphurous vapors, and when he re-turned to the monastery, the monks recognized him only by his voice. Another time, Sabas and his disciple Agapetus observed Lent by walking along the Jor-dan River to one of the sources of the river situated in Paneas (Banyas). Stephen Sabaites, who lived in the Great Laura during the eighth century, would walk around the entire periphery of the Dead Sea during Lent. On other occasions he observed Lent in deserted caves around the monastery of Castellion or in the laura of Douka.[7]

Wandering was a common practice among Palestinian monks. Sometimes they set out with a specific goal, such as visiting other monks or going on a pilgrimage to a holy place. But sometimes their wandering was for its own sake, roaming about under difficult conditions with no possessions and depending entirely on charity for food being considered a form of asceticism.[8] This practice originated in Syrian monasticism, which in its beginnings, at least, advocated life without a roof or even a fixed dwelling place.[9]

This practice was strongly censured by the Church, and by the fifth and sixth centuries, Church and State had joined in opposing wandering monks.[10] Even the founders of the desert monasteries tried to at least curtail this habit; and Euthymius even went so far as to condemn it, forbidding the monks to leave the monastery without permission from the abbot (*V. Euth.* 19, 30. 7–9). But the wanderlust of the monks could not be curbed. Moschus tells of a hermit in the area of Socho, on the western slopes of the Judean hills, who would go to pray in the most remote places in Sinai, Syria, and elsewhere (*Pratum* 180, 3052B). Moschus himself walked considerable distances, reaching Sinai, Egypt, Syria, and finally Rome.[11] Another monk with strong wanderlust was Peter the Iberian, who went as far as Tyre, Sidon, Mount Nebo, and the Dead Sea (*V. Pet. Ib.* 78, 76).

Caves provided natural dwellings for hermits in the Judean desert. When Sabas came to the Kidron valley, he lived in a cave high up in the cliffs above the stream. To facilitate the climb, he tied a rope to the mouth of the cave. Hermits were also drawn to abandoned fortresses from the Second Temple period. Euthymius, Domitian, and others took shelter among such ruins, obtaining water from the cisterns left on the sites.[12]

The hermits, often known as "grazers," subsisted on a minimal diet of dry bread, kidney beans, wild plants, and water. As already mentioned, when Sabas and his disciple went out wandering during Lent, they took a leather rucksack containing ten loaves of dry bread, which were meant to supply their needs for the entire forty days. Moschus tells of a female hermit who lived for seventeen years in a cave near the Jordan River, eating the kidney beans she had brought with her from Jerusalem, which miraculously did not run out.[13] As noted in chapter 3, the plants most commonly eaten by the hermits were *melagria* (identified as asphodel), *kardias kalamon* ("reed hearts"), and saltbushes.

Some hermits seem to have had gardens, but the sources seldom mention such, and few hermitages with remains of garden plots have been found. An exception is Cyriac's vegetable garden at Sousakim. The garden, traces of which were found at the site, is mentioned by Cyril. According to the story, a lion lived with the saint and protected the garden from wild goats (*V. Cyr.* 16, 232. 13). Another example is the small vegetable plot found next to the hermitage near 'Ein er-Rashash in the northern Judean desert. Occasionally, the hermits received fresh food from benefactors in the vicinity (see ch. 3).

The hermits generally used natural supplies of water (springs and depressions that collected rainwater). Occasionally, they used cisterns in the area near their hermitages. When Sabas was in the ravine of the Kidron valley, for example, he drew his water from the cistern called Heptastomos (*V. Sab.* 15, 98. 19–20). According to Cyril, the cistern was 15 stadia (about 2.8 km) from his cave. This information helped to identify the cistern as Bir Sabsab, about 3.5 km northwest of Mar Saba,[14] which is a large cistern used to this day by the residents of the area. The cistern is fed by long canals that drain the runoff from the slopes situated south of it. Next to it are the mouths of other cisterns, which have become clogged over the years; they probably inspired the cistern's Byzantine name, Heptastomos, which means "with seven mouths."

Another means of obtaining water was by digging down to the water table with a small trowel. Cyril's writings inform us of the use of the high water table in the desert. One Lent, Euthymius, Domitian, and Sabas set out for the Dead Sea. On the way, Sabas became faint with thirst. Euthymius quickly dug a little trench with the trowel in his hand, and it filled up with water fit to drink.[15]

A supply of water was vital, and for that reason the hermits equipped themselves with various vessels for storing water. The female hermit Maria the harp-player took a pitcher with her to the desert (*V. Cyr.* 19, 234. 2).

In several instances, the hermitages of exemplary monks became the nucleus around which a monastery got started. After Sabas had secluded himself in a cave in the Kidron valley for five years (*V. Sab.* 16, 99. 5–7), monks and hermits began to gather around him, until there were enough of them to found a laura. This pattern was repeated in the founding of the monasteries of Euthymius, Theodosius, and Zannus.

The sites of hermitages were chosen in accordance with the desires and abilities of the individual hermits. Some hermits chose to seclude themselves for many years in total isolation in the depths of the desert. Others lived in hermitages outside a monastery, but near it. For example, when Euthymius arrived at the laura of Pharan, he chose a "place of seclusion" outside the monastery. At a certain stage Sabas also took a "secluded cell" for himself, some 15 stadia (about 2.8 km) from the Great Laura.[16]

Living in caves or nooks in the rocks, feeding on wild plants, and using what water was available, most hermits left little impression on the landscape.[17] For example, in the survey carried out among the cliffs in the interior of the Judean desert, a Byzantine jug was discovered buried in the floor of a cave above 'Ein Turabi.[18] On the basis of this find, the cave was identified as the hermitage of a Byzantine monk; but if the jug had not been found, we would never have known about the use of the cave as a place of seclusion.

To date, only a few sites in the Judean desert have been identified with a high degree of certainty as hermitages of monks from the Byzantine period.[19] One is the natural cave discovered in a tributary of Wadi Fasayil, near the spring of 'Ein er-Rashash.[20] The cave runs northward along the middle of a cliff rising about 20 m above the wadi (fig. 117). A steep, narrow trail descends to the cave from the direction of the spring and ends on a narrow rock ledge leading to the cave complex. The approach to the cave is through a narrow corridor 3 m long (fig. 118).

At the entrance to the corridor, a small indentation was made in the ground, apparently for placing a pitcher of drinking water. The corridor ends in a small opening 0.6 m wide and only 0.8 m high, equipped with slots and sockets for a wooden door. In this way the hermit could lock himself into the cave to protect

Figure 117 Cave hermitage near 'Ein er-Rashash (looking north)

himself from wild animals or other uninvited guests. The cave itself is roomy and high enough to stand in, 4.5 m long and 3.5 m wide. On the stone walls of the cave, four roughly carved crosses were found, which indicates that the cave was used as a hermitage during the Byzantine period. A large natural opening in the cliff face provided light and air for the interior. In the northeastern wall of the cave a small niche 0.6 m wide and a small slot for an oil lamp were carved

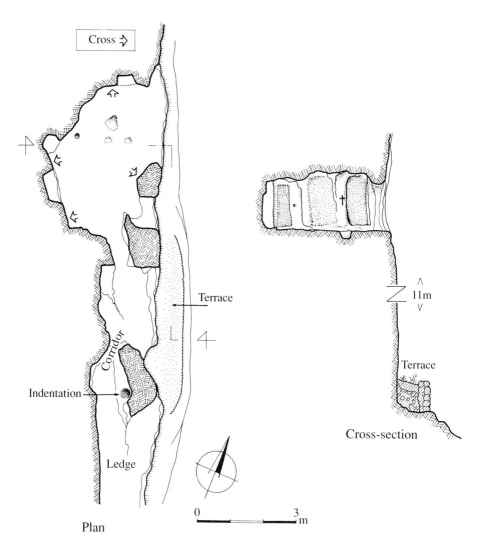

Cross ⤳

Terrace

Corridor

Indentation

Ledge

Plan

0 ⸻ 3
m

11m

Terrace

Cross-section

Figure 118 Plan and cross-section of a natural cave hermitage found near 'Ein
er-Rashash

out of the rock; next to them is one of the previously mentioned four crosses. Judging from these features, this may have been a prayer niche.

At the bottom of the cliff is the retaining wall of a terrace for the garden cultivated by the hermit. The garden plot was 5.5 m long and 1.2 m wide, and the wall of the terrace has been preserved to a height of about 1 m. The water for irrigating the plot apparently came from a nearby spring.

A second well-preserved hermitage is that of Cyriac, about 10 km east of Tekoa. It is mentioned in the works of Cyril, who states that the site of the hermitage, Sousakim, was at the junction of two streams: the stream descending from the Nea Laura and the one coming from the area of the monastery of Chariton (*V. Cyr.* 10, 288. 25–8). In the mid-sixth century, Cyril walked to Sousakim to meet the holy man, whom he venerated. He began his journey at the monastery of Chariton, and from there he went down to Sousakim with John, Cyriac's disciple. On their way, the two encountered the lion who was the saint's companion and who protected the vegetable garden from wild goats. Later Cyril mentions that, since there was no cistern, Cyriac had made "indentations in the rocks in which he collected water in the winter that supplied all his needs plentifully both for drinking and for watering his vegetables all summer long" (*V. Cyr.* 15–16, 232).

Two stages of use were discernible in a survey I made of the site: an early stage, in which the hermit settled in a natural cave, and a later stage (still during Cyriac's lifetime), when a chapel was built, with cisterns to supply its needs.[21] The cave is situated beside a narrow ridge, some 30 m above the intersection of Wadi el-Quseir and Wadi Maqta' el-Juss.[22] It is a relatively large cave, with two levels: an entrance level and above it another level, the entrance to which is blocked by a chapel (fig. 119). The mouth of the lower level is fenced with a

Figure 119 Chapel built at the mouth of Cyriac's cave at Sousakim

wall, which is preserved to a height of 1 m. In this way the hermit protected his dwelling from unwanted visitors.

The lower chamber of the cave is irregular in shape, measuring 4 × 5 m, with an average height of about 2 m (fig. 120). A narrow opening in the rear of the cave permitted passage to the upper level. Here, too, there was apparently a functional division between an entrance area, for visitors, and a rear area, for the personal use of the hermit. The inner chamber of the cave is also irregular, measuring about 4 × 4.5 m, 2.2 m high in the front part, but becoming as low as 0.8 m in the rear. Near the rear wall of the cave is a natural rock ledge, about 1 m wide and 1.6 m long. This ledge was probably used as a sleeping platform.

Near the cave, the remains of a cistern and a small garden plot were found. These elements were probably installed by Cyriac while he lived there. The cistern is oval and measures approximately 2 × 4 m; it is fed by runoff from the rocks above it. The garden plot, located beneath the cave, has been leveled off by means of a retaining wall built of fieldstone, preserved to a height of about 2.5 m. The plot covered about 25 m². Another garden plot extending over an area of 40 or 50 m² was found about 250 m southwest of the hermitage. A cistern was installed in its center for irrigation of the garden.

A chapel was built at the upper entrance to the cave. The quality of construction and the dimensions of the stones forming the wall show that it was erected by professional builders. The chapel is preserved to the full height of its walls, about 3.3 m above floor level. The presence of such a fine edifice in a hermitage is unusual but can be explained by the fact that Cyriac was a holy man and was much venerated.

The building is almost square, with exterior dimensions of 3.6 × 4.1 m; the walls are 0.8 m thick. The entrance is in the southern wall, and the interior space is lit by three small windows in three different walls. The lintel above the eastern window is decorated with a cross painted black. The presence of a cross in a window facing east shows that the room was used for prayer; and indeed, a square prayer niche, 0.7 m wide and 1.4 m high, can be found under that window.

The chapel was roofed with a stone dome. The base of the dome, which has remained in situ, forms a perfect circle 1.4 m in diameter (fig. 121). The transition from the square chapel building to the round dome was achieved by corbeling: the two upper courses of stone in the walls were graduated toward the interior. For this purpose, the builders used stone beams as long as 2.5 m. The fact that two stages are in evidence at the site points to the process mentioned earlier, of monasteries being established around the hermitages of exemplary monks.

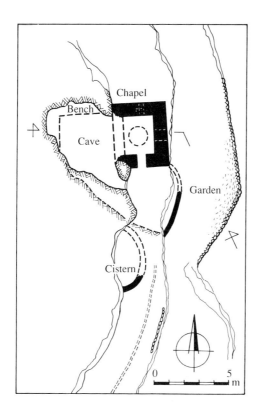

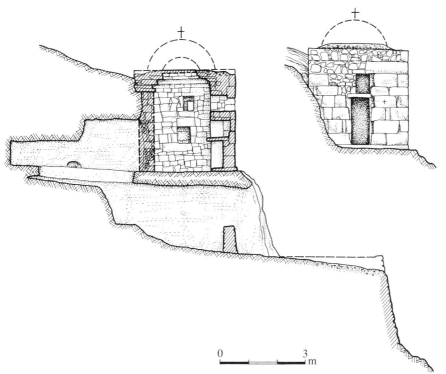

Figure 120 Plan, cross-section, and elevation of Cyriac's hermitage at Sousakim

Figure 121 Base of the dome of Cyriac's hermitage chapel (looking east)

CHAPTER EIGHT

Holy Sites in
the Judean Desert

The phenomenon of holy sites is described in the pilgrim Egeria's account of her visit to the Holy Land at the end of the fourth century. She was met in many places by monks and priests who lived on the site or in the vicinity and served as guides. According to Egeria, the monks, both at their own initiative and upon her request, pointed out various holy places, at each of which the group would stop to read an appropriate passage from Scripture and pray.[1]

This procedure is described in detail, particularly in Egeria's account of her visit to the southern mountains of Sinai. The holy places she visited there were located along the pilgrim route that led to the peak traditionally identified as Mount Sinai, today Jebel Mussa.[2] A survey of the monastic remains on the mountain range south of the monastery of St. Catherine substantiated the information provided by Egeria and added to it.[3]

Along the path leading to Jebel Mussa, about twelve semicircular prayer niches were discovered. The niches face east and were built about 1 m above ground level. Their average size is 2×2.5 m. The positions of these niches along the path to the holy mountain indicate that, as Egeria reports, each marked a spot traditionally associated with the giving of the Ten Commandments to Moses. Further archaeological surveys carried out in the area uncovered similar prayer niches.

Did the monks of the Judean desert set up special sites on the roads to their monasteries? Recent surveys in the area have revealed a number of religious sites that are too far from any settlement to be connected with village religious life; on the other hand, they are not monasteries.[4] Their religious purpose is attested by the remains of a chapel and/or dedicatory inscriptions and crosses found at them. A common feature of these sites is their location along paths leading to desert monasteries.

The holy sites within the confines of the Judean desert may be divided into two types. The first functioned as a station on the path to a monastery or a pilgrimage site. Such was the place where the empress Eudocia built the church dedicated to St. Peter. The church was built on the road from Jerusalem to Jericho at the spot where travelers first caught sight of the laura of Euthymius in Mishor Adummim. According to Cyril, the empress had come to watch the construction of a reservoir on this spot. Seeing the laura from there, she had then uttered a blessing and ordered the building of a church on the site (*V. Euth.* 35, 53. 10–13). Pilgrims who took the same route could pray in the church and rest awhile on their way. The ruins of Qasr ʿAli, about 6 km northeast of Jerusalem, have been identified as the reservoir and church built by Eudocia.

A remarkable example of a holy site on the way to a monastery is "the Rock of the Crosses." This site was discovered during a survey in the area of the monastery of Chariton. It is situated on the northern bank of Wadi Khureitun, about 2 km east of the laura.[5]

The Rock of the Crosses is an enormous niche, 8.4 m long, 3.5 m deep, and 3 m high, cut out of the rock and facing northeast (fig. 122). There are no indications on the sides of the niche of its having been roofed over, which suggests that it was open to the sky. Five crosses were carved on its walls, each of the Greek type, with arms that broaden gradually from the center outward (fig. 123). The arms of the central and largest cross are nearly 1 m long (fig. 124).

East of this ornamented rock were approximately twenty-five carved steps leading down to a cave. A drainage channel leading to a water cistern at the mouth of the cave ran alongside the steps. The cave is enormous: its width at the opening comes to 22 m, its maximum depth to 25 m, and its height is approximately 9 m. The water cistern at the opening was carved out of the rock and was lined with hydraulic plaster containing large quantities of Byzantine crushed pottery.

On the eastern side of the cave, a semicircular niche can be discerned. Its diameter is 1.9 m and its height 2.3 m. Its well-defined form and eastern orientation point to its use as a prayer niche or apse. This discovery lends weight to the hypothesis that the Rock of the Crosses was a holy site commemorating some event in the history of the area.

The site is approached by one of three footpaths. The first descends steeply from the plateau on the northern side of the ravine; along it, the surveyors found impressive segments of retaining walls of the type found elsewhere beside Byzantine monastic paths. This route links the site with Byzantine churches

Figure 122 The Rock of the Crosses (looking northeast)

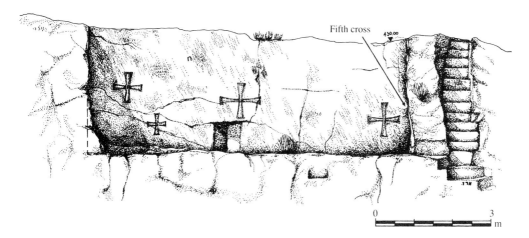

Figure 123 Elevation of the Rock of the Crosses

Figure 124 Central cross of the Rock of the Crosses

in Herodium and continues to Bethlehem. The second path comes from the monastery of Chariton, and the third crosses the wadi and then branches off into paths leading to Tekoa and to several monasteries in the area. The location of the site, at a junction of footpaths, suggests its connection with pilgrim traffic in the Byzantine period.

Open religious sites, such as this and the above-mentioned prayer niches in southern Sinai, seem to have been extremely rare in early Christianity. Ceremonies were usually carried out under a roof of some sort (in a church, a crypt, a cave, or whatever).

A further example of a commemorative site established by monks is a large stone block that stands between the monastery of Kursi, on the eastern side of the Sea of Galilee, and the cliff to the east of the monastery.[6] According to tradition, the miracle of the Gadarene swine (Matt. 8:28–32) took place beside this block. Protective walls surround the block, and a small chapel was built beside it. The excavators leave open the question of whether the stone block was roofed or not. In any case, this is one of the most beautiful and best preserved memorial sites constructed by monks during the Byzantine period.

Another religious site on the way to a monastery was discovered near the monastery of Theoctistus.[7] The site is located about 100 m west of the monastery gate. The fact that it is a holy place is indicated by a dominant cross carved high up on the face of the cliff that rises to the north of the wadi; several other crosses and inscriptions were scratched on the rock face below it (fig. 125). The main cross was very carefully carved. It is large, measuring 1 m in height and 0.7 m in width. Between its arms is inscribed a Greek monogram signifying "Jesus Christ," and beneath the cross are the first and last letters of the Greek alphabet, *alpha* and *omega,* alluding to John 22:13. The cross and the monogram were probably carved by the monks when they built the bench and the cistern that were found next to the rock. The other crosses and inscriptions at the site were carved by pilgrims. The names of two women appear in the inscriptions, leading to the conclusion that this was a meeting place for the monks with

Figure 125 Plan and cross-section
of a religious site near
the monastery of Theoctistus

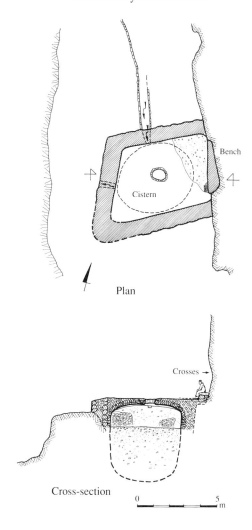

Bench

Cistern

Plan

Crosses →

Cross-section

0   5
m

women pilgrims, who were not allowed to enter the monastery. (As noted, the only monastery in the Judean desert that permitted women to enter was that of Choziba.)

The most interesting inscription reads: "Holy (man), help Za(nnos)." Unlike the other inscriptions, this one relates directly to a particular holy man. His name is not mentioned, but it seems reasonable to assume that he was Theoctistus, who was venerated after his death, or possibly Euthymius, who was recognized as a holy man during his lifetime. Euthymius was the founder of the monastery and was the spiritual leader of the community until his death in 473. In any case, it is clear that the site was used by people who venerated Theoctistus and Euthymius and who came in search of personal salvation.

The second type of holy site in the Judean desert was a place near a monastery connected with a venerated monk. The hagiographical literature of the Judean desert mentions several sites dedicated to saintly monks or celebrated hermits. One of the earliest is Chariton's hermitage, a small alcove high up on a cliff known in Chariton's day as "the Hanging Cave of Chariton" (*V. Char.* 24, 34. 6–7). At the time when Chariton's biography was being written, two hundred years later, the cave still served as a holy place. Cyril's biography of Cyriac illustrates the reverence in which it was held at that later period. At the age of seventy-seven, Cyriac left the monastery of Chariton to lead a solitary life at Sousakim. At this stage of his life, he was already recognized as a holy man and a miracle-worker. According to Cyril, when an epidemic of bubonic plague erupted in 542, the fathers of the monastery of Chariton came to Cyriac and begged him to come back to the monastery to protect them from disaster. As a sign of their veneration and in recognition of his wish for solitude, they settled him in the Hanging Cave of Chariton, where he lived for five years.[8] This implies that the cave was usually empty and that it was given to Cyriac only because he was recognized as a holy man.

The niche identified as the Hanging Cave of Chariton was discovered in the southern bank of Wadi Khureitun about 800 m south of the laura.[9] Two footpaths lead to it: one from the monastery of Chariton, the other from Tekoa in the southwest. The niche opens approximately 15 m above ground level—hence its name (fig. 126). Access to it is by means of a ladder, via two caves located beneath it. The first cave, which is at ground level, is bell-shaped and measures about 7 × 15 m. Three water cisterns were dug inside the cave. At the mouth of the cave, a small pool shaped like a bathtub was found (fig. 127). This was probably used as a baptismal font. Along the well-paved path that leads to the font is a large shelf in the cliff, which gave shelter to visitors. An opening in the ceiling of the cave, about 4 m from the floor, leads to the second cave, on the middle level (fig. 128). In this cave, the remains of a small chapel were found (fig. 129).

Figure 126 The Hanging Cave of Chariton on the southern bank of the Wadi Khureitun (marked with an arrow; looking south)

These remains include a semicircular niche 1.1 m in diameter, a number of other niches cut out of the cave walls, and an additional water cistern on the eastern side of the cave. The opening leading to Chariton's alcove was cut out of the uppermost corner of the cave, 3.5 m above floor level. From the opening, an extremely narrow passage, somewhat like a shelf, led to the uppermost level.

Chariton's alcove is pear-shaped and measures 1 × 2 m, with a maximum height of 1.9 m. Its walls were carved out of the rock and were lined with a well-smoothed yellowish plaster and adorned with painted Greek monograms and drawings of two crosses executed in black, red, and yellow paint. An abbreviation of the phrase "Jesus Christ, Son of God" was painted next to the arms of the main cross on the eastern wall of the niche. The niche's decoration and its location high up on the rock face enable us to identify it as the Hanging Cave (fig. 130).

Thus, it seems that the Hanging Cave had two stages of use. Initially it served as Chariton's place of seclusion, suspended high up on the rock face. This type of asceticism resembles that of the stylites, who lived atop pillars, a

Figure 127 Entrance to the bottom level of the Hanging Cave of Chariton

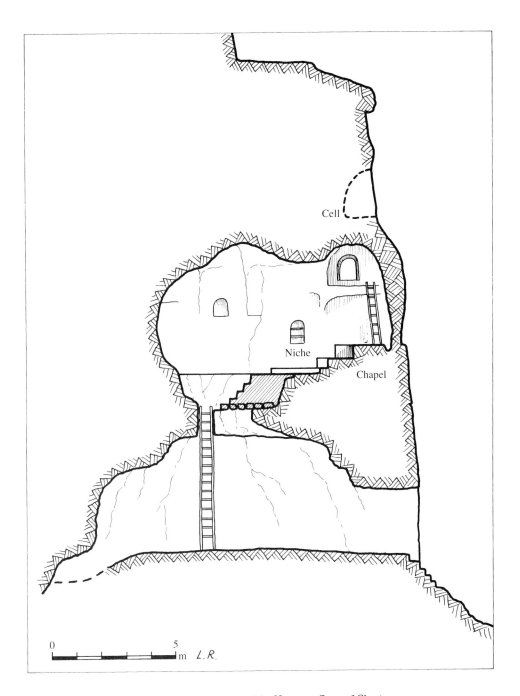

Cell

Niche

Chapel

0   5
m   *L.R.*

Figure 128 Cross-section of the Hanging Cave of Chariton

Figure 129 Chapel below Chariton's cell in the Hanging Cave

practice that became widespread later in the Byzantine period. After Chariton's death, the cave became a venerated spot for the monks. It was then that the chapel in the intermediate cave was carved and the cisterns were dug, probably to provide water for visitors.

Another holy place of this type, known only from the written sources, is the abode of Mary the harp-player, whose story is told by Cyril of Scythopolis (*V. Cyr.* 17–19, 233. 4). Cyril heard the story from Cyriac's disciple John, the monk who accompanied Cyril on his visit to Cyriac's hermitage at Sousakim. On the way back from Sousakim, John pointed out the place where Mary had been buried, in the cave that had served as her hermitage for eighteen years. According to John, Mary was a harp-player in the Church of Anastasius in Jerusalem. Fearing for her soul, she decided to leave her position and went to the desert to live in solitude. This account includes many of the themes commonly found in hagiographic literature; but it appears that the story has a solid basis that reflects some historical reality. John related that it was he and his friend Paramon from the Old Laura who found the dead body of the saintly woman.

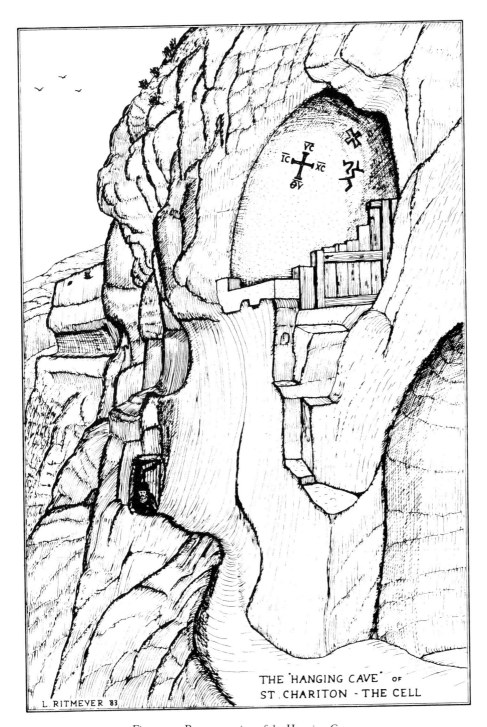

THE "HANGING CAVE" OF
ST. CHARITON - THE CELL

L. RITMEYER 83

Figure 130 Reconstruction of the Hanging Cave

Lacking the necessities to prepare the body for burial, the two monks returned to the monastery of Chariton to obtain them. They then buried her in her own cave and sealed the entrance with stones.[10] Cyril notes that the site was pointed out to passersby.

Another source that mentions a holy place in the vicinity of the Great Laura is the text known as "The Passion of St. Michael the Sabaite." This text was written by an anonymous monk who lived in the Great Laura toward the end of the eighth or the beginning of the ninth century.[11] According to the author, the monks of the Great Laura would celebrate the Annunciation (25 March) in a certain place 2 stadia (370 m) east of the laura. This was the spot where, according to tradition, Sabas saw a vision of the Virgin Mary and vowed to dedicate the main church of the laura to her. The monks gathered at the site with crosses and icons, chanting hymns, praying to the Virgin Mary, and reading from Scripture. Although this text is late, the proceedings described are almost identical with those reported by Egeria in the fourth century. Therefore it may be assumed that this was the kind of thing that went on at all holy sites in the vicinity of the Judean desert monasteries during and after the Byzantine period.

Conclusions

This study of the archaeological evidence and the literary sources leads to several conclusions about Judean desert monasticism. First, monastic society in the Judean desert had a distinct organizational framework, which evolved over a long period of time and attained its final form only in the time of Sabas and Theodosius. Both the written sources and the archaeological finds indicate that during the period under discussion there were about twenty lauras and forty-five coenobia in the Judean desert. There were also hermits, most of whom were affiliated with a mother monastery. The coenobia, especially the larger ones, provided charity and shelter for the needy; so the monks, apart from their communal and private prayer, were engaged in providing social services. The monks of the lauras, on the other hand, spent most of their time in contemplation and in reading spiritual books. Consequently, it was the aspiration of many monks to join a laura. However, a regulation instituted during the time of Euthymius and adopted by his successors specified that lauras were only for experienced monks who had undergone a long period of training in a coenobium. This regulation ensured that lauritic life maintained a high level. In fact, the large lauras—for example, the Great Laura and the monastery of Chariton—became major centers of spiritual and literary activity during the Byzantine period and later.

Second, most Judean desert monasteries of the Byzantine period had the resources to invest in the best materials and the finest construction. Special attention was lavished on the common buildings: the church and the refectory. Their remains usually include evidence of expensive materials and fittings, such as marble, stucco, fresco, colorful mosaics, and glass windowpanes, and the church (and often the refectory) was usually roofed with tiles. These materials were not readily available and had to be purchased outside the desert and transported to the building sites. Most parts of a monastery were built relatively simply, however, albeit with great efficiency. A utilitarian architecture was used for the water systems, gardens, storerooms, ovens, living quarters, and other elements associated with the more mundane activities. The remains of cells in the lauras also indicate simplicity, the modest dimensions and construction reflecting a humble way of life.

Yet in many respects, the standard of living in the Judean desert monasteries seems to have been higher than that of most people in the Byzantine Empire. The coenobia were usually built in the style of a country house, with spacious buildings surrounded by a wall and with interior courtyards. Written sources and archaeological finds indicate that most of the religious communities in the Judean desert were small, with no more than twenty members. Thus, the monasteries were not crowded, and it is probable that monks from lower- and middle-class strata of society improved their standard of living by joining a monastery.

The result of the monks' activity was to turn the Judean desert into part of the settled world of the Byzantine period. Indeed, the many remains of monastery buildings, elaborate water systems, gardens, and footpaths found there attest to the monks' success in settling the wilderness.

In addition, the monks of the Judean desert were experts when it came to living off the natural resources of the land. It can be assumed that they acquired their knowledge of the wild plants which featured significantly in their diet from the long-time inhabitants of the desert: the Saracens and the shepherds from the villages on the desert fringe. Indeed, cooperation between the monks and the desert-dwellers is alluded to in the written sources. But the ability of the monks to harness the resources of their desert environment is seen primarily in the water installations found in their monasteries.

We may also conclude that the monastic movement in the Judean desert had strong ties with the Church establishment in Palestine, especially in Jerusalem. From the time of Euthymius onward, desert monks were often appointed to ecclesiastical positions. Owing to its location in a major center of pilgrimage, the Church of Jerusalem was much exposed to external influences and was thus quite open to incorporating foreigners in its ranks. Many of the Judean desert monks were originally pilgrims to the holy places. Indeed, the monastic movement in the Judean desert may be regarded as a direct continuation of the mass pilgrimage movement to Palestine. The latter was the main source of manpower for the monasteries, and the donations of pilgrims were the main source of funds for building and maintaining monasteries. As long as security conditions in the Byzantine Empire remained unchanged, desert monasticism flourished unrestricted. However, the geopolitical changes that took place in the wake of the Muslim conquest in 638 and the severance of Palestine from the main centers of the Byzantine Empire led to a drastic decline in the number of pilgrims, and consequently in the capability of many of the monasteries to survive.

Finally, during the Byzantine period, the monks of the Judean desert developed a way of life that has survived—albeit with a number of changes—to this day. In the late nineteenth century, there was a revival of desert monasticism, and several monasteries were rebuilt: some, such as the monastery of Choziba (St. George) in Wadi Qilt and the monastery of Douka (Deir Quruntul) west of Jericho, utilizing the construction techniques of the Byzantine period. This restoration, as well as the uninterrupted presence of monks in the Judean desert throughout the centuries, are indications of the profound cultural heritage of monasticism in this region.

A Who's Who of Judean Desert Monasticism

Brief Biographies of the Major Figures

ANTHONY OF CHOZIBA (CHOZIBITES)

A monk who lived in the monastery of Choziba and biographer of George of Choziba. Our sole source of information about Anthony is an autobiographical section in the biography.

Anthony arrived at the monastery of Choziba toward the end of the sixth century or at the beginning of the seventh century (in any case, prior to the Persian invasion of 614). His first position in the monastery was that of candlelighter in the church. During the Persian invasion, he did not join the abbot, who fled with most of the monks to Transjordan, but with George, his mentor, hid in a ravine near the monastery, apparently Wadi Qilt. Various anecdotes attest to the strong bond that developed between Anthony and George during this time. When the monks returned, Anthony came back as well and was put in charge of the storeroom.

After George's death, Anthony wrote his biography; he also wrote a history of the monastery from its foundation in the fifth century, as well as accounts of various miracles credited to the monastery's patron saint, the Virgin Mary.

CHARITON

Monk, holy man (a title usually given to miracle-workers), and father of Judean desert monasticism. He was born in Iconium (Konya today), in Asia Minor, at the end of the third century and died in the laura of Pharan in the middle of the fourth century. The sole source of information about Chariton is a biography written by an anonymous monk who lived in one of Chariton's monasteries in the second half of the sixth century.

239

Chariton was born into an aristocratic family that was a target of anti-Christian persecution. After the Edict of Constantine the Great (the first Christian emperor), Chariton came to Jerusalem as a pilgrim. He then visited the Dead Sea region and settled in Pharan, where he founded a laura, the first monastery in the Judean desert and the first of its kind in the world. He went on to establish two more lauras: Douka and Souka (the Old Laura).

He lived an exemplary life and was known for his strict asceticism. He would take short naps on the ground, spend most of the night chanting psalms, and habitually wore a hair shirt. But he was most famous for his lifelong quest for solitude. Indeed, he left each of the monasteries that grew up around his places of seclusion. His final dwelling place was a cave near the Old Laura, his third and most important monastery, at the top of a steep cliff; because of its location it was called "the Hanging Cave."

Shortly before his death, he returned to his first monastery, the laura of Pharan. There he assembled the elders of all three of his monasteries and spoke to them about monastic principles. He appears to have been buried in that monastery. At the end of the Byzantine period, or perhaps later, his remains were reinterred in the Old Laura, which was then renamed the monastery of Chariton.

CYRIAC

Monk and holy man of the Judean desert. Cyriac was born in Corinth, in Greece, in 449 and died in the Old Laura in 557. The sole source of information about him is a biography written by Cyril of Scythopolis, who knew him personally and received the details of his life directly from him.

Cyriac was born into a respected family related to the local bishop. As a child, he was a reader in the church. In 467 he arrived at the laura of Euthymius. Its founder admitted him to the brotherhood but because of his youth sent him to the monastery of Gerasimus for a novitiate.

After nine years in the monastery of Gerasimus, Cyriac returned to the laura of Euthymius for nine years. Then, in 485, he moved to the Old Laura, where he spent thirty-one years. During this time, he held various positions in the monastery and lived a life of extreme asceticism. By his own account, the sun never saw him eating or showing anger during the years he spent in the Old Laura.

In 526, he left the monastery and went to live as a hermit in the interior of the desert. He gradually became famous as a miracle-worker, and admirers flocked to his door. His first miracle was the healing of the lunatic son of a dignitary in the nearby village of Tekoa. In search of solitude, he then moved to a more remote site, known as Sousakim, where he lived alone for seven years. He was then asked by the elders of the Old Laura to return to the monastery, in the hopes that his presence (as a holy man) would protect them from the bubonic plague that had broken out in 542. He spent five years there as an honored guest in the Hanging Cave of Chariton and then resumed his solitary life at Sousakim.

Eight years later he again complied with a request from the elders of the Old Laura to return to the monastery, where he lived until his death at the age of 108. Cyril reports that despite his advanced age, Cyriac remained strong and vigorous. He would stand throughout the church services and attend to his many guests himself. He was buried in the Old Laura.

CYRIL OF SCYTHOPOLIS

Monk and hagiographer. Cyril was born ca. 525 in Scythopolis (Beit She'an) and died sometime after 560 in the Great Laura. His work, which includes seven biographies, contains autobiographical details that enable us to reconstruct his life story.

He was born into a prominent family in Beit She'an. His parents were devout Christians and knew Sabas, who was perhaps the leading figure in Judean desert monasticism at the time. Cyril reports that his parents gave hospitality to Sabas's disciples and sent yearly contributions to his monasteries.

In 543 Cyril joined a monastery in the vicinity of Beit She'an. Shortly thereafter, he left for the Judean desert. Guided by his spiritual mentor, John Hesychast of the Great Laura, Cyril settled in the coenobium of Euthymius. During the nearly ten years he spent there, Cyril occasionally roamed the desert roads and visited monks he admired. He was thus able to collect anecdotes and information about their lives. He began writing only after he arrived at the Nea Laura in 554 as one of the 120 monks sent to replace the supporters of Origenism, who had been excommunicated and banished from the site. During his residence there, he kept to his cell, where he apparently completed the first of his biographies, that of Euthymius. Two years later, he joined the community of the Great Laura, where he completed his other biographies. He was then at the height of his career and was ordained a priest. The latest date mentioned in his work is 559.

Thanks to his writings, which reflect his broad education, we know more about monasticism in the Judean desert than about any of the other monastic movements in Palestine.

ELIAS

Monk, founder of a monastery, and patriarch of Jerusalem from 494 until 516. The main source of information about him is Cyril of Scythopolis.

Elias was born in Transjordan. In 457 he and his friend Martyrius arrived at the laura of Euthymius. Since they had both spent several years at the monastery on Mount Nitria, in Egypt, and were thus experienced monks, they were accepted right away into the laura's community. They were even invited to join the chosen few who roamed the depths of the desert with Euthymius during Lent. Later, they left the laura and went their separate ways. Elias moved to the Jericho region, where he founded two coenobia which bore his name and were under the leadership of a single abbot. In 474, he and Martyrius were ordained priests in the Church of the Holy Sepulchre in Jerusalem.

In 494, Elias was appointed patriarch of Jerusalem, the highest-ranking position in the Church hierarchy. During his term of office, he gave much assistance to the Judean desert monks, particularly for construction. On account of his opposition to the religious policy of the emperor Anastasius, he was exiled to Aila (Eilat) in 516. He died there two years later. In his will, he instructed that his two monasteries in the Jericho region remain united, under the jurisdiction of a single abbot. However, this instruction was ignored. In 528, one of the monasteries was purchased by a group of wealthy eunuchs from Constantinople and was renamed "the monastery of the Eunuchs."

EUDOCIA

Empress, philanthropist, and one of the great builders of ancient Palestine. Eudocia was the daughter of the Athenian philosopher Leontius and was originally named Athenais. After receiving a classical education, she converted to Christianity; was baptized, taking a new name, Elia Eudocia; and in 421 married the emperor Theodosius II. In 441 or 442, Theodosius was separated from her; but he allowed her to retain her status as empress, and she settled in Jerusalem. Until her death about twenty years later, she was a leading figure in the city and a benefactor of the holy places. Despite her wealth and position, however, she lived a life of asceticism and Christian piety.

She initiated many building projects in Palestine, including the southern wall of Jerusalem, hospices for the poor and the aged, and St. Stephen's Church, north of the city. In her last years, she became a fervent supporter of Euthymius and built a tower in his honor at the top of Mount Muntar, where she met with him on one occasion for spiritual direction. She also built St. Peter's Church, on the Jerusalem–Jericho road. In 460, a year after its completion, she died in Jerusalem.

EUTHYMIUS

A holy man, one of the most prominent leaders of monasticism in the Judean desert, founder of three monasteries, and the only Palestinian monk to be acclaimed as "the Great." Euthymius was born in Melitene, Armenia, in 377 and died in 473 in the laura that bore his name. He is the subject of the first biography written by Cyril of Scythopolis.

Cyril emphasizes that Euthymius was a formative influence on the monastic movement in the Judean desert. He arrived there at a relatively mature age (twenty-nine), after having been ordained a priest in his homeland and having experienced monastic life there. He founded the first coenobia in the Judean desert, the monasteries of Theoctistus and Caparbaricha, as well as the laura of Euthymius. As abbot, he gave much spiritual guidance to his monks—in fact, Cyril often refers to him as "the great teacher."

Euthymius's many admirers included villagers and nomads living in the vicinity of his monasteries. Among the converts to his credit were a Saracen tribe who had settled in the Judean desert and several inhabitants of villages on the desert fringe.

Euthymius avoided becoming actively involved in public life. Unlike other Judean desert leaders, such as Sabas and Theodosius, he stayed away from Jerusalem and kept his contacts with the religious establishment to a minimum. In the years after the Council of Chalcedon in 451, Euthymius, who was alone in his support of the council's resolutions, decided to leave his monastery and live in solitude in the interior of the desert. Eudocia, who venerated him and later became a supporter of the Chalcedonian Creed, sent messengers begging him to meet her once in the tower she had built in his honor on Mount Muntar; he complied with her request.

Cyril describes Euthymius as a pleasant man, very short in stature, with a round face, sharp eyes, and a flowing white beard. He remained strong and vigorous throughout his life and died on 20 January 473. His funeral was attended by a multitude of devoted followers. His tomb, in the monastery that bears his name, continued to be venerated long after his death.

GABRIEL

Monk of the Judean desert and abbot of the monastery beside St. Stephen's Church in Jerusalem. The limited information available about him is mainly from the writings of Cyril of Scythopolis.

Gabriel was one of the first monks to join Euthymius's community. He arrived at the laura in 428, together with his two older brothers, Cosmas and Chrysippus. The three brothers came from Cappadocia, in Asia Minor. Gabriel was a eunuch from birth and had a feminine appearance; he was therefore instructed by Euthymius never to leave his cell, for fear of "the temptations of the Devil."

In about 456, Eudocia invited Gabriel to serve as abbot of the monastery of St. Stephen's Church, a position he held for twenty-four years. During this period, he established a small coenobium of his own to the east of Jerusalem, where he would spend Lent in solitude. According to Cyril, Gabriel was famous for his love of learning and was fluent in Latin, Greek, and Syriac.

GEORGE OF CHOZIBA (CHOZIBITES)

Monk and holy man at the monastery of Choziba at the end of the sixth century and during the early seventh century. Because of his fame, the monastery is known to this day as the monastery of St. George. His life story is recounted at length by his disciple Anthony of Choziba.

George was born into a devout Christian family in Cyprus. His uncle was abbot of a monastery there, and his brother Heraclides was a monk in the laura of Calamon, in the Jordan valley. George followed in his brother's footsteps, but, because of his youth, was sent to the monastery of Choziba for a novitiate. His first position in the monastery was that of gardener's helper.

Some time later he became famous as a miracle-worker and, in order to avoid becoming an object of adulation among his fellow monks, decided to join his brother at the laura of Calamon. The two brothers spent about twenty years together in the laura, living on scraps of cooked food and cultivating the monastery's date-palm plantation. After Heraclides died, George returned to the monastery of Choziba. As an experienced monk, he was permitted to live in the Cells of Choziba, a laura-style arrangement connected with the monastery. During this period, he served as spiritual guide to the community, although he never became abbot. On Sundays, when he and the other cell-dwellers went to the monastery for common prayer, the monks in charge of the various offices would consult him and ask his blessing. George set an example for the community, volunteering for arduous tasks such as baking bread and dispensing water to pilgrims en route to Jericho.

After the Persian invasion of 614, he left his cell and moved into the main complex of the monastery. He was buried in the tomb of the monastery's founding fathers, where his remains are displayed to this day.

GERASIMUS

Monk and founder of the first monastery in the Jordan valley. Gerasimus was born in Lycia, in Asia Minor, and died in 475 in his monastery. The main source of information about him is a work written by an anonymous monk in his monastery during the second half of the sixth century.

Gerasimus was born into a devout Christian family and entered monastic life at an early age. After spending some time in a coenobium, he began to live as a hermit, subsisting on wild plants. His first experience as a hermit was in the Dead Sea region. Thus, when he arrived in the Judean desert and joined Euthymius, who left his monastery in 451 and secluded himself in the depths of the desert, he was already familiar with various forms of monastic life.

The laura of Gerasimus combined solitude with communal life, and Gerasimus may be viewed as one of the important formative influences on Judean desert monasticism. He provided the monks of the laura with detailed regulations. He also continued to maintain ties with his spiritual mentor, Euthymius, and according to the account we have, learned of the latter's death through a divine revelation.

The biographies of most of the important Judean desert monks contain the classic theme of the lion who is devoted to the hero. But the most famous of these stories is that of the friendship that developed between Gerasimus and the lion he named "Jordan." In 470 Gerasimus extracted a long thorn from the lion's foot, and from then on, the lion followed him everywhere. Five years later, when Gerasimus died, the grief-stricken lion succumbed as well, on the site of Gerasimus's tomb. To this day, icons and frescoes depict Gerasimus with a lion at his feet.

JOHN HESYCHAST

One of the most famous monks of the Great Laura and its spiritual leader during the Origenist controversy. John Hesychast was born in 454 in Nicopolis, in Armenia, and died in the Great Laura in 559. His biography was the third written by Cyril of Scythopolis, following those of Euthymius and Sabas.

He was born into a noble family, many of whose members occupied high positions in government. At the age of twenty-eight, he was appointed bishop of Colonia, but as a result of disputes with his brother-in-law, who was governor of the province, he decided to leave this post and live as a monk in the Judean desert. Ten years later, in 491, he arrived at the Great Laura, incognito.

He was diligent in his appointed tasks and was notable for his ascetic practices. After John had served as steward of the laura for three years, Sabas, the abbot, not knowing his background, wanted to ordain him a priest. After learning, through a revelation, his true identity and his former position as bishop, Sabas permitted John to live in solitude in his cell, without participating in the weekly communal prayers. John lived in seclusion for more than fifty years—hence his appellation "Hesychast" ("the Contemplative Recluse").

During his long years of solitude, numerous people came to his cell to receive his blessing. Although he never served as abbot, many of the laura's monks, including Cyril, sought his advice and confided in him. During the Origenist controversy of 532–54, he headed the anti-Origenist movement in the Great Laura. He died on 8 January 559 at the age of 105 and was buried in the tomb of the leading monks of the Great Laura. According to tradition, the cell he inhabited is on the eastern bank of the Kidron valley.

MARTYRIUS

Monk, founder of a monastery, and patriarch of Jerusalem from 478 to 486. Most of the biographical information available about him is found in the work of Cyril of Scythopolis.

Martyrius was born in Cappadocia. After spending several years in the monastery on Mount Nitria, in Egypt, he arrived at the laura of Euthymius with Elias, his friend and colleague, in the summer of 457. Some time later, the two left the laura and founded their own monasteries. Martyrius founded the monastery not far from Jerusalem that bears his name. After the death of Euthymius in 473, Martyrius, like Elias, was asked to serve as a priest in the Church of the Holy Sepulchre.

Five years later, in 478, Martyrius was appointed patriarch of Jerusalem. One of his first acts as patriarch was to convert the laura of Euthymius into a coenobium. This act, which was unprecedented, proved to be extremely important for the history of the monastic movement in the Judean desert, because it raised the status of the coenobitic form of monasticism relative to the lauritic form. Yet, he also appears to have assisted Sabas in the early years of the Great Laura. Judging by the impressive ruins of the monastery of Martyrius, it is probable that he extended special assistance to his monastery during his term as patriarch.

He died in 486 and was apparently buried in the cemetery for Christian patriarchs in Jerusalem.

JOHN MOSCHUS

Monk and compiler of a collection of anecdotes concerning the lives of monks, known as *Pratum spirituale* (*Lemonarion*, "The Meadow"). John Moschus lived from ca. 550 to ca. 620, and his work includes a few autobiographical details.

His country of origin is not mentioned explicitly, but it is known that he was not a Palestinian. In about 575, he was accepted as a monk at the monastery of Theodosius. After a novitiate that was probably lengthy (the novitiate of monks in the coenobitic monasteries of the Judean desert was usually about ten years), Moschus moved to a cell in the laura of Pharan. He spent about ten years there, and his anecdotes from this period make special mention of several ascetics who lived on a weekly diet of one piece of bread. He then moved to the relatively new laura of the Aeliotes, in the Jordan valley, and his reminiscences from this sojourn provide numerous details about monastic life in that area.

After ten years at the monastery of the Aeliotes, he moved to the Nea Laura and then began wandering outside the Judean desert. In the course of his travels, he visited the great centers of monasticism: Egypt, Mount Sinai, Antioch, Cyprus, and Rome, where he died ca. 620. His body was brought back to Palestine by his friend Sophronius, later patriarch of Jerusalem. He was entombed in the monastery of Theodosius, where he had begun his monastic life.

SABAS

Monk and holy man, founder of many monasteries, and religious leader of the Church in Palestine. Sabas was born in Cappadocia, in Asia Minor, in 439 and died in 532 in the laura he had founded in the Kidron valley. The biography of Sabas written by Cyril of Scythopolis provides a detailed history of the man he says was "divinely commanded to turn the desert into a city."

Sabas was born into a prominent Christian family in a small village named Mutalaska near the Cappadocian city of Caesarea. His father was a high-ranking officer in the army. At the age of eight, Sabas was sent to a coenobium near the village, where he lived for about ten years. At an early age, he was appointed reader in the church. When he was eighteen, he decided to join the monks of the Judean desert. He arrived in Jerusalem in the winter of 456–7 and later went to the laura of Euthymius. Because of his youth, he was sent to the monastery of Theoctistus, although he already had experience of monastic life.

Three main periods may be distinguished in Sabas's long career as a monk in the Judean desert (about seventy-five years): first, the period between 457 and 483, when he lived as a monk in a coenobium and later as a hermit near the coenobium and in the inner desert; second, the period between 483 and 512, during which he founded the Great Laura in the Kidron valley and most of his other monasteries; and third, the period between 512 and 532, when he served not only as abbot at various monasteries but also as the spiritual leader of the Church of Palestine as a whole.

The most notable aspect of Sabas's career was his establishment of monasteries. Over the years, he founded no less than eight monasteries within the confines of the Judean desert (as well as two others outside the desert), and four more monasteries were founded by his disciples.

Sabas developed close ties with the Church establishment in Jerusalem and enjoyed the moral and financial support of the various patriarchs. In 490 he was ordained a priest and in 494 was elected archimandrite in charge of the lauritic monks and hermits throughout Palestine. His ordination to the priesthood came relatively late in his career, perhaps because he was cross-eyed. (Physical defects usually disqualified candidates for the priesthood.) The fact is, however, that the patriarch of Jerusalem ordained him in response to his opponents' claim that he could not lead such a large laura without being a priest.

From his beginnings as a novice at the monastery of Theoctistus, he was outstanding for his industriousness, asceticism, and piety. He was always the first to arrive for prayers and the last to leave. According to Cyril, he was physically strong and was renowned for his ability to survive under harsh conditions. Sabas often spent Lent roaming in the desert. He would wander as far afield as Zoar (south of the Dead Sea) and the sources of the Jordan River in the north. He is described as a holy man, whose miracles included rain-making and healing the sick.

When Sabas was sent by the patriarch to the emperor in Constantinople in 511, his rags led the guards to drive him away, on the supposition that he was a beggar; but later he was received royally and was greatly revered by the noblewomen of the court.

He died on 5 December 532 and was buried in the central courtyard of the laura, where his tomb stands to this day.

THE SENATOR'S DAUGHTER ("SYNCLETICA")

A hermit in the Jordan valley in the sixth century. Of her story, told by an anonymous monk in the Judean desert, we have few details.

She was the daughter of a wealthy senator in Constantinople. At the age of eighteen, wishing to lead an ascetic life, she asked her father's permission to make a pilgrimage to Jerusalem. He supplied her with a retinue of attendants and three thousand gold coins. After praying at the holy places in Jerusalem, she traveled to the Jordan River, where she met some monks from the laura of the Egyptians (Coprotha). On her return to Jerusalem, she slipped away from her attendants and went to see a hermit she had met in the Jordan valley. After presenting him with three hundred gold coins, she received a monk's habit and a Bible that he had in his possession. She then lived in solitude for twenty-eight years in a cave in the Jordan valley.

This story is rich in conventional themes, but most of the details with regard to monastic life in the Jordan valley are realistic.

STEPHEN SABAITES

Monk and holy man in the Great Laura. Stephen Sabaites was born in 725 in a village near Ashkelon and died in 794. His biography (preserved partly in Greek, partly in Arabic) was written by his disciple Leontius. Stephen was renowned for his miracles and was therefore given the Greek appellation "Thaumaturgos," or miracle-worker.

He was born into a devout Christian family, but at the age of nine he was orphaned and was then adopted by his uncle Zacharias, a monk in the Great Laura. He lived with his uncle as a novice for fifteen years.

In 749, Zacharias was appointed abbot of the monasteries of Spelaion and Castellion, which were affiliated with the Great Laura. Stephen remained in his uncle's cell, now as a regular cell-dweller, and held various service positions—in the bakery, the infirmary, the library, and so on. He was also appointed deacon and leader of the communal prayers in the church. By then, he had become a spiritual guide, and other monks would consult him on various matters. Seeking more peace and quiet, he requested and received a more secluded cell.

During Lent, he would roam the interior of the desert. On several of these journeys, he circled the Dead Sea, reaching a number of monasteries that had already been deserted. His biography is thus one of the most important sources regarding monastic life in the Judean desert after the Byzantine period.

THEOCTISTUS

Monk and abbot of the first coenobium in the Judean desert. The sparse details we have about his life come from the works of Cyril of Scythopolis (mainly the biography of Euthymius).

Theoctistus was a monk in the laura of Pharan when Euthymius arrived there in 405. The two became friends and would go together into the interior of the desert during Lent. On their fifth trip, they discovered a cave fit for habitation, which became the nucleus of the monastery of Theoctistus. About ten years later, Euthymius left the monastery, but Theoctistus remained as sole leader until his death in 466, at a "ripe old age."

THEODOSIUS

Monk, holy man, and founder of the largest and most important coenobium in the Judean desert. Theodosius was born in 423 in Cappadocia and died in his monastery in 529, at the age of 105. The main source of information is a work by Theodore of Petra, a monk in his monastery. Additional details are provided by Cyril of Scythopolis.

Theodosius was born into a devout Christian family in the Cappadocian village of Mogarissus. As a boy, he was appointed reader in the church of the nearby town of Comana. In 451 he arrived in Jerusalem with the intention of leading a solitary life in the Judean desert. He spent about twenty years in the monastery of Cathisma, between Jerusalem and Bethlehem, and then received instruction in the eremitical life from Marinus and Lucas, hermits who had been disciples of Euthymius, in the desert region east of Cathisma. These years prepared him for his later role as leader of coenobitic monasticism in the Judean desert. In about 479 he founded his large monastery east of Bethlehem.

According to Cyril, Theodosius was famous for his extreme asceticism, his charity and hospitality, and his strict observance of ritual. His monastery, described in detail by Theodore of Petra, was founded on, and functioned according to, these principles and was particularly renowned for its hospices.

In 494, he and his friend Sabas were elected to the position of archimandrite. Theodosius was given responsibility for the coenobitic monasteries in the Jerusalem district and was then given the appellation "Coenobiarch."

According to Theodore of Petra, Theodosius worked many miracles, and his fame as a holy man spread. He was venerated by villagers on the fringe of the desert, as well as by the many pilgrims who came to the monastery and made donations to it. With Sabas, he led the Jerusalem Church in its struggle against the Monophysite policy of the emperor Anastasius.

Theodosius died on 11 January 529 and was buried in his cell, which can be seen in the center of his monastery to this day.

THEOGNIUS

Monk, founder of a monastery, and bishop of the town of Bethulion, near Gaza. His life is recounted by Paul of Elusa, a monk in his monastery. Additional details are given by Cyril of Scythopolis.

Theognius was born in Cappadocia, in Asia Minor, and became a monk as a youth. In 455, he arrived in Jerusalem and joined a monastery on the Mount of Olives, where he lived for about thirty years. He then joined the monastery of Theodosius. A few years later, suffering from an infection in his thumb, he was advised to move to the drier region near Jericho. He accordingly spent some time in the laura of Calamon, until his finger had healed. When he returned to the monastery of Theodosius, it struck him as too large and he decided to leave and to establish his own monastery.

After building a monastery near that of Theodosius, he was asked to serve as bishop of Bethulion. At the close of his life, he returned to his monastery, where he died in 526.

Notes

INTRODUCTION

1. For the historical background of the Essenes and the Therapeutae, see Schürer 1979, 593–7. The main studies of pre-Christian monasticism and the rise of Christian monasticism are Heussi 1936 and Guillaumont 1979.

2. This theory was developed by Vööbus 1958, 109–13, 158–69.

3. Narcissus, bishop of Jerusalem, fled "into a remote and desert area" (Eusebius, *HE* 6, 9.8), having been falsely accused of unspecified crimes by several members of his own flock. His flight took place either toward the end of the second century or in the early third century (Chitty 1966, 14). Lampe 1961, 129 gives the context of the usage of the word *anachoresis*. For the use of the term in Egypt, see Marrou 1964, 270 and Patlagean 1977, 334.

4. In the late third or early fourth century, men fleeing from persecution found refuge in the caves of Calamon, on the west bank of the Jordan River. An obscure tradition concerning these early anchorites is brought to our attention by the biographer of Chariton (*V. Char.* 13, 26.3–4).

5. Marrou 1964, 269–70. For the concept of the monk as successor to the martyr, see Malone 1950, 46–7, 121–6.

6. Swiss and French teams have explored thousands of hermitages in Kellia (Kasser 1967) and Esna (Sauneron and Jacquet 1972). The vast material concerning Egypt has been summarized by Walters (1974) and Badawy (1978). For Pachomius and his system, see Veilleux 1980–2 and Rousseau 1985.

7. For a study based on written sources, see Vööbus 1958, 1960. In the archaeological field, H. C. Butler's surveys (1903, 1919) are still the most valuable sources for the ancient monasteries of Syria. Further evidence has been gathered by Tchalenko (1953) and more recently by Peña, Castellana, and Fernandez (1983). The ecclesiastical archaeology of Syria has been summarized by H. C. Butler (1929) and Lassus (1947).

8. Vailhé's repertory (1899–1900) includes 137 names of monasteries and monastic sites all over Palestine. This list is based on his monastic studies, published as a series of articles between 1897 and 1909.

9. See Chitty 1966. Additional information can be found in Corbo 1958 and Rubin 1982. The first

of these deals with the material culture of the monasteries in Palestine, the second with the lauras of the Judean desert. An updated list of monastic sites within the confines of the Judean desert was published by me in 1990 (Hirschfeld 1990b).

10. E. C. Butler (1911, 529) writes: "In the fifth century, the Holy Land became the head centre of Greek monachism." See also Chitty 1929, 79, 114.

11. Chitty 1966, 130–2; Flusin 1983, 83–6. Schwartz's Greek edition (1939) was translated into French by Festugière in three volumes (1962, 1962a, 1963). An English translation by R. M. Price is due to be published soon. For Cyril's career as monk and hagiographer in the Judean desert, see Vailhé 1907, 298–302; Génier 1909, xii; Flusin 1983, 12–40; and Hirschfeld 1989c.

12. See Vailhé 1901–2 and Chitty 1966, 143–9. The Greek text published by Migne is based on a seventeenth-century edition; the Latin translation that accompanies it is early and based on an independent text. Thus the Latin translation may be of great value in establishing the true text. An annotated translation into French was published by de Journel in 1946. Regarding the historical value of the *Pratum*, see Baynes 1947 and Chadwick 1974.

13. Garitte 1941, 10. Garitte's edition is based on a manuscript containing the sixth-century biography. Until 1941, Chariton's biography was known only in the tenth-century abstract prepared by Simeon Metaphrastes, on which the Migne edition is based (*PG* 115, 899–918). The original work is rich in literary hyperbole, but the factual descriptions are authentic (Hirschfeld 1990a). An English translation of the biography has been prepared by Di Segni (1990).

14. Quasten 1963, 176–7. The Greek edition of *Historia Lausiaca*, which was edited by C. Butler (1898–1904), has been criticized by Flusin (1983, 43–4).

15. Chitty 1966, 99, n. 62 and Flusin 1983, 35–7, 226–7. The edition used was published by Koikylides (1902).

16. Chitty 1966, 151–2. The text with its Latin translation was published by House in 1888. A Hebrew translation has been published by Di Segni (1986–7). Schneider (1931) compared the details of this source with the monastic remains at Choziba.

17. The panegyric devoted to Theodosius and his monastery was delivered by Theodore on the first anniversary of his hero's death in 530 (Festugière 1963, 86). But there is evidence that the text was published only later, about eighty years after Theodosius had founded his monastery, ca. 556 or 557 (Theod. Petr., *V. Theod.* 18, 46. 17–18). This assumes that Génier (1909, 36) is correct in dating the founding of the monastery as 476. Paul's laudatory discourse was composed for the first anniversary of Theognius's death in 526 (Vailhé 1897–8a, 381).

18. The text (*De syn.*), with introduction and commentaries, was published by Flusin and Paramelle in 1982.

19. Procopius's work, with an English translation, was edited by Dewing and published in 1940.

20. Archaeological study of Judean desert monasteries has resulted in about two hundred different publications. The most important are those of Féderlin (1902–4) on the lauras and monasteries in the Jericho region. Féderlin surveyed many sites in this region and suggested various identifications, which he presented on a detailed map. His studies are invaluable, since most of the sites he describes were destroyed in the twentieth century. Most of the publications concerning Judean desert monasteries are mentioned in the dissertations of Patrich (1989) and Hirschfeld (1987b).

21. Preliminary reports were published by Chitty and Jones (1928) and Chitty (1930, 1932).

22. Corbo 1955 described his excavations at several monastic sites northeast and east of Bethlehem. For the surveys conducted by Corbo and Bagatti, see Bibliography.

23. Bar-Adon 1972.

24. For the excavations at Khirbet ed-Deir, see Hirschfeld and Birger 1986; Hirschfeld and Schmutz 1987; and Di Segni and Hirschfeld 1987. The excavation of the monastery of Martyrius was carried out by Magen and Hizmi (1985). Further information has been published in the Corbo volume by Magen (on the excavation), Di Segni (on the inscriptions), and Talgam (on the mosaics). I recently published a general discussion of Yadin's monastic finds on Masada (the laura of Marda) (Hirschfeld 1989).

25. The geographical data given here are based on several studies, including those of Nir (1965 and 1975, 19–20, 142–4); Orni and Efrat (1966, 56–7, 85–6), and Karmon (1971, 331–3).

26. The difference between the average temperature in summer (approx. 32°C) and in winter (approx. 15°C) throughout the Judean desert is also worth mentioning.

27. This name is found in various independent sources, such as the title of Cyril of Scythopolis's biography of Sabas (*V. Sab.* 85. 5–6), Procopius (*Buildings* V, 9. 7), and *Apoph. Pat.* (*PG* 65, 43A). Another version of this name, "The Desert of the Holy City," appears in Moschus's *Pratum* 92, 2949B, among other sources.

28. For a definition of *laura,* see Vailhé 1908, 226–7 and Festugière 1962, 69, n. 31. Most scholars believe that the first examples of this type of monastery were the lauras founded by Chariton in the Judean desert; see Schiwietz 1913, 138–9; Leclercq 1929, 1966–7; Corbo 1958, 232; Chitty 1966, 15; and Rubin 1982, 25.

29. See Festugière 1962, 69, n. 37.

30. For the historical background of Chariton and his peregrinations in the Judean desert, see Vailhé and Pétridès 1904; Schiwietz 1913, 131–43; and Garitte's introduction to *V. Char.*, 11–12. For an analysis of Chariton's life, see Hirschfeld 1990a.

31. Chitty 1966, 48 and Perrone 1980, 34, 37–8, 43–5.

32. Vailhé 1898–9a and Chitty 1929, 77.

33. The region of Byzantine Jericho has been studied by Augustinovič (1951).

34. Lent falls in the season when life in the desert is less difficult; see Chitty 1929, 77–8; Rubin 1982, 45–6.

35. Euthymius's career has been described in detail by Vailhé (1907–9) and Génier (1909).

36. Chitty 1966, 85; Schwartz 1939, 359; Perrone 1980, 37; and Hunt 1982, 244.

37. *V. Euth.* 27, 44. 20 (Lycia); *V. Euth.* 48, 69. 16 (Galatia); *V. Euth.* 50, 72. 10 (Cilicia); *V. Sab.* 20, 105. 4 (Armenia); *V. Sab.* 32, 117. 2 (Isauria); *V. Sab.* 43, 133. 8 (Bithynia); and *V. Sab.* 44, 134. 9 (Asia). Moschus mentions a monk from Pontus (*Pratum* 108, 2957D). Other monks mentioned were from Cyprus (*V. Geor.* 1, 97. 4), Greece (*V. Cyr.* 1, 223. 2), and Italy (*V. Euth.* 24, 36. 13; *Pratum* 101, 2960B). There were also monks from the eastern provinces, such as Mesopotamia (*V. Ger.* 4. 99. 6), Syria (*V. Euth.* 47, 68. 18), Arabia (*Pratum* 96, 2953B), and Egypt (*V. Sab.* 44, 134. 19). A few were from places in Palestine, such as Jerusalem (*V. Euth.* 57, 178. 4). The list is not complete.

38. Chitty 1966, 85. Examples include two of the first disciples of Euthymius, Stephen and Cosmas, who were appointed deacons of the Church of the Holy Sepulchre in Jerusalem. After the Council of Ephesus in 431, Stephen was appointed bishop of Jamnia (Yavne, on the coastal plain), and Cosmas was nominated "Guardian of the Cross" in Jerusalem (*V. Euth.* 20, 32–3). Later, after the Council of Chalcedon, Chrysippus and Gabriel, Cosmas's brothers, were appointed priests in the Church of the Holy Sepulchre, and Andrew, Stephen's brother, was installed as abbot of the monastery founded by Bassa, a Roman matron (*V. Euth.* 30, 49. 19–20).

39. See Flusin 1983, 38 and Chitty 1966, 90. The monastic setup of the laura of Gerasimus is

described by Gerasimus's biographer (*V. Ger.* 2.2) and by Cyril of Scythopolis (*V. Cyr.* 4, 224–5).

40. Vailhé 1898–9a, 107–10.
41. *V. Sab.* 30, 115. 17–26 and *V. Theod.* 239. 6–12. For the title "archimandrite" in general, see Meimaris 1986, 239–40; for specific developments in Jerusalem, see Chitty 1966, 86.
42. Chitty 1966, 114 and Charanis 1974, 98–102.
43. Theodosius regularly read Basil's rules to his monks (Theod. Petr., *V. Theod.* 20, 50. 15–16).
44. *V. Sab.* 58, 158. 19–20. The historical development of the Great Laura has been described by Vailhé (1897, 1898–9); Phokylides (1927); Leclercq (1929); and recently by Patrich (1988, 1989).
45. Vailhé 1898–9, 339. The dates of Sabas's foundations have been revised by Patrich (1988, 133–4, n. 4).
46. Diekamp 1899 is still the best study of the Origenist controversy; for a more recent discussion, see Perrone 1980, 175–222.
47. Hirschfeld 1989c, 32.
48. Chitty 1966, 150.
49. Theod., *De Situ* 20, 121. 21–8. According to the description provided by Antoninus of Placentia (ca. 570), the monastery of St. John the Baptist was a very large one, with several hospices (*Ant. Plac.* 12, 136. 6–11). The history of this monastery and its remains in the nineteenth century (before it was rebuilt by the Greek patriarchate of Jerusalem) have been described by Guérin 1874, 111–16.
50. See n. 6 above.
51. This is well expressed in a letter sent by Zacharias, the patriarch exiled to Babylon, to Modestus in Jerusalem (*PG* 86. 2, 3227–34, esp. 3231).
52. This question is discussed by Schick 1987, 153–4, 180–2, 213–16. For a more detailed discussion, see Hirschfeld 1987b, 118–23.
53. Griffith 1986 has many references to the literary activities of the monks at these monasteries.

CHAPTER ONE: TYPES OF MONASTERIES

1. *V. Sab.* 30, 115. 20–6 and *V. Theod.* 239. 4–12. On the significance of this event, see Corbo 1958, 235–6; Chitty 1966, 109–10; and Flusin 1983, 140–2.
2. Vailhé 1908, 226–7 and Festugière 1962, 69, n. 31.
3. For the expression "cell-dwellers," see *V. Sab.* 47, 138. 9.
4. Cyriac was in charge of the symandron when he was a prayer leader in the Old Laura (*V. Cyr.* 8, 227. 5).
5. For descriptions of the construction of Euthymius's laura and the Nea Laura, see *V. Euth.* 15, 24. 19 and *V. Sab.* 36, 123. 27, respectively.
6. See *V. Euth.* 17, 27. 14 for Euthymius's laura; *Pratum* 5, 2857A for the laura of the Towers; and *V. Sab.* 58, 160. 6 for the Great Laura. From the context, we know that the steward's office served as a storeroom for household articles as well as food.
7. Contra Rubin (1982, 30–1), who lists the refectory as one of the usual components of the laura.
8. E.g., *V. Sab.* 44, 135. 67. Most hermits had cooking and eating implements in their cells; living without them was considered an exceptional measure of asceticism. See *V. Sab.* 40, 131. 6 and 44, 135. 1–2.

9. See *V. Ger.* 2, 3; 5, 5 and *V. Cyr.* 4, 225. 2–6 for Gerasimus's laura; *V. Sab.* 40, 130. 29–30; 48, 138. 15–16 and *V. John Hes.* 6, 205. 28 for the Great Laura.

10. *V. Euth.* 43, 64. 18. According to Cyril, the refectory of the converted monastery was built beneath the new church. Its location in the central vault under the church has been identified by Chitty and Jones (1928, 175) and Chitty (1930, 46–7).

11. Patrich 1990.

12. The first attempt to classify monasteries in the Judean desert was that of Féderlin (1903, 182–3), who distinguished between one type of laura characteristic of the Jericho area and another type characteristic of the high plateau of the desert. This classification by topography is also used by Chitty, who refers to Chariton's lauras as "cliff lauras" (Chitty 1929, 77) and Firminus's laura as a "cliff-top building" (Marcoff and Chitty 1929, 170). Similarly, the monastic remains at Khirbet ed-Deir are described as those of a "cliff-side coenobium" (ibid. 178). This classification was further developed by Corbo (1958, 236; 1958b, 171; and 1960, 139–40), who distinguished between a "ravine type" (*il tipo di gola*) of laura and a "plain type" (*il tipo di pianura*). Another system of classifying Judean desert monasteries has been proposed by Norris (1950–1), but it is too general; see Rubin's comment (1982, 32, n. 27).

13. See Hirschfeld 1987b, 23–81, and 1990b for an updated list of monasteries.

14. See Rubin 1982, which hardly mentions level lauras at all.

15. See Vailhé 1897–8, 41–4, and 1899–1900, 42, no. 94; Vailhé and Pétridès 1904, 335–40; Schiwietz 1913, 136–8; Abel 1938, 404; etc. The identification of the site, first made by Marti (1880, 7–11), is universally accepted. The site was first investigated by Guérin (1869, 71–3) and Jullien (1896). Additional details are given in Bagatti 1969; Meinardus 1964–5, 227–9; and Hirschfeld 1989a, 72–3; 1988–9, 95–7; and 1990b, no. 1.

16. About nineteen caves in the cliffs along the wadi bed have been surveyed by Patrich (1985a). Most of these caves were created and used as hiding places during the Second Temple period. Vailhé and Pétridès (1904, 338) claimed that there were about fifty monks' caves in the Byzantine period, but in fact, most of these caves show no signs of human habitation dating from that time.

17. Vailhé and Pétridès 1904, 335–40 describe the findings of this excavation, which was carried out by the White Fathers of Jerusalem. Other scholars who have described this excavation are Schiwietz (1913, 136–8); Leclercq (1929, 1966–8); and Ovadiah and de Silva (1981, 204, no. 1).

18. Dinur and Feig 1986.

19. The laura of Jeremias has been identified as Khirbet ez-Zaraniq (Vailhé 1899–1900, 23, no. 64). The archaeological remains of the laura were excavated by Farmer (1957) and Patrich (1988, 163–4). See also Hirschfeld 1990b, no. 31. For the Cells of Choziba, see Meinardus 1966; Meimaris 1978; and Patrich 1990. The remains near 'Ein el-Fawwar were excavated by Hamilton (1932) and surveyed by Meinardus (1964–5, 229–30), and Hirschfeld (1988–9, 97–8; 1990b, no. 32).

20. A summary of the history of the monastery of Chariton was published by Vailhé and Pétridès (1904, 343–58). See also Vailhé 1897–8, 50–8; 1899–1900, 524–5, no. 21; Schiwietz 1913, 141–2; and Bagatti 1971. The first systematic description of the remains was provided by Conder and Kitchener (1883, 357). For a detailed description with a comprehensive plan of the site, see Hirschfeld 1985, 36–48, no. 17, and 1990b, no. 3.

21. *V. Sab.* 18, 102. 9. We can assume that the population subsequently became even larger. The history of the monastery of Sabas was presented in several articles by Vailhé (1897; 1898–

9; and 1899–1900, 274–6, no. 106). The most detailed work concerning the history of the monastery was published by Phokylides (1927).

22. Patrich (1988) presents a detailed description of the cells and dwelling complexes that he surveyed on the site. One of the first scholars to describe the cells was Corbo (1958c). Meinardus 1965–6, 342–55 devotes a long chapter to the remains of the cells, but he mistakenly treats each prayer room and dwelling complex as a separate monastery, and Ovadiah and de Silva 1981, 253–4, nos. 69, 70 repeat Meinardus's error.

23. The present monastery of Mar Saba has been described by Guérin 1869, 92–101; Conder and Kitchener 1883, 219–20; Frances 1963; Mann 1969; etc.

24. Patrich 1989, 68.

25. This coenobium was founded by Sabas in 493 as part of the Great Laura (Vailhé 1899–1900, 39, no. 88). The site was identified by Corbo (1958c, 109–10) but was actually discovered earlier by Marcoff and Chitty (1929, 176–7), who erroneously identified it as the tower marking the northern boundary of the Great Laura. See also Hirschfeld 1990b, no. 19.

26. For the identification and description of the Nea Laura, see Hirschfeld 1985, 99–105, no. 87 and 1990b, no. 22.

27. The laura of Firminus was first identified by Lagrange (1895, 94). The remains have been studied by several scholars: Marcoff and Chitty (1929, 167–71); Corbo (1960); Desreumaux, Humbert, and Nodet (1978); Patrich and Rubin (1984); Patrich (1989a); and Hirschfeld (1988–9, 97–8; 1990b, no. 28). A large cliff-type laura was discovered recently at Khallet Danabiya by Goldfus (1990).

28. Féderlin (1903, 134, 148), who discovered these remains, believes that the present monastery was built of ancient stones taken from the core of the laura. Deir Hajla is described by Guérin (1874, 53–6); Conder and Kitchener (1883, 178); and Schneider (1938). Augustinović 1951, 109–10 mentions remains of cells around the existing monastery. See also Hirschfeld 1988–9, 100–1 and 1990b, no. 7.

29. Delau (1899–1900, 269–70) was the first to identify the remains of Khirbet Jinjas as the laura of Heptastomos. The site was surveyed again by Féderlin (1903, 137), who emphasized the symmetry of the laura. Corbo (1958a, 85–8) confirmed this identification and suggested that the water cistern named "Heptastomos" could be Bib Sabsab, in the Kidron valley. Our survey is described briefly, in Hirschfeld 1983, 59 and 1990, no. 25. For the history of the laura, see Vailhé 1897–8, 349–51 and 1899–1900, 539, no. 54.

30. Festugière 1962, 69, n. 31. According to Corbo 1955, 1, a coenobium is a type of monastery in which each component is connected to the next.

31. Corbo 1955, 2. The same conclusion was reached by studying the Byzantine monasteries of Syria (H. C. Butler 1919, 99; Lassus 1947, 272).

32. See Theod. Petr., *V. Theod.* 13, 34–5, and 16–17, 41–2, for a general description of the monastery, and ibid., 18, 45–8, and *V. Theod.* 240. 23–4, for a description of the churches.

33. See *V. Geor.* 28, 12. 8–9 and *Miracula* 1, 362.1 for the two gates of the monastery and its inner courtyard, and *V. Geor.* 4, 99–100 for the location of the refectory and kitchen. Schneider 1931, 305–14 described the shape of the monastery of Choziba according to the historical sources.

34. It was Corbo (1958, 248–9) who first divided the coenobia this way.

35. Hirschfeld 1987b, 144–6.

36. Féderlin (1894, 82–3) was the first to identify the remains of Deir Mukallik as the monastery of Theoctistus. The history of the monastery was presented by Vailhé 1898 and 1907, 342–8. See also Leclercq 1929, 1986–8. Systematic descriptions of the remains were provided by Con-

der and Kitchener 1883, 189–90; Fast 1913; Meinardus 1964–5, 246–50; and Hirschfeld 1988–9, 99–100 and 1990b, no. 4. Patrich and Di Segni (1987) found crosses and Greek inscriptions on the path leading to the monastery.

37. The remains of the cave church, including the Greek inscriptions and frescoes, have been described by several scholars: Chitty (1928, 139–45); Ovadiah (1970, 47–8, no. 34); Blomme and Nodet (1979); Kühnel (1984); and Patrich and Di Segni (1987, 277–8).

38. Chitty 1928, 139.

39. The history of the monastery from its founding to the end of the Byzantine period was summarized by Vailhé (1897–8) and Schneider (1931). Schneider also described the physical structures and burial caves of the monastery. Detailed descriptions of the churches have been published by Ovadiah (1970, 50, no. 37), and Ovadiah and de Silva (1981–2, 213–14, no. 14). The cell where John of Thebes is said to have resided has been described by Meimaris (1978).

40. Conder and Kitchener 1883, 192–9.

41. For this monastery, see Hirschfeld 1985, 58–9, no. 28 and 1990b, no. 56.

42. The site was discovered and identified as a monastery by Conder and Kitchener (1883, 327). Marcoff and Chitty (1929, 178) identified it as the monastery of Severianus, but without any proof. For preliminary descriptions of the remains, see Hirschfeld and Birger 1986; Hirschfeld and Schmutz 1987, 42–8; and Di Segni and Hirschfeld 1987.

43. The identification of Khirbet el-Murassas as the monastery of Martyrius was first suggested by van Kasteren (1890, 84–9). Its remains were surveyed and reported on by Tobler (1854, 763–5); Marti (1880, 28–9); Furrer (1880, 235); Conder and Kitchener (1883, 121–2); and von Riess (1892, 226–8). See also Ovadiah 1970, 113–14, no. 111. The excavations were initiated by Damati (1979 and 1989) and continued on a larger scale by Magen and Hizmi (1985). See also Magen 1984; Magen and Talgam 1990; and Di Segni 1990.

44. The monastery of Jeremias in Saqqara (Egypt), e.g., was divided by means of an orthogonal arrangement of passageways into a communal area and a separate dwelling area (Quibell 1912, 1–2 and Badawy 1978, 47–8). The same arrangement can be seen in several monasteries in Palestine, such as the one excavated at Kursi on the eastern shore of the Sea of Galilee (Tzaferis 1983) and the well-preserved monastery known as Deir Qalʿa on the western slope of the Samaria hills, which dates from the time of Justinian (Guérin 1875, 126–9; Conder and Kitchener 1883, 315–19; and Hirschfeld 1989b, 40–3).

45. Magen and Hizmi (1985, 70) say that the inscription of Paul's name on the tombstone proves that he was the dominant figure in the history of the monastery, even though it was named after Martyrius. But it is possible that Paul was merely the first abbot to be buried within the monastery. Martyrius was probably buried in the Byzantine patriarchs' tombs in Jerusalem; thus Paul's name was meant to mark the abbots' burial place, since ten skeletons were found in the grave. The abbots' tomb was indeed a focal point in monasteries where its place is known, such as the monasteries of Theodosius and Khirbet ed-Deir or the Great Laura.

46. An idea of the crowds of visitors who came to a famous monastery on special occasions may be obtained from Theodore of Petra's biography of Theodosius, which describes the reception of pilgrims and local visitors at the monastery of Theodosius at Easter and at the feast of the triumph of the Cross (14 September). The monks laid one hundred tables on each of these days, which means that at least eight hundred people were served (Theod. Petr., *V. Theod.* 13, 36. 11).

47. The remains of the monastery of Theodosius were first described by Marti (1880, 36–7). Theodosius's burial cave was cleaned out during the construction of the present monastery,

and the plan of it was published by Weigand (1914–19). For the monastery of Euthymius, see Hirschfeld 1990b, no. 7.

48. Corbo (1951) was the first to identify the site. The remains of the site were described by van Kasteren (1890, 116–17) and more systematically by Schneider (1934, 224–5) and Ovadiah (1970, 181–2, no. 179). The site was surveyed again later by Kallai (1972, 188, no. 157) and by Patrich (1984, 62). See also Hirschfeld 1990b, no. 12.

49. For Khirbet el-Quneitira, see Hirschfeld 1985a and 1990b, no. 63. For the monastery of Severianus, identified as El-Qasrein, see Hirschfeld 1990b, no. 27. The site of Khirbet et-Tina was discovered by Corbo (1962), who wrongly identified it as the Nea Laura. For further details, see Hirschfeld 1985, 94–7, no. 81 and 1990b, no. 59. El-Qasr was surveyed by Hirschfeld (1988–9, 149–50 and 1990b, no. 43).

50. For Masada and Hyrcania, see n. 54 and 56, respectively. Re Doq (Dagon), the site has been identified as the laura of Douka. It is located at the caves of Mount Quruntul, known as Deir el-Quruntul, 3 km northwest of Jericho. It was first described by Tristram (1866, 212–17). Further descriptions were given by Guérin (1874, 41–5); Conder and Kitchener (1883, 200–4); Marti (1880, 13–14); Vailhé (1897–8, 45–9); Leclercq (1929, 1968–70); Meinardus (1969) and Hirschfeld (1990b, no. 2). Re Herodium, Corbo (1967, 116–19) was the first to point out the existence of a monastery among the remains of Herodium, Herod's palace, about 5 km southeast of Bethlehem. The remains of the monastery include a chapel and several cells on top of the artificial mound of Herodium. Testa (1982, 118) advances the hypothesis that the monastery was inhabited by Monophysite monks. In the course of excavations at lower Herodium, additional Byzantine structures were discovered, including three chapels: see Netzer 1990 and Ovadiah and de Silva 1981–2, 218–19, nos. 19 and 20. Zias (1986) suggests identification of the Byzantine remains at Herodium with the leprosarium founded by the empress Eudocia at a place called Furdisia. Re Cypros, the site, known as Tel ʿAqaba, is on a high, conical hill southwest of Jericho. Most of the remains have been identified as the palace built by King Herod and named for his mother, Cypros (Netzer 1975). A small Byzantine structure found on the lower terrace of the palace was probably a hermitage for one or two monks. See also Ovadiah and de Silva 1981, 211–12, no. 11 and Hirschfeld 1990b Hermitage. Re Nuseib el-ʾAweishireh, the site, located on a small conical hill west of Jericho, was excavated by Netzer, who found remains of a fortress from the Second Temple period and, above it, remains of a Byzantine monastery (Netzer and Birger 1990). For the Greek inscription found in the church, see Di Segni 1990b and Hirschfeld 1990b, no. 50. For a general discussion of the Judean desert fortresses, see Tsafrir 1982.

51. For Khirbet el-Qasr, see n. 57. For Khirbet el-Kilya, see Magen 1990. I have surveyed a number of early Byzantine forts along the fringe of the Judean desert (Hirschfeld 1979).

52. See Aharoni 1962, 2–4. Other examples include the Roman fortress near Kibbutz Yehiam in western Galilee, among whose ruins the remains of a small Byzantine monastery were found (Foerster 1978, 11), and Tel ʿIra in the northern Beersheba valley, on whose peak a Byzantine monastery was built on the foundations of Herodian tower (Beit Arieh 1981). It should be pointed out that the monks settled not only in fortresses but also in burial caves and even in abandoned quarries. Indications of the presence of hermits have been found in burial caves from the Second Temple period in the village of Silwan, east of Jerusalem (Ussishkin 1986, 298–306). The monastic remains discovered in Khirbet el-Masanʿi, northwest of Jerusalem, were built in the remains of an ancient quarry (Mazor 1984).

53. MacMullen (1963, 140) stresses that the phenomenon was largely responsible for the semi-military layout of the coenobia during the Byzantine period. See also Peña, Castellana, and Fernandez 1983, 54.

54. Yadin 1965, 111–14 and 1966, 111–15. The first descriptions of the Byzantine remains at Masada were provided by Conder 1875, 137–8 and Conder and Kitchener 1883, 420–1. The church was described in detail by Schneider (1931a). For the identification of Masada as Marda, see Lagrange 1894, 271–2; Delau 1899–1900, 280–1; and Abel 1911, 122–3. For a more recent paper on Byzantine Masada, see Hirschfeld 1989.

55. Chitty 1966, 120, n. 77 suggested that the building had a double vault with a B-shaped cross-section.

56. Wright 1961. The monastic site of Hyrcania has been surveyed and reported on by many scholars: Conder and Kitchener (1883, 121); Marti (1880, 19–24); Furrer (1880, 235); van Kasteren (1890, 108); Mader (1929); Bagatti (1954); Ovadiah (1970, 111–12, no. 109); Ovadiah and de Silva (1982, 149, no. 34); and Patrich (1986). For the history of the site, see Milik 1961; Vailhé 1899–1900, 522–3, no. 19; and Hirschfeld 1990b, no. 18.

57. Hirschfeld and Kloner 1988–9.

58. Hirschfeld 1979.

59. Magen 1990.

60. Patrich and Rubin 1984; Patrich 1985a.

61. Patrich 1984 and 1989a.

62. Patrich 1984, 62 and 1985a.

63. Patrich 1984, 62 and 1990.

64. Forsyth and Weitzmann 1970.

65. Testini 1964. Other impressive examples of monasteries beside memorial churches are the monastery of Kursi, east of the Sea of Galilee (Tzaferis 1983), and the monastic complex erected on the peak of Mount Nebo, from which Moses looked out at the Promised Land (Saller 1941; Saller and Bagatti 1949).

66. St. Adam's Church was excavated by Prignaud (1963). The identification of the site as St. Adam's Church was suggested by Milik (1960, 590). See also Hirschfeld 1990b, no. 34. Excavations at Ghalghala (Jaljulieh), identified as Byzantine Galgala, were undertaken by Baramki (1949–51). See also Ovadiah and de Silva 1981, 216–17, no. 17 and Hirschfeld 1990b, no. 33. The monastery of St. John the Baptist remained in continuous use, albeit with many changes, until the Middle Ages. Literary sources reveal that the original monastery was damaged by earthquakes and floods and was then rebuilt (Guérin 1869, 111–16; Vailhé 1899–1900, 19–22, no. 61). The plan of the ruins accompanying the description provided by Conder and Kitchener 1883, 177, 217–18 does not indicate the original form of the monastery. See also Ovadiah and de Silva 1981, 249, no. 63 and Hirschfeld 1990b, no. 20.

67. The site was discovered and identified by Schneider (1934, 221–3). The first scholar to describe the site, although he did not identify it, was van Kasteren (1890, 94–5). In 1984, I carried out a systematic survey and test excavations (Hirschfeld 1984; see also idem, 1990b, no. 8). For descriptions of the Roman road from Jerusalem to Jericho, see Beauvery 1957 and Wilkinson 1975. The remains of Qasr ʿAli were identified as "Embetoara," which is mentioned in the Georgian calendar as being "four miles" from Jerusalem (Milik 1960, 580).

68. Similar features are found at the monastery of Kathisma, near Bethlehem, where the various monastic components were dispersed beside the church building (see n. 65). Two sources from

the seventh and eighth centuries describe the monastery of St. John the Baptist as completely separate from the church. See *V. Steph. Sab.* 85, 537B and Wilkinson 1977, 107 for a translation of Adamnanus, *De locis sanctis* 11. 16, 7–8.

69. The services provided by the monks along the Jericho road included supplying drinking water, repairing shoes, helping to carry loads, and the like. See Moschus, *Pratum* 24, 2869B–C, and *V. Geor.* 23, 122. 11–12.

CHAPTER TWO: HOW MONASTERIES WERE BUILT

1. Zeisel 1975, 340, n. 57 stresses the importance of the beast of burden in monastic life.
2. *V. Sab.* 36, 123. 11–28. For Theodosius, see *V. Theod.* 238. 17. According to Cyril, the pack animals of the Great Laura were sent to Jericho to bring timber for the construction of the hospice (*V. Sab.* 26, 109. 19–20). Anthony of Choziba tells of a monk loading a donkey with lime from a kiln (*V. Geor.* 26, 125. 8–10).
3. *V. Sab.* 37, 126. 18. The coenobium of the Cave has been identified as Bir el-Qattar, about 3 km northeast of Mar Saba. According to Patrich 1983, 66, it was a small coenobium meant for no more than ten to fifteen monks. For the history of the monastery, see Vailhé 1899–1900, 283–4, no. 173, and for its location, see Hirschfeld 1990b, no. 23.
4. *V. Sab.* 42, 132. 20–133. 6. I have identified the monastery of Zannus as El-Bourj, 2 km west of Mar Saba. It was a small coenobium, for only a few monks. For a short description and plan, see Hirschfeld 1983, 58 and 1990b, no. 26. Vailhé 1899–1900, 292, no. 137 suggested that the monastery was founded in 513, but I favor Patrich's (1988, 133, n. 4) dating—that is, 511.
5. Paul. El., *V. Theog.* 9–10, 87–9. Corbo 1955, 149, 155 suggested that the remains he excavated at Khirbet Makhrum, about 2.5 km southwest of the monastery of Theodosius, were from the monastery of Theognius. It was a medium-sized coenobium, covering an area of about 1,500 m² (larger than the coenobia of Spelaion and Zannus). Vailhé 1897–98 describes the history of Theognius and his monastery. See also Hirschfeld 1990b, no. 17.
6. Theod. Petr., *V. Theod.* 13, 34. 8. According to Cyril, the fifth church of the monastery of Theodosius was built under Sophronius, Theodosius's successor as head of the monastery (*V. Theod.* 240, 23–4).
7. *V. Sab.* 25, 109. 15. Another hospice was built in Jericho.
8. Magen and Hizmi 1985, 65–7. Building in stages also characterizes large monasteries situated beyond the borders of the Judean desert.
9. *V. Euth.* 39, 59. 1–2. This was not Euthymius's first try as an amateur architect: ca. 427, when the Saracens, led by Peter Aspebet, settled in the vicinity of his two monasteries, Euthymius himself chose the position of their encampment, planned its layout, and even outlined the plan of the church, marking it on the ground (*V. Euth.* 15, 24. 24–7). The term *mechanikos* was used for the greatest architects of the Byzantine period (see Mango 1974, 24).
10. Magen and Hizmi 1985, 66.
11. Hirschfeld 1985a, 247.
12. Tsafrir 1985, 393 discusses the use of "round numbers" in Byzantine architecture in Palestine.
13. *V. Euth.* 12, 222. 19–20. The bailiff of an estate near Nicopolis (Emmaus, on the way to Jerusalem) did the same for Sabas when he settled near there (*V. Sab.* 35, 120. 27–8), and a priest of the Church of the Holy Sepulchre in Jerusalem came with his sons to help Sabas build the coenobium of the Cave (*V. Sab.* 37, 127. 5–9).
14. *V. Sab.* 26, 109. 19. Sabas's construction efforts were greatly furthered by the assistance he re-

ceived from the monks of the Great Laura. In the construction of the monastery of Castellion, e.g., Sabas took a group of fathers and worked together with them (*V. Sab.* 27, 111. 18).

15. The cells of the Great Laura, which in many cases had mosaic floors, stucco work, and high-quality construction, were an exception. Patrich 1988, 161–2 concluded that those cells were constructed by professional masons.

16. *V. Sab.* 37, 126. 16. An inscription in the monastery of St. Catherine at the foot of Mount Sinai, carved in a window frame in the refectory, mentions a monk who was also a professional stone-dresser (see Forsyth and Weitzmann 1970, Pl. 102A).

17. See *V. Euth.* 15, 24. 17 for the laura of Euthymius; *V. John. Hes.* 6, 206. 12 for the builders of the Small Coenobium.

18. For the functions of rural masons, see Krautheimer 1965, 102.

19. See *V. Euth.* 43, 64. 15–21 for the rebuilding of the monastery of Euthymius; *V. Cyr.* 6, 225. 25–6 for Cyriac's participation.

20. Hirschfeld 1985, 45–6 and 1989a, 306.

21. The cross and the inscription under the Nea Church in Jerusalem were discovered by Avigad (1977 and 1980, 245).

22. Construction in stone is typical of the monasteries in the mountainous areas of Palestine, Syria, and Asia Minor (see H. C. Butler 1929, 25 for Syria; Restle 1979, 137–8 for Asia Minor). In Egypt, most of the monasteries were built of mud brick, and only special elements, such as the entrance or sometimes the surrounding walls, were of limestone (Quibell 1912, 1–2).

23. Magen and Hizmi 1985, 83. Guérin (1875, 128) came to a similar conclusion regarding the huge cisterns at Deir Qalʿa in the western slopes of the Samarian hills.

24. Féderlin 1903, 133.

25. Forsyth and Weitzmann (1970) and Forsyth 1968, 9.

26. *V. Sab.* 26, 109. 19. The use of palmwood beams for roofing was common in Palestine (see Hirschfeld 1987b, 147). Traces of sockets in the cliff face of several monasteries are also evidence of the use of wooden beams.

27. This information was supplied by Ehud Netzer, architect of the excavations at Masada, whom I wish to thank.

28. See Hirschfeld 1985a, 250 for Khirbet el-Quneitira; idem 1985, 101–2 for the Nea Laura; and Patrich 1988, 154–5 for the Great Laura.

29. Yadin 1965, 114 and Hirschfeld 1989, 268.

30. Hirschfeld and Birger 1986, 280. Bricks of the same type were found in the monastery of Theognius (Khirbet Makhrum), east of Bethlehem (see Corbo 1955, 4).

31. Féderlin 1903, 133.

32. Magen and Hizmi 1985, 69–70.

33. Yadin 1965, 31, 36. For glass panes at the monastery of Martyrius, see Magen and Hizmi 1985, 73. Complete, greenish panes of glass have been found in excavations of Khirbet Siyar el-Ghanam near Bethlehem (see Corbo 1955, 75).

34. Hirschfeld and Birger 1986, 279–80 and Di Segni and Hirschfeld 1987, 373, 386.

35. Magen and Hizmi 1985, 65.

36. Hirschfeld 1985, 102, Fig. 78.

37. Hirschfeld 1985, 45. The same method was used throughout Palestine.

38. Hirschfeld 1987b, 143.

39. Magen and Hizmi 1985, 67. An excellent example of a Byzantine roller stone exists to this day at Khirbet ed-Deir, west of Hebron (see Kopp and Steve 1946, 564). At Khirbet Bureikut,

southeast of Jerusalem, I discovered remains of a similar roller stone (see Hirschfeld 1990b, no. 30).

40. See Hirschfeld 1985, 88, Fig. 67 for Khirbet Umm el-'Amed, and idem 1985a, 247, Fig. 6B for Khirbet el-Quneitira.

41. A photograph of this window appears in Yadin 1966, 110.

42. See Magen and Hizmi 1985, 66 for stone rollers; Paul. El., *V. Theog.* 24, 111. 3–4 for wooden ceiling planks.

43. Avi-Yonah 1954, 19.

44. Hirschfeld 1987, 37, n. 73.

CHAPTER THREE: THE DAILY LIFE OF THE MONKS

1. The phenomenon of pilgrimage to the Holy Land at this time has been described by Hunt (1982).

2. For Cyril's biography, see Flusin 1983, 11–32 and Hirschfeld (1989c).

3. See *V. Geor.* 15–19, 115–19 for the boxer; *De syn.* for the Senator's daughter.

4. Zeisel 1975, 296 and Patrich 1989, 251, n. 2. The Egyptian model of authority was accepted in most monasteries, including those in the Judean desert. For Egypt, see White 1932–3, 178; Rousseau 1978, 24–5, 52; and Veilleux 1980–2, 416, n. 1, in his commentary on the Pachomian *koinonia*. The term *hegoumenos* also appears in Syria (Canivet 1977, 227–9), together with *archimandrites* and its parallel in Syriac, *riš daira* (Vööbus 1960a). The term *archimandrites*, meaning "chief of *mandra* (monastic community)," also appears in Palestine in inscriptions from the Byzantine period; these inscriptions bear witness to its use as a synonym for *hegoumenos*, notwithstanding the special usage of "archimandrite" in Cyril's writings. In the legal usage of Justinian's edicts, hegumen and archimandrite are synonyms (Meimaris 1986, 239–40, 248). In the writings of Basil of Cappadocia, on the other hand, the regular term for abbot is *proestos* (Pujol 1958, 67–71). An exceptional phenomenon may be noted in the federation of Sabas's monasteries in and around the Kidron valley; there, Cyril reserves the title of hegumen for Sabas, while the abbots of his other monasteries are referred to as administrators (*dioketai*). This reflects the subordination of the lesser monasteries to the leadership of Sabas (Patrich 1989, 151–3).

5. *V. Sab.* 39, 129–30. See Festugière 1962a, 84, n. 60 and compare Clematius's story above. The question of obedience to the commands of the abbot is raised repeatedly in Pachomius's regulations for the communal monasteries of Egypt—e.g., rules 23, 27, 30, 47, etc. (Veilleux 1980–2, 149–52). The obligation not to leave the monastery without the permission of the abbot is mentioned repeatedly in the rules of the Syrian monasteries (Vööbus 1960a, 83, no. 19; 91, no. 14; and 171, no. 14).

6. *V. Geor.* 4, 99. 1–3. This ceremony is mentioned several times in the hagiographical literature of the Judean desert—e.g., *V. Ger.* 5, 6 (compare *V. Cyr.* 4. 224. 22–3). The abbot's responsibility to accept a new monk only after having investigated his background is treated in detail in Maruta's rules (Vööbus 1960a, 143–4, nos. 26–33).

7. See Paul. El., *V. Theog.* 7, 86. 3–4 for the laura of Calamon; *V. Sab.* 16, 99. 27–100. 2 for the Great Laura.

8. *V. Euth.* 39, 58. 24–5. For a further example of election of an abbot by the "elders" (*pateres*) of a monastery, see *V. Sab.* 36, 124. 12–14; 125. 16–17.

9. See *V. Geor.* 11, 106. 18 for the laura of Calamon; *Pratum* 7, 2857B–C for the laura of the Towers.

10. The Greek term *hegoumeneion* is defined in Lampe 1961, 60 as "the superior's cell."

11. See *V. Sab.* 18, 102. 25–6 for Sabas; Theod. Petr., *V. Theod.* 18, 48. 13–14 for Theodosius.

12. For the inscription at the monastery of Martyrius, see Di Segni 1990a; for that at the monastery of Theognius, see Corbo 1955, 152–3. Another example of an inscription involving the name and title of an abbot was discovered at the monastic site known as Khan Saliba, between Jerusalem and Jericho (Prignaud 1963, 251–2). The mosaic floor of the refectory at Bir el-Qatt contains a Georgian inscription with the name of Anthony, abbot of the monastery (Tarchnis-vili 1955, 136–7). At the monastery of Kursi, a dedicatory inscription found in the floor of the baptistry mentions Stephen, the priest and abbot of the monastery (Tzaferis 1983, 28–9). For a general discussion, see Meimaris 1986, 239–49.

13. *V. Theod.* 240. 13–14. Another example is Leontius, at the coenobium of Euthymius, who was deputy until 542, when he was elected abbot of the monastery (*V. Euth.* 48, 70. 13). This kind of succession appears to have been more or less the norm, although it was by no means legislated; in fact, Justinian expressly forbade the automatic succession of deputies to abbacies. Deputies could be elected if worthy, but their position was not to confer on them the status of presumed successor. See *Codex Iust.* 1–3: 46. 13. The subject has been discussed by Patrich 1989, 156–60.

14. The positions of steward and deputy and the character of these offices in the Judean desert monasteries are discussed at length by Patrich 1989, 154–60.

15. For instance, Cyril mentions the nomination of the steward of the laura of Euthymius by Euthymius himself (*V. Euth.* 17, 27. 7). The same custom is mentioned in Egyptian papyri (Barison 1938, 38–9). Zeisel 1975, 273 describes the general functions of the steward in Byzantine monasteries.

16. See *V. Cyr.* 7–8, 226. 22–227. 4 for Cyriac's career; *V. John Hes.* 7–8, 206. 15–207. 7 for John's career. The chronology of John's career is discussed by Patrich 1989, 330–1, n. 21.

17. *V. Euth.* 18, 28. 16. When John Hesychast arrived at the Great Laura, he was placed under the supervision of the steward, who assigned him various jobs (*V. John Hes.* 5, 205. 6–7). The steward of the monastery of Euthymius purchased pack animals for the community (*V. Euth.* 18, 28. 13–14), whereas the steward of the Great Laura arranged for the transportation of wheat (purchased in Transjordan) from the Dead Sea coast to the monastery (*V. Sab.* 80, 186. 15–17).

18. The *oikonomeion* of the laura of the Towers is mentioned by Moschus (*Pratum* 5, 2857A); see also Lampe 1961, 940.

19. This raises a number of questions. For example, while a monk was serving as steward, did his cell remain vacant, or was it assigned to another monk? After completing his term as steward, did he return to the cell in which he had lived previously? It would seem likely that if a monk were required to move to a different cell while filling a certain post, he would retain his original cell for use after his term of office had ended. It is known that Zannus and Benjamin retained their cells in the Great Laura while they were engaged in converting a vacant hermitage into a coenobium at some distance from the laura (*V. Sab.* 42, 132) and that Theognius kept his old cell in the monastery he founded in the Judean desert after he was appointed bishop of Bitulion, a small town near Gaza (Paul. El., *V. Theog.* 10, 89. 8–10).

20. For example, Cosmas, a Cappadocian monk and one of Euthymius's first disciples in the laura at Mishor Adummim, was first ordained deacon and assigned to the Church of the Holy

Sepulchre in Jerusalem; then he was made guardian of the Cross; finally he was appointed metropolitan of Scythopolis (*V. Euth.* 20, 3203; 33, 55–6).

21. Therefore, a community could have Mass only when a priest came to visit them (*V. Sab.* 16, 100. 12–14). This situation prevailed from the founding of the laura in 483 until 490, when the patriarch of Jerusalem, Sallust, ordained Sabas to the priesthood (*V. Sab.* 19, 103–4).

22. The leader of the prayers is mentioned in *V. Sab.* 43, 134. 1 and 58, 159. 29; *Pratum* 11, 2860C; and esp. in Theod. Petr., *V. Theod.* 19, 49. 2–10.

23. *V. Geor.* 34, 133. 9. The same job in the same monastery is mentioned in *Miracula* 6, 368. 14.

24. Patrich 1989, 155–6.

25. *V. John Hes.* 7, 206. 15–16, and Cyriac, who is known to have held four posts at the Old Laura in four years, probably also held each for exactly a year (*V. Cyr.* 7, 226. 22–4; 8, 227. 18). In other places, like the monastery of Hypatius in Asia Minor, the rotation of personnel took place every week; see Call., *V. Hyp.* 5, 248. On the other hand, there are indications that in at least some monasteries in Syria, the rotation was annual (see Vööbus 1960a, 83, no. 23).

26. For the cook, see *V. Sab.* 40, 130. 30 and 48, 138. 11 and *V. John Hes.* 6, 205.

27. Paul. El., *V. Theog.* 22, 105. 13–17; the monk in charge of the storeroom is also mentioned in *V. Geor.* 12, 108. 8 and 23, 122. 8. One of the dedicatory inscriptions in the burial cave of the monastery of Choziba mentions a storeroom-keeper (Schneider 1931, 328, no. 210).

28. See *V. Euth.* 17, 27. 22–3 for the laura of Euthymius; Theod. Petr., *V. Theod.* 14, 37 for the coenobium of Theodosius; and Paul. El., *V. Theog.* 22, 105. 15–106. 4 for the coenobium of Theognius.

29. See *V. Sab.* 8, 92. 12 for Sabas; *V. Cyr.* 4, 225. 2 for Cyriac; and Cass., *Con.* 6.1, 153.

30. *V. Sab.* 8, 92. 13. The function of looking after the pack animals is mentioned by Moschus (*Pratum* 101, 2960B).

31. *V. Geor.* 4, 99. 4 and *Miracula* 4, 264. 6. Leontius "the gardener" is mentioned in one of the dedicatory inscriptions in the burial cave of Choziba (Schneider 1931, 327, no. 183).

32. *V. Geor.* 20, 119. 19; 25, 125. 3; and 28, 126. 6; *Miracula* 1, 361. 18. Sometimes two gatekeepers were on duty at the same time.

33. *V. Geor.* 25, 124–5. In the regulations given to the monasteries of Syria by Maruta, several chapters are devoted to the virtues required of the gatekeeper (see Vööbus 1960a, 89, no. 4; 131, no. 1; 132, nos 2–5).

34. *V. John Hes.* 6, 205. 28. Anthony of Choziba was a hospice-keeper, and he gives us a vivid description of his job (*V. Geor.* 57, 355–6). A large hospice was discovered at the monastery of Martyrius, and there also seems to have been a sizable hospice at the monastery of Theodosius.

35. The doctor at the Great Laura is mentioned by Cyril (*V. Sab.* 41, 131. 26); and for infirmaries at the lauras of Calamon and the Towers, see *V. John Hes.* 20, 216. 24 and *Pratum* 10, 2860B, respectively. A hospital is mentioned only in connection with the larger monasteries, like the Great Laura (*V. Sab.* 32, 117. 8) and the monastery of Theodosius (Theod. Petr., *V. Theod.* 16, 40–1). The monastery of Theodosius also ran a hospital in Jericho.

36. *V. Euth.* 50, 72. 8–10. Cyril was an eyewitness to this incident when he lived at the monastery of Euthymius. The "possessed" monk came from the nearby monastery of Martyrius.

37. The writing and copying of books was a regular occupation in the monasteries of Egypt (White 1932, 184–5) and Syria (Vööbus 1960, 389–93).

38. An archive would be needed in every monastery, small and large alike, for the filing of bills, personal documents belonging to the monks, letters from church authorities, pamphlets from

theologians, the founder's instructions, etc. Regarding book production and libraries, see Schwartz 1939, 254–6; Festugière 1962a, 43; Chitty 1966, 131; Flusin 1983, 41–3; and Patrich 1989, 169–72. The library of the Great Laura is mentioned in the biography of Stephen Sabaites (*V. Steph. Sab.* 10. 6, 355).

39. Rubin 1982, 32–3. Charanis 1971, 69–72 offers similar figures for the monasteries of Asia Minor and Syria. This points to a sharp contrast between the monasteries of those areas and the over-populated monasteries of Egypt (White 1932, 84; Jones 1964, 930; and Rousseau 1978, 21).

40. Zeisel 1975, 268 applies the same assumption to monasteries beyond the Judean desert.

41. Theod. Petr., *V. Theod.* 18, 46. 9. The figure 400 may be an approximation meant to emphasize that the community was flourishing. This number is repeated several times in descriptions of large monasteries in Syria (Vööbus 1960a, 146, 187, 232). Nevertheless, what we have here are reliable data, probably coming from the archive of Theodosius's monastery. According to Theodore of Petra, up to the year of Theodosius's death (529), 693 monks had lived in the monastery at one time or other, including monks who had since died and former members of the community who had been called away to head other monasteries or to take up other church posts.

42. Magen 1984, 42.

43. Another monastery with a large population was the coenobium of Romanus, south of Tekoa, founded in the first half of the fifth century (Vailhé 1899–1900, 272–3 no. 102). According to John Rufus, this monastery had six hundred monks (see *Pler.* 25, 58.5). Khirbet er-Rubei'a, a monastic site about 5 km southwest of Tekoa that has been identified as the coenobium of Romanus, covers a large area (35 × 60 m) (Hirschfeld 1988–9, 102–4), but it is certainly not large enough to accommodate six hundred monks. However, the monks under Romanus's leadership may also have included hermits living in cells outside the enclosed area of the monastery. Cyril hints at an arrangement of this sort in his description of the founding of the Nea Laura (*V. Sab.* 36, 123. 6).

44. See *V. Sab.* 18, 102. 9 for the Great Laura; 90, 199. 18 for the Nea Laura.

45. For example, Qasr el-Banat, a relatively large monastery in southern Syria, was inhabited by fifty monks according to Lassus 1947, 267. (See also n. 40.)

46. See *V. Euth.* 18, 28. 11 for the laura of Euthymius; *V. Ger.* 7, 16 for the laura of Gerasimus. At the latter, in addition to the seventy cell-dwellers, there were monks living in the coenobium that constituted the core of the laura. It should also be said that the round number seventy is suspect. The same number appears in Cyril's biography of Sabas (*V. Sab.* 16, 100. 3). It was, as Cyril himself notes, the number of the larger group of Jesus's disciples, a number itself inspired in all probability by Moses' appointment of seventy elders to lead the children of Israel (Num. 11:16, 24), the number of members of the Sanhedrin, and the number of translators of the Septuagint. The hagiographers probably considered it the perfect number for a brotherhood of saintly men. But the actual number of monks in the laura of Gerasimus may not have been very different, given that the biographer was writing for readers with direct knowledge of the size of the monastery.

47. See *V. Euth.* 16, 26. 14 for the laura of Euthymius; *V. Sab.* 37, 126. 15–16 for the coenobium of the Cave.

48. At first, Yadin 1965, 114 estimated that there had been between thirty and fifty monks at Masada. However, in informal discussion, Yadin proposed reducing this estimate to between twenty and twenty-five (Hirschfeld 1985a, 253, n. 3). In fact, judging from the number of

cells, the size of the community at Marda must have been even smaller than this (Hirschfeld 1989). A similar number of cells has been found in other lauras, such as 'Ein el-Fawwar, the Cells of Choziba, and the laura of Jeremias (Patrich 1989, 101). For the coenobium of the Cave (Spelaion), see Patrich 1989, 122–31, and for Khirbet et-Tina, see Hirschfeld 1985, 94–7, no. 81.

49. These figures are based on a careful examination of each site (Hirschfeld 1987b, 214–17; 1990b).

50. Flusin (1983, 141) suggested that because of the many lauras in the Judean desert, the number of hermits—that is, recluses living outside any community—was relatively small. The number of "ghost" monasteries, those known only from the sources, is about nine (Hirschfeld 1990b).

51. Cyril mentions that ten thousand pro-Chalcedonian monks gathered in the Church of St. Stephen in Jerusalem in 516 (*V. Sab.* 56, 151. 10). He also notes, however, that they came from all over the Jerusalem diocese. According to Patrich (1989, 10, English summary), at least half the monks in the diocese must have lived in desert monasteries, since it was probably the desert monks who gave Sabas and Theodosius the majorities they needed to be elected archimandrites. But power is not always based on numbers, and in any case the total number of ten thousand is probably an exaggeration disseminated by the pro-Chalcedonian source on which Cyril's report is based.

52. Vööbus 1960a, 143, nos. 23, 24. The "Seventy-Three Canons of Maruta," bishop of Maipherqat, were composed during the fifth century in the monasteries of northern Syria. On monastic rules, see also Savramis 1962, 19; Chitty 1966, 21; Rousseau 1978, 38–9, 69–70; and Veilleux 1980–2, 7, 12.

53. *V. Sab.* 74, 179. 22 and 76, 182. 21–2. The earliest version of Sabas's rules is found in a manuscript from the twelfth or thirteenth century (published by Kurtz in 1894). According to Génier 1909, 227 and Festugière 1962a, 71, n. 35, Sabas's rules were influenced by the oral instructions given by Euthymius.

54. *Pratum* 136, 3000B. Seven gatherings for prayer a day are mentioned in Theod. Petr., *V. Theod.* 18, 45. 19–20, for the monastery of Theodosius. For the Cappadocian tradition, see Mateos 1963, 87 and Patrich 1989, 205–12.

55. *V. Geor.* 26, 126. 9. The custom of striking a symandron before prayer is also mentioned by Moschus (*Pratum* 104, 2961A–B). The symandron was also struck on important occasions, such as at the death of one of the monks (*V. Sab.* 43, 134. 1 and *Pratum* 11, 2860C).

56. A photo of the symandron at St. Catherine's was published by Forsyth and Weitzmann 1970, Pl. 39A. For the use of the symandron in general, see Lenoir 1852–6, 153–4).

57. *V. Euth.* 9, 18. 2–3. Among the rules attributed to Rabbula, bishop of Edessa in northern Syria (d. 435), we find one similar to that of Euthymius. His rule no. 25 instructs: "No one shall talk during the worship and prayer—not even the abbot—and not at the dinner table, without necessity" (Vööbus 1960a, 84).

58. In the Pachomian monasteries of Egypt, two meals per day were common (see Veilleux 1980–2, 184, n. 13 and Rousseau 1985, 84). The custom of serving two meals a day in coenobia in Syria is mentioned explicitly in the sources (Vööbus 1960a, 141, no. 18).

59. For a thorough discussion of the evidence on this issue, see Patrich 1989, 216–28.

60. Mader 1929, 123–6. A similar sundial was found in the eastern church in Mamshit. Eleven lines were inscribed in it, dividing it into twelve strips, one for each hour of the day. A cross was carved in the stone, with palm branches on either side (Negev 1983, 170).

61. Magen and Hizmi 1985, 86.

62. See *V. Cyr.* 20, 234. 31 for Cyriac; *V. John Hes.* 16, 214. 4–5 for John Hesychast; *V. Euth.* 40,

60. 12 for Euthymius; and *V. Sab.* 77, 183. 14–17 for Sabas. For more details, see Festugière 1962, 68–9, n. 29.

63. Cyril provides a description of the area surrounding the monastery of Euthymius. The place was "beautiful to see, due to the excellent evenness of the terrain, and suitable for [the practice of asceticism], because of its mild and temperate climate" (*V. Euth.* 43, 64. 21–4).

64. *V. Char.* 16, 28. 17. The custom of eating bread with salt was common. It is also mentioned in a homily of Euthymius to his disciples (*V. Euth.* 39, 58. 6) and in the rules of Pachomius (Veilleux 1980–2, 159, no. 79). The importance of bread in the monastic diet is discussed at length by Dembinska 1985, 438. But, as has been shown by Patlegean 1977, 38–44, bread was equally significant in the diet of ordinary people in Byzantine society.

65. *Pratum* 41, 2896B. The same is told of Gerasimus (*V. Ger.* 4, 5). De Journel 1946, 85, n. 2 remarks that the Communion wafer in the Orient was larger than that used in the West. We must not forget, however, that these stories reflect, not the regular diet, but exceptional practices of ascetic monks.

66. *V. Euth.* 17, 27. 20. At Choziba the guests were supplied with bread and wine (*V. Geor.* 37, 136. 19) and at the monastery of Theodosius with bread and cooked food (Theod. Petr., *V. Theod.* 15, 39. 8).

67. Theod. Petr., *V. Theod.* 15, 37. 6. The custom of using a balance for weighing bread is mentioned by Theodoret of Cyrrhus (see *Hist. relig.* 5, 1353A).

68. *V. Cyr.* 9, 228. 3 and 16, 232. 17. Palladius tells of a hermit near Jericho who had three loaves in his cell; he offered two of them to twenty-eight visitors and ate the third over a period of twenty-five days (*Hist. Laus.* 51, 144. 20–2). A monk from the laura of Pharan would take along some small loaves and some kidney beans when he went to visit other monks in the Jordan valley (*De syn.* 1, 306. 9).

69. This story is found twice: once in Theodore of Petra's biography of Theodosius (Theod. Petr., *V. Theod.*, 74–5) and again in the *Pratum* of Moschus (ed. Nau and Clugnet 7. 1, 49–50). In the latter, the monks are said to have served a cooked dish of lentils and fresh vegetables and to have put spoons on the table, probably for eating the cooked dish.

70. Jones 1964, 441. In estimating the quantity of bread needed in the monasteries, the testimony of Dorotheus of Gaza should be taken into account. As a novice, his disciple Dositheus would eat six pounds (about 1.5 kg) of bread every day. Later he gradually reduced the quantity, and ultimately he ate only a little over half a pound (about 220 g) a day (Doroth. 5, 128–30).

71. *V. Geor.* 25, 124. 2. This job, translated by Lampe 1961, 1132 as "buyer of stores," does not appear in any other source on Judean desert monasteries.

72. Theod. Petr., *V. Theod.* 75. 5. See n. 69.

73. See photograph in Forsyth and Weitzmann 1970, Pl. 18A. For Khirbet ed-Deir, see Hirschfeld and Birger (1986).

74. Hand-operated flour mills have been found in several monasteries, both in the Judean desert and elsewhere. At Khirbet Siyar el-Ghanam, northeast of Bethlehem, Corbo (1955, 9) discovered a two-coned basalt flour mill. A similar mill was found in the monastery excavated near Beit She'an (Aharoni 1954, 210).

75. *V. Sab.* 36, 123. 27. The bakery of the Great Laura, on the other hand, was built only at the second stage of construction, in the early sixth century (*V. Sab.* 32, 117. 7); it may therefore be assumed that at first the monks of the Great Laura baked their bread by simpler means, without a special bakery building, as is still done by Bedouins in the desert.

76. *V. Sab.* 8, 92. 11–12. Cassian, writing in the early fifth century, tells of monks from the vicinity

of Bethlehem who, lacking firewood, were forced to go down into the desert, sometimes as far as the Dead Sea, in order to gather wood for the oven of their monastery (Cass., *De Inst.* 4. 21, 61). In a later source, from the Middle Ages, we learn of the transportation of wood for cooking and baking at the monastery of Euthymius (Chitty and Jones 1928, 138).

77. Forsyth and Weitzmann 1970, Pl. 22A.

78. See, e.g., the well-known picture showing a basket of bread in the Church of Heptapegon, north of the Sea of Galilee. Bread of the same size and shape appears in mosaic floors in Judean desert monasteries—e.g., at Marda (Yadin 1966, color picture on p. 113) and at Khirbet ed-Deir (Hirschfeld, unpub.).

79. Some bread stamps have been found at the monastery of Dominus Flevit on the Mount of Olives in Jerusalem (Bagatti 1955–6, 256–7).

80. This rule (no. 116) was translated by Veilleux (1980–2, 163) and is further discussed by Dembińska (1985, 439).

81. *V. Geor.* 43, 336. 10.

82. On the importance of pulses in the monks' diet in Egypt and Europe, see Dembińska 1985, 440.

83. *De syn.* 1, 306. 9 and *V. Cyr.* 19, 234. 3. It was also said of Theodosius that he would eat "soaked kidney beans" (Theod. Petr., *V. Theod.* 7, 19. 25).

84. *V. Sab.* 48, 131. 11. The *pisarion* is mentioned by Cyril (*V. Sab.* 40, 130. 31–2) and the *phakos* by Theodore of Petra (Theod. Petr., *V. Theod.* 74. 3).

85. *V. Sab.* 76, 182. 10. The same is told of Theodosius (Theod. Petr., *V. Theod.* 7, 19. 25–6). Eating only dates and carobs was a sign of asceticism. Anthony mentions a young monk at the monastery of Choziba who would eat only dates and carobs for several days (*V. Geor.* 19, 118. 16–17).

86. For Theognius, see Paul. El., *V. Theog.* 8, 86. 16; for the laura of Gerasimus, *V. Ger.* 2, 2 and 3, 3.

87. *V. Geor.* 7, 102. 5–13. The importance of the date palm to the subsistence of the monks is discussed by Dembińska 1985, 435–6.

88. *V. John Hes.* 25, 220. 5–21. The remains of John's cell were described by Patrich 1988, 144–9.

89. *V. Steph. Sab.* 40, 520B. The rules may have been stricter in the sixth century, however. Abstention from meat was also the rule among Syrian monks. The rules attributed to Maruta state explicitly that "they [the monks] shall not eat meat in their monasteries" (Vööbus 1960a, 148, no. 2). The Egyptian monks occasionally ate meat and fish on holidays (Dembińska 1985, 435).

90. When Cyriac was a novice at the monastery of Gerasimus, he never used oil or wine (*V. Cyr.* 5, 225. 7). The same is said of George of Choziba, who had neither wine nor oil in his cell (*V. Geor.* 12, 108. 4).

91. Palladius, *Hist. Laus.* 48, 143. 3–7. Vine growing is still a feature of Mediterranean culture and can be found in any traditional settlement, including monasteries.

92. *V. John Hes.* 19, 216. 1; *V. Sab.* 44, 135. 2 and 60, 161. 25; *V. Cyr.* 5, 225. 7; and *V. Ger.* 4, 4. Moschus mentions the custom in Egypt of drinking *eukration* (*Pratum* 184, 3057B–C). For the nature of this drink, see Festugière 1962a, 61, n. 99 and Patrich 1989, 187.

93. *V. Sab.* 8, 92. 8. According to Cyril, the monks of the Great Laura would take food with them when they went out to gather *manouthia* (*V. Sab.* 40, 130. 30), which implies that this task required them to be absent from the monastery for a whole day. Elsewhere Cyril mentions that he used to go into the desert with his companions from the monastery of Euthymius to

gather manouthion bushes (*V. Euth.* 50, 72. 19). For a detailed discussion of this subject, see Hirschfeld 1990.

94. Hirschfeld 1990. According to Danin 1983, 124, boiled young flower clusters of tumble thistle have a taste similar to artichoke. Among present-day Arabs, ʿaqub is so prized as a food that it is exported to Saudi Arabia and the Gulf Emirates.

95. *De syn.* 2, 307. 8–10 (see the recension below the text). The saltbush is mentioned several times in the literary sources as a plant eaten by hermits. While living on Masada, Euthymius and Domitian subsisted on the saltbushes they found there (*V. Euth.* 11, 22. 6).

96. Danin 1983, 124 and Dafni 1985, 81.

97. Danin 1983 and Dafni 1985, 103.

98. *V. Geor.* 12, 108. 7–12. According to Anthony, when George lived with his brother in the laura of Calamon, they would collect the scraps and eat them (see *V. Geor.* 6, 101. 14).

99. *V. John Hes.* 12, 211. 3–4. In a similar case, a man from Tekoa visiting Cyriac in the interior of the desert brought him fresh bread (*V. Cyr.* 9, 227. 21–2).

100. *V. Sab.* 13, 96. 18 and 15, 99. 3.

101. *V. Theod.* 240. 8. Other examples include *V. Cyr.* 4, 224. 22–3; *Pratum* 166, 3033A; and *De syn.* 11, 314. 2.

102. Vööbus 1960a, 106, no. 1.

103. *V. Sym. Sal.* 13, 1688. This custom existed in Syrian monasteries as well (Vööbus 1960a, 182, no. 19) and probably originated from the custom of giving newly baptized adults a white garment, which was worn for a week after the baptism ceremony.

104. *V. Euth.* 50, 73. 13. According to Festugière (1962a, 129, n. 166), this seems to be the only explicit mention of the black color of the monks' habit in the Judean desert. Another indication is found in Theodore's work, which notes that Theodosius's attire was exceptional, for his hood was white (Theod. Petr., *V. Theod.* 71. 23–4)—which suggests that the dominant colors of the monks' dress were dark. Visual evidence of this is found in a mosaic in the Church of the Holy Bush, preserved at the monastery of St. Catherine in Sinai. On the edges of the mosaic are several medallions enclosing figures of prophets, saints, and two monks: the abbot of the monastery and his deacon. Whereas the prophets and saints are shown wearing light-colored clothing, the two monks are depicted in dark garments (Forsyth and Weitzmann 1970, Pl. 120, 121).

105. See *V. Geor.* 12, 100. 5–6 for George's dress; *V. Ger.* 4, 3 for the garments of the cell-dwellers at the laura of Gerasimus. For a detailed discussion, see Patrich 1989, 190–4.

106. Kühnel 1984, 188, n. 50. Patrich 1989, 118–19 favors an earlier date (seventh or eighth century).

107. *V. Geor.* 4, 99. 10. Another monk notable for his austerity would wear a "straw cape" (*Pratum* 92, 2942C). Straw did not provide sufficient protection from the cold, and it scratched the skin; its use was thus intended for mortification.

108. Doroth. 15, 168. 1–2.

109. Vööbus 1960a, 148, no. 4.

110. Fritz 1975, 110.

111. Forsyth and Weitzmann 1970, Pl. 126.

112. Vööbus 1960a, 142, no. 22. Another Syrian regulation stated that the monks were to sleep without "loosening their girdles or taking off [their] clothes" (ibid., 90, no. 8, and 141, no. 19).

113. Vööbus 1960a, 106, no. 3: "He shall not sleep on his sides and also not on his back, but sitting, and his face shall look toward the East."

114. *V. Euth.* 21, 34. 6–7. In one of the cave cells of the laura of Firminus, Marcoff and Chitty 1929, 169 found a small hole in a protrusion from the ceiling. In their opinion, a rope was fastened to it to support the cell-dweller while he was asleep, following Euthymius's example.

115. *Pratum* 63, 2916A. Another anecdote mentions a monk of the same laura who would sleep on a chair (*Pratum* 68, 2917D).

116. See Magen and Hizmi 1985, 68 for the couches at the monastery of Martyrius. A room with two beds discovered at the monastery of Euthymius but not yet reported is dated to the later stage of the monastery (the Middle Ages); but its construction and its two beds preserve the building tradition of the Byzantine period.

117. At the monastery of Martyrius, e.g., the stone couch was probably reserved for the gatekeeper; the other monks probably slept on mattresses laid on the ground, as indicated in the sources.

118. Private cells of a priest and an elder in the coenobium of Theodosius are mentioned in *Pratum* 104, 2961A–B. Anthony of Choziba had his own cell when he was keeper of the storerooms in the coenobium (*V. Geor.* 40, 142. 6; 35, 135; and 37, 136). Even in Egypt, elders in coenobia had private cells (*Pratum* 184, 3057D).

119. *Codex Iust.*, Novella V, III. 3–40. This question was discussed by Gerostergios 1982, 170–1.

120. Deir Qalʿa was first discovered and described by Guérin (1875, 126–9) and then by Conder and Kitchener 1883, 315–19. I surveyed the site and published my conclusions, including a new plan of the site (Hirschfeld 1989b, 40–3). Another example of the influence of Justinian's Codex may be observed at the coenobium of Khirbet ed-Deir, where foundations of large halls were discovered in the living quarters, whereas on the lower level a few cells were excavated. Reports on the new discoveries have not yet been published.

121. *Pratum* 3, 2856A. Sabas also kept a rucksack in his cell (*V. Sab.* 13, 96. 14).

122. See *V. Geor.* 13, 109. 14 for George's cell; Paul. El., *V. Theog.* 8, 87. 1 for Theognius's cell.

123. *Miracula* 4, 364. 10. A picture of a scythe of this kind appears in the mosaic floor of the church at Khirbet ed-Deir. A notion of the variety of tools available to the monks emerges from the archaeological finds at the monastery of Kyria Maria in Beit Sheʾan (Fitzgerald 1939, Pl. 37). In the course of excavations, various bronze tools were found in the monastery, including knives, a double-bladed axe, a scythe, a hoe with a pointed blade, and a spade (Tsafrir 1984, 352).

124. *V. Ger.* 3, 3. The candlelight used by Theodosius is mentioned by Theod. Petr., *V. Theod.* 18, 48. 20, and the lanterns of the Great Laura's hostel in Jericho by Cyril (*V. Sab.* 46, 137. 7). Candles on a candelabrum lit the church at Choziba (*V. Geor.* 23, 122. 18 and 34, 133. 9). Oil lamps were found by Baramki and Stephen (1935, 82) in the niches in the wall of the Nestorian hermitage near Jericho. A splendid bronze lamp was found in one of the cells of the laura of Marda (Yadin 1965, 58). Bronze lamps are often depicted in mosaics, e.g., in the mosaic pavement in front of the church in the monastery of Martyrius.

125. Magen and Hizmi 1985, 84–6.

126. Moschus tells the story of a monk who borrowed a book belonging to a presbyter in Jerusalem (*Pratum* 46, 2901B). Another story tells of a monk in a laura in southern Palestine, near Gaza, who obtained "The Sayings of the Desert Fathers" (*Apoph. Pat.*) from the laura's abbot (*Pratum* 55, 2909A). The library of the Great Laura is mentioned in the biography of Stephen Sabaites (*V. Steph. Sab.* 10. 6, 355).

127. Magen and Hizmi 1985, 68.

128. *V. Geor.* 12, 108. 5; see also Lampe 1961, 768.

129. See Theod. Petr., *V. Theod.* 13, 36. 11 for the tables in the monastery of Theodosius; *V. Geor.* 12, 108. 8 and 43, 336. 10 for the tables at the monastery of Choziba.

130. Magen and Hizmi 1985, 74. The photographs accompanying their article show many of the ceramic finds.

131. The photographs accompanying Magen and Hizmi 1985, 80 show more than eighty such bowls found at the monastery of Martyrius. Bowls of this type found at Khirbet Siyar el-Ghanam, northeast of Bethlehem, were reported by Corbo 1955, 72.

132. *Pratum* 107, 2968B. In the monasteries excavated by Corbo (1955, 9) east and north of Bethlehem, pottery vessels of various kinds were found, including eating utensils (plates, bowls, and cups), storage vessels (pitchers and small-mouthed jugs), lamps, etc. Pottery vessels with more ornamental shapes were used for church purposes. Large clay and stone utensils for grinding were also found, as well as basalt flour mills.

133. Festugière 1963, 79.

134. Weitzmann 1935, 163–8, Pl. 25.

CHAPTER FOUR: SOURCES OF LIVELIHOOD

1. Bury 1931, 287; Avi-Yonah 1958, 43–7; Savramis 1962, 46–9; Hunt 1982, 137; Patrich 1989, 33–44, 46–7. Donations were also an important source of income for the monasteries in Egypt (Hardy 1931, 142–3; Jones 1964, 931) and Syria (Vööbus 1960, 162–73).

2. Mango 1974, 27.

3. See *Pratum* 157, 3025B–C for the donation to the three monasteries near the Jordan. In *Miracula* 1, 360–1 we read of a wealthy matron who toured all the monasteries near the Holy City and the Jordan River, leaving offerings, and finally came to Choziba. According to Anthony of Choziba, a donation of sixty golden coins was brought by another woman who came to the gate of the monastery and then disappeared (*V. Geor.* 25, 124. 19). Cyril tells of Aitherius, who came to Jerusalem from Asia Minor and made donations "to the poor and the monasteries" (*V. John Hes.* 15, 213. 6–7). Anastasius's nephew, Hypatius, gave one hundred pounds of gold to Theodosius and Sabas, to be distributed among the monks (*V. Sab.* 56, 152).

4. See *V. Sab.* 25, 109. 6–9 for Sophia's legacy; *V. Cyr.* 7, 226. 11–13 for Terebon's.

5. *V. Euth.* 10, 21. 11–15. Monks' property was an important issue in the Justinian Codex (Orestano 1956). Until then, and even after the time of Justinian, disposal of a monk's property was left to his own discretion. This practice may be seen in the story of the Senator's daughter, who paid an enormous sum of gold (three hundred coins) in order to be given the monastic habit (*De syn.* 11, 314. 1). According to a story in the *Pratum*, a prospective monk brought a bag of gold into one of the monasteries in the Jordan area, but the abbot, a very prudent man, accepted this money only conditionally, until the man's fitness for monastic life had been satisfactorily proved (*Pratum*, ed. Nissen, 13, 368–71).

6. *V. Sab.* 28. 113. 20–3.

7. *V. Sab.* 74, 179. 12–13. For Procopius's list, see *Buildings* V, XI. 1–13, 356–8. The imperial support for the Holy Land has been discussed by Hunt 1982.

8. See Theod. Petr., *V. Theod.* 78. 19–24 for the woman's donation of food; ibid., 80. 24–7 for the village's contribution. The monastery of Theodosius received many donations, more than any other monastery in the Judean desert. Theodore of Petra mentions some of these gifts (ibid., 11, 27. 8–10; 12, 29. 1–3; 16, 41. 6–9; 18. 10–13).

9. *Pratum* 92, 2949–52. It is not impossible that St. Cyricus was the patron of the army commander.

10. *V. Euth.* 10, 21. 13–15; *V. Cyr.* 6, 226. 10–15. For more details, see Festugière 1962a, 72, n. 139. For monastic property in Egypt, see Johnson and West 1967, 66–72.

11. Magen and Hizmi 1985, 86.

12. Chitty 1966, 3; Rubin 1982, 36. For raw materials near the oasis of Jericho, see Avi-Yonah 1937, 252–3.

13. *Apoph. Pat.* 436A, Eng. trans. in Ward 1975, 242.

14. See Paul. Fl., *V. Theog.* 7, 86. 4 5 for Theognius; Theod. Petr., *V. Theod.* 15, 38. 20 for the monastery of Theodosius. Patlegean 1977, 316, 319 calls these monks "les artisans du 'desert.'"

15. Fitzgerald 1939, 41–2, Pl. 37–8. Depictions of baskets are found in the mosaic floor in the church of the monastery of Kursi (Tzaferis 1983, Pl. 105). One of the loveliest and most detailed depictions of a wicker basket appears in the mosaic floor in the Church of St. George at Khirbet el-Mekhayyat, Transjordan (Saller and Bagatti 1949, 67–77).

16. See *V. Geor.* 7, 102. 5–13 for Calamon; *V. Ger.* 3, 3 for the laura of Gerasimus.

17. Corbo 1958a, 246 and Rubin 1982, 37–8. Patlegean 1977, 321 calls these monasteries "les monastères agricoles."

18. Corbo 1955, 4–5; 1958, 254–5. Winepresses and/or oil presses have been found at the following monasteries: the monastery found on the French hill in northern Jerusalem, described as a "monks' farm" (Oren 1971); the monastery of Ras Tawil, north of Shuʿafat in northern Jerusalem (Gibson 1985–6, 72); the monastery complex discovered near Khirbet el-Bira, in western Samaria (Dar and Safrai 1982, 11–13); the monastery of Beit Hashita, near Beit Sheʾan (Scythopolis), described as a "Byzantine monastery farm" (Aharoni 1954, 210); the monastery discovered in Mevo Modiʿin, on the coastal plain (Eisenberg 1977, 27); the monastery called "monks' farm," near Kibbutz Ruhama, in the northern Negev (Gophna 1962). Winepresses were also found in several monasteries in southern Sinai, such as Deir Antush (Finkelstein and Tepper 1982) and in ʿEin Najila (Dahari 1983, 10). Winepresses and oil presses were found in many monasteries in Transjordan, indicating that there, too, monks were engaged in agriculture and the production of olive oil and wine (Piccirillo 1985, 258–9). For winepresses and oil presses in the Byzantine monasteries of Syria, see Lassus 1947, 282.

19. According to Oren (1971), the gathering vat of the winepress on French Hill was decorated with two crosses, painted red. The winepresses near the YMCA were discovered by Iliffe (1935, 76–7). He identified the installation as a "bathhouse," though it was undoubtedly the monastery winepress.

20. I have surveyed the monastic site of Khirbet el-Quneitira (Hirschfeld 1985a).

21. Hirschfeld and Kloner 1988–9.

22. *Pratum* 134, 2997B–C. Some scholars believe this story refers to the construction of a cistern somewhere in Sinai (Chitty 1966, 149), but this seems unlikely.

CHAPTER FIVE: ARCHITECTURAL COMPONENTS: SACRED ELEMENTS

1. *V. Sab.* 36, 123. 17–18. This inconvenient situation was exceptional and lasted only for a short time.

2. See Theod. Petr., *V. Theod.* 18, 45 for the first four churches of the monastery of Theodosius and *V. Theod.* 240. 23–4 for the fifth. For the churches of the Great Laura, see *V. Sab.* 16, 100. 11 for the small chapel, 18, 102. 2–6 for the cave church, and 32, 117. 8–10 for the central church.

3. Other square apses were found in the churches in Herodium (Netzer 1990) and the church at Tel Masos, in the Beersheba valley (Fritz 1975, 112).

4. This phenomenon is found in various monasteries beyond the Judean desert as well. In a remote monastery surveyed by Glueck (1933–4, 60) in Wadi Mujib, east of the Dead Sea, the church faces southeast. The chapel of the monastery at ʿEin Najila, in southern Sinai, faces northeast because of the steep topography of the site (Dahari 1983, 9–10).

5. See *V. Euth.* 48, 69. 12–17 for the diaconicon in the coenobitic stage of the monastery of Euthymius.

6. *V. Euth.* 10, 20. 28. For a detailed discussion of baptistries in monasteries, see Ben-Peshat 1990.

7. Corbo 1958, 257. This type is also common among the monasteries beyond the Jordan desert— e.g., the church of Dominus Flevit on the Mount of Olives in Jerusalem (Bagatti 1955–6, 240–1) and the church of Kyria Maria in Beit Sheʾan (Fitzgerald 1939, 3–4).

8. Magen and Hizmi 1985, 71.

9. Another example of a large monastery with a narrow prayer room is Deir Qalʿa on the western slopes of Samaria (Conder and Kitchener 1882, 315–19 and Hirschfeld 1989b, 40–3).

10. Yadin 1965, 111–12. A plan of the church on Masada was published by Schneider (1931a). For a discussion of the monastic remains on Masada, see Hirschfeld 1989. A church similar to the one on Masada was found at Nuseib el-ʾAweishireh, west of Jericho. The church at Nuseib and its mosaic floors—one of which contains an inscription—are discussed by Netzer and Birger (1990) and by Di Segni (1990b).

11. Wright 1961, 10 and Patrich 1989, 113–19.

12. Corbo 1960, 141 and Hirschfeld 1990b, no. 28.

13. The cave church of the Great Laura was discovered by Vailhé (1897, 117), who also published its plan.

14. Patrich 1985a, 60–1 and Hirschfeld 1988–9, 95–7. Until the 1970s, a small Russian Orthodox monastery existed here. A photograph from that period published by Compagnoni (1978, Pl. 16) shows that Chariton's cave was used as a church. The altar seen in the photograph stands where the four sockets of the original altar were found. The site was abandoned in 1978 (van den Heyden 1986, 78–9).

15. Chitty 1928, 139–45; Meinardus 1964–5, 249–50; Blomme and Nodet 1979; Kühnel 1984; and Patrich and Di Segni 1987, 277–8.

16. Goldfus (1990) discusses the cave church at Khallet Danabiya at length.

17. Di Segni and Hirschfeld 1987, 368–73, inscription no. 1.

18. Negev 1983, 352.

19. Two other churches of the basilica type in the Judean desert either are not Byzantine or do not belong to a monastery. The first is the church of the monastery of Euthymius. Chitty 1930, 44–5 and 1932, 195–200 dates this building to the Byzantine period, but excavations that Birger and I performed at the site show it to be not earlier than 660. The other basilica church was discovered at Khirbet Umm el-ʿAmed, east of Tekoa. Following the survey, I suggested that the site be identified as a monastery (Hirschfeld 1985, 86–9, no. 69), but on reevaluating the evidence, I have concluded that it was not a monastic complex, but a lay settlement in the desert.

20. Hirschfeld 1990b, no. 9.

21. Patrich 1983, 66 and 1989, 135.

22. For the significance of the founder's tomb to the community, see Flusin 1983, 132–3.

23. *V. Ger.* 9, 9 and *Pratum* 107, 2969A.

24. Chitty 1928, 151.

25. Patrich and Di Segni (1987), 277–8. This practice also existed outside the Judean desert. In a group of monasteries in Syria, the tombs of the heads of the monastery and the priests have been found, while the simple monks were buried in an area outside the monastery (see Lassus 1947, 276).

26. See *Pratum* 91, 2949A for the laura of Coprotha; ibid. 92, 2952A for the church of St. Cyricus.

27. *Pratum* 93, 2952C. For a description of the simple grave of a monk in the laura of the Aeliotes in the Jordan valley, see *Pratum* 6, 2857B–C. The same custom existed in Syria and Arabia (Transjordan). Moschus tells of an old monk and his disciple who lived in solitude on a mountain in Syria. When the disciple died, the old man wished to bury him but, lacking proper tools for digging, was forced to seek help (*Pratum* 91, 2948C). For burial of a monk in the ground in Transjordan, see *Pratum* 123, 2985B.

28. See *V. Sab.* 41, 132. 16–19 for a monk's death in the Great Laura; ibid. 76, 183. 1–2 for Sabas's death after taking Communion. See also *V. Cyr.* 21, 235. 18–19 for Cyriac's death in the Old Laura. Additional details on the funeral ceremony can be found in Moschus—e.g., *Pratum* 11, 2860D–2861A for the death of monks in Syria. For the funeral of George of Choziba, see *V. Geor.* 57, 356–7.

29. *Pratum* 92, 2949–52. Burial in Syria in a tunic and an upper garment and with a cross is also mentioned by Moschus (*Pratum* 87, 2945A).

30. *Pratum* 170, 3037A. Graves of monks were excavated in Egypt in which the bodies had been deposed in full monk's dress (Walters 1974, 231–4).

31. See *Pratum* 11, 2860C for a funeral in the laura of Gerasimus; ibid. 86, 2944B for one in Syria.

32. See *V. Geor.* 36, 135. 6–8 for George's deep meditation; ibid. 57, 357. 12 for his death.

33. *Pratum* 87, 2945A and 92, 2952A.

34. Theod. Petr., *V. Theod.* 18, 46. 12. This number was probably taken from the archive of the monastery.

35. Schneider 1931, 315–30.

36. In the burial place of the monastery of Euthymius, more than a hundred complete skeletons were found, all in the position of a first burial. Since the monastery of Euthymius functioned until the thirteenth century, we can conclude that the custom of separating the skulls from the rest of the bones developed later, at least in the Judean desert. A similar custom apparently exists in the monastery of St. Catherine in Sinai, but the date of its origin is unknown (Tsafrir 1971).

37. Chitty 1930, 150–2; 1932, 200–1; and Barrois 1930.

38. Meimaris (1977) suggests that this chamber was originally the tomb of Peter-Aspebet, chief of the Saracen tribe that was converted to Christianity; but there is no evidence to support this hypothesis.

39. Magen and Hizmi (1985). See Di Segni 1990b for the inscriptions and Magen and Talgam 1990 for the mosaic floors.

40. Patrich and Di Segni 1987, 277–8.

41. *V. Euth.* 36, 55. 18. In a survey of the cave carried out by Chitty, a fragment of a sarcophagus with a funerary inscription was found. Chitty 1928, 151 suggested that it might have been the tomb of Theoctistus, but this does not accord with the account of Stephen Sabaites.

42. Di Segni and Hirschfeld 1987, 377–83, inscription no. 3.

43. Ibid. 383–5, inscription no. 4.

44. According to Kühnel 1984, 188, n. 50, the drawings should be dated to the Middle Ages (the

twelfth century); but it is not impossible that they are earlier (Patrich 1989, 118–19). Since the cave occupied a central position and drawings decorate the walls, Milik 1961, 26 surmised that the heads of the monastery and their followers were buried there.

45. Hirschfeld 1988–9, 149–50 and 1990b, no. 43.

46. Patrich 1989, 103–4 and 1990.

47. Dinur and Feig 1986.

48. We may point to two other examples. Among the Cells of Choziba in Wadi Qilt, a cave church was found. Judging from the large quantity of bones in it, we raised the possibility of its being a burial crypt. On the eastern side of the laura of 'Ein el-Fawwar, the remains of a public building were found. It is a hall built next to the natural cliff, with two adjoining cells. The dimensions of the hall are 8.5 × 14.5 m. The rock wall contains two horizontal rows of depressions for wooden beams, which indicates that it was a two-story building. Several threshold stones found beneath the ruins indicate the quality of the construction, and sections of a mosaic floor remain in situ. Since it is situated in the eastern part of the monastery, it can be surmised that this building was used for burial (Hirschfeld 1988–9, 97).

49. Moschus mentions monks in the coenobium of Theodosius who would pray privately, one in front of the main church of the monastery, the other in the burial crypt (*Pratum* 104–5, 2961A–B). A monk in the coenobium of Choziba would spend most of the night in prayer in the chapel of the Five Saints (*V. Geor.* 19, 118. 19–20).

50. *V. Char.* 16–17, 28–9. Moschus mentions prayers in a laura cell or in a hermitage (see *Pratum* 63, 2917A for the laura of the Aeliotes; ibid. 160, 3028B about an anchorite).

51. *Pratum* 45, 2900B and 180, 3082A.

52. *V. Geor.* 13, 109. 4–5. The sources testify to the habit of some monks, especially those living in remote places, of keeping ritual articles in their cells and using them from time to time.

53. See *V. Euth.* 8, 15. 21 for the cave church in the monastery of Theoctistus; 11, 22. 7 for the chapel on Masada; and 15, 24. 19–20 for the chapel in Mishor Adummim (see also 16, 26. 15–16).

54. A list of the community's tools is mentioned by Cyril (*V. Sab.* 36, 122. 25–6). With regard to monks requesting help from local peasants, see *V. Sab.* 84, 130. 18–20.

55. *V. Sab.* 28, 113. 21–3. Cyril himself followed Sabas's dictum and had his cell built in the Great Laura, probably at his own expense (*V. Sab.* 75, 181. 11–12).

56. Patrich 1988 and 1989, 70–83. Meinardus 1965–6, followed by Ovadiah and de Silva 1981, 240–1, 253–4, mistakenly considered some of the hermitages to be separate monasteries. The reason for this mistake may have been the existence of prayer rooms in these cells.

57. Patrich 1989, 81, nos. 15, 42.

58. *V. John Hes.* 10, 208 and 14, 229. For the remains of the cell thought to have belonged to John Hesychast, see Patrich 1989, 74–5, no. 29.

59. Hirschfeld 1988–9, 100–1. Not far from the laura of Gerasimus, at a site called 'Ein Abu Makhmud, several other cells with prayer rooms were discovered by Patrich. These prayer rooms, too, were carved in the soft Lissan marl of the Jordan valley region. A report on this discovery has not yet been published.

CHAPTER SIX: ARCHITECTURAL COMPONENTS:
SECULAR ELEMENTS

1. See *V. Euth.* 38, 57. 7–9 for Euthymius; *V. Sab.* 17, 101 for Sabas.

2. See *V. Sab.* 8, 92. 11–12 for Sabas; *V. Cyr.* 4, 225. 2 for Cyriac; and *V. Geor.* 4, 99. 7 for George of Choziba.

3. *V. John Hes.* 5, 205. Sabas did not know that John was a priest and a bishop, but he must have been a learned, dignified figure, who could hardly have been taken for an unskilled laborer. Nevertheless, and despite his age, he was employed in carrying water, picking up stones, and cooking.

4. As in the case of the Nea Laura (*V. Sab.* 36, 123. 6–7) and the monastery of Castellion, which the monks helped Sabas to build (*V. Sab.* 27, 111. 19–22).

5. Paul. El., *V. Theog.* 22, 105. 9–10. The monastery of Theognius is identified as Khirbet el-Makhrum, east of Bethlehem (Hirschfeld 1990b, no. 17).

6. See *V. Sab.* 27, 111. 24–6 for the monastery of Castellion; *V. Euth.* 44, 65. 18–23 for the monastery of Euthymius.

7. Magen and Hizmi 1985, 76.

8. Hirschfeld 1989b, 39.

9. Hirschfeld 1985a, 251.

10. Magen and Hizmi 1985, 83. This estimate is probably exaggerated, though the water storage capacity of the Monastery of Martyrius was indeed extraordinary.

11. For a detailed discussion, see Hirschfeld 1989d.

12. See Marcoff and Chitty 1929, 169–70 for the laura of Firminus; Tinelli 1973, 98 for the reservoir beneath the Church of the Holy Sepulchre. A number of other cisterns and reservoirs decorated with crosses have been found in monastic complexes in Jerusalem and the Judean desert. A cross in high relief was found on the upper edge of a large reservoir in the area of the "third wall" north of Jerusalem (Ben-Arieh and Netzer 1974, 106). The reservoir was part of the complex of St. Stephen's Church. A vaulted cistern found in Rujum Mugheifir, one of Elias's monasteries near Jericho, contained a cross surrounded by a medallion (Conder and Kitchener 1883, 221). A similarly decorated cistern was found at the monastery of Euthymius by Chitty (1932, 190). To these examples we can add the crosses found on winepresses at monastic sites (see ch. 4).

13. Avigad 1980, 244–5. Another cross, whose existence has not yet been reported officially, was found in a reservoir beneath the other end of the annex of the Nea Church. This reservoir was found during the laying of the foundations of the Seibenberg house in the Jewish quarter of Jerusalem's Old City.

14. Hirschfeld 1988–9, 101–2.

15. We noted the existence of a device for preventing evaporation in our investigation of the remains of the cisterns at Khirbet ed-Deir.

16. See Paul. El., *V. Theog.* 22, 105. 22 for the monastery of Theognius; Theod. Petr., *V. Theod.* 14, 37. 16 for the monastery of Theodosius.

17. See *V. Geor.* 28, 126. 9–10 for the main gate; 27, 125. 18 for the side gate.

18. See *V. Euth.* 56, 77. 19–20 for the gatekeeper; *V. Geor.* 20, 119. 19 for his cell. For the importance of the gatekeeper, see Gorce 1972, 75–6.

19. Cyril mentions, e.g., the closed cell of John Hesychast in the Great Laura (*V. John Hes.* 19, 216. 1–2 and 23, 219. 7–8). A similar description of a hermit's cave near the Jordan River is given by Moschus (see *Pratum* 19, 2865B).

20. *V. Euth.* 56, 77. 14–15. For female visitors near the monastery gate, see *V. Euth.* 54, 76. 18–27. This subject is discussed in detail by Patrich and Di Segni 1987, 275–7.

21. Magen and Hizmi 1985, 67.

22. I discovered and identified Khirbet Bureikut as a monastery in 1982 (Hirschfeld 1987b, 58–9 and 1990b, no. 30). The Khirbet ed-Deir that lies west of Hebron was described by Kopp and Steve 1946, 562. It is worth mentioning that a similar round stone was installed in the entrance to the synagogue complex at Khirbet Susiya, southeast of Hebron (Magen and Hizmi 1985, 67).

23. Magen and Hizmi 1985, 68.

24. Another good example of a monastery with gates and gatekeepers' cells is the monastery of Theognius. According to the excavator (Corbo 1955, 149–53), the monastery had two gates: one in the northern wall, which led to the central courtyard, and one in the eastern wall, which led to the living quarters. Both opened onto passageways leading to the interior of the monastery. The eastern gate was about 2.5 m wide, and its passageway was 3.8 m wide. On the northern side of the passageway—i.e., to the right of someone entering the gate—was the gatekeeper's cell, measuring 4.5 × 5.8 m (interior dimensions). Opposite the cell, next to the wall of the passageway, a bench was placed. The northern gate was narrower (1.8 m wide), as was the corridor leading from it (also 1.8 m wide). The gatekeeper's cell was found on the western side of the passageway—i.e., to the right upon entering.

25. The "Byzantine gate" on Masada was first described by Conder (1875) following his visit to the site in 1875. For Conder's photographs of the gate, see Hirschfeld 1989, 264.

26. For a general discussion of the courtyard, see Corbo (1955), 3.

27. *Miracula* 1, 362. 1 and *V. Geor.* 19, 119. 1–2.

28. The courtyard at the monastic site of Bir el-Qatt, near Bethlehem, was paved with a mosaic floor (Corbo 1955, 8), as was the courtyard at the monastery of Lady Mary in Beit She'an (Fitzgerald 1939, 2), which, according to Fitzgerald, was roofed. However, judging from its dimensions (9.7 × 16.4 m) and the absence of any means of supporting the ceiling, it seems more likely that it was an open courtyard.

29. Hirschfeld 1990b, no. 27. Another example of an irregular courtyard of a cliff coenobium, albeit beyond the Judean desert, was found at the small monastic site discovered by Glueck (1933–4, 60) in one of the tributaries descending to Wadi Mujib, east of the Dead Sea.

30. In the early sixth century, the monks of the Judean desert were warned by the military authorities to protect themselves against an invasion of Saracens (*V. John Hes.* 13, 211. 15–22). For the historical background, see Festugière 1963, 23, n. 43. This danger was the reason invoked by Sabas when, on his second visit to Constantinople in 531, he asked Justinian to build a fort in the desert near his monasteries (*V. Sab.* 72, 175. 16–19). Anthony of Choziba mentions a band of robbers who tried to gain entrance to the monastery (*V. Geor.* 28, 126–7). Later, after the Persian invasion of Palestine in 614, the hermits could not live beyond the walls of this monastery (*V. Geor.* 42, 143. 9–11). For the historical evidence, see Isaac 1984 and Mayerson 1986.

31. The nucleus of the laura of Calamon was called "the Castrum" ("the Fortress") (*V. Geor.* 6, 101. 13). The monastery of St. John the Baptist on the Jordan River is also called a *castrum* by Epiphanius Monachus; see Wilkinson 1977, 121. For the influence of military architecture and the role of the tower in late antiquity, see MacMullen 1963, 140–2.

32. This hypothesis was put forward by Ben-Dov 1973. The arguments against it were presented by Rubin 1982, 34, n. 76.

33. See *V. Euth.* 30, 48. 10 for Eudocia's tower; *V. Sab.* 38, 127 for the founding of the monastery of John Scholarius around it.

34. *Pratum* 9, 2860A, and 10, 2860B.

35. Patrich 1989, 61.

36. This is the assumption proposed by Desreumaux, Humbert, and Nodet 1978, 418–19. A description of the tower, accompanied by a plan, was presented by Lombardi 1958–9, 276.

37. Chitty 1932, 198 mentions the existence of these remains, which appear in British Mandate maps as Qasr el-Khan. Today the remains have been completely destroyed, and since no description appears in the sources, it is impossible to give any further information.

38. In Egypt, where monks faced the pressure of attacks by "barbarians," fortified towers were built in most monasteries. At Kellia two towers, two or three stories high, were added to the monastery in the fifth century; and in the monastery of Epiphanius a massive tower was erected at the end of the sixth century (Arkell 1959, 117; Walters 1974, 86, 96; and Badawy 1978, 41).

39. See n. 31.

40. *Pratum* 104, 2961B. Describing the new building of the monastery of Peter the Iberian near Maiuma, on the southern coastal plain, Peter's biographer says that the cells were built on the lower and upper levels of the monastery (*V. Pet. Ib.* 144). For a detailed discussion of this important description, see Hirschfeld 1985a, 247.

41. I surveyed and excavated the site (Hirschfeld 1985, 94–7, no. 81).

42. See, e.g., *V. Sab.* 41, 131. 1 for Jacob's cell; 43, 133. 9 for Anthimos's cell; and 44, 134. 24 for Aphrodisios's cell. Theognius lived in his own cell in the laura of Calamon (Paul. El., *V. Theog.* 7, 85–6). The custom of living in separate cells is reflected repeatedly in the regulations given to the Byzantine monastic communities of Syria (Vööbus 1960a, 218, s.v. "Cells").

43. See *V. Sab.* 42, 132. 28 for Zannus and his brother; *V. Geor.* 6, 101. 10 for George and his brother. Moschus tells of an old monk in the laura of Calamon who lived with another monk in the same cell for several years (*Pratum* 26, 2873A). The eighth-century monk Stephen Sabaites lived in his uncle's cell as his disciple; later, when he had disciples of his own, they lived on the ground floor of his dwelling while he lived on the upper floor (*V. Steph. Sab.* 10. 1, 354).

44. Kurtz 1894, 169. However, we have an explicit statement to the contrary in the biography of Stephen Sabaites, whose uncle gave him his cell when he left the Great Laura to become head of the monasteries of Castellion and Spelaion. It may be argued, though, that the dwelling already belonged in part to Stephen, who had been living there for some years with his uncle (see n. 43).

45. This is mentioned explicitly in the description of the laura of the Towers (*Pratum* 5, 2857A).

46. The small dimensions of the cells of the laura of Euthymius are mentioned by Cyril twice (*V. Euth.* 12, 26. 15 and 32, 51. 15–16).

47. Patrich 1988, 135–7 and 1989, 71.

48. *Pratum* 163, 3029C. Moschus also mentions cave dwellings in the lauras of Petrus (*Pratum* 17, 2865A) and Koprotha (*Pratum* 20, 2868A–B), both in the Jordan valley.

49. Hirschfeld 1988–9, 100–1.

50. This phrase appears in Cyril's writings twice (*V. Sab.* 16, 100. 1–2; 20, 105. 8).

51. Xenophon and his sons first became monks at the monastery of Chariton (*V. Xen.*, 389. 5–6). "Xenophon's cell" at Mar Saba was surveyed by Patrich (1988, 140–2 and 1989, 72–3, no. 39).

52. For the Cells of Choziba, see Meinardus 1966; Meimaris 1978; and Patrich 1990.

53. Féderlin 1903, 133.

54. Hirschfeld 1985, 99–105, no. 87.

55. See *V. Euth.* 19, 31. 16–17 for Euthymius's cell; *V. Geor.* 13, 109. 14 for George's cell.

56. Patrich 1988 and 1989, 70–86. A previous survey of the cells of the Great Laura was conducted by Corbo (1958, 237–9. One of the most elaborate cells was mistakenly identified by Corbo (1958c, 109–10) as the monastery of Zannus.

57. Patrich 1988, 144 calls it a terrace or a balcony, which refers to an open or semi-open space. In my opinion, however, it is more likely that a dwelling cell occupied the level area created by the towerlike structure.

58. This hypothesis, based on the written sources, was proposed by Patrich 1988, 134.

59. The custom of using a pebble for knocking at a door is mentioned by the biographer of Stephen Sabaites (*V. Steph. Sab.* 2, 513A). The custom of knocking on the door of a hermitage is mentioned by Moschus several times (see *Pratum* 53, 2908C for the Great Laura; 19, 2865B and 163, 3039A for the Jordan valley; and 129, 2993C for Transjordan, near Petra).

60. Stories of other monks and even lions entering hermits' caves are sometimes told, but always with an emphasis on the exceptional nature of such occurrences (*V. Sab.* 24, 108. 4; *V. Cyr.* 18, 233. 19; and *De syn.* 2, 307. 9–10). For the story of a lion entering Sabas's cave near Scythopolis, see *V. Sab.* 33, 119. 8–10. Paul of Elusa tells of a snake entering Theognius's cave in the laura of Calamon (Paul. El., *V. Theog.* 7, 85–6).

61. *V. John Hes.* 19, 216. 1; 21, 218. 2; and 23, 219. 7.

62. *V. Sab.* 58, 160. 6–7. Special feasts held by the monks of the Great Laura and its dependencies (i.e., the laura of Heptastomos) are mentioned by Cyril (*V. Sab.* 39, 130. 25–6). A communal meal on Sundays is mentioned in connection with the laura of Gerasimus (*V. Ger.* 2, 3) and the Cells of Choziba (*V. Geor.* 12, 108. 14–15). It may be assumed that a communal weekly meal was the custom in other lauras too, although it must be borne in mind that, unlike other lauras, as far as we know, the laura of Gerasimus and the Cells of Choziba each had a coenobium, with a refectory where the cell-dwellers could dine together.

63. See *V. Sab.* 40, 130. 28–30 and *V. John Hes.* 6, 205. 28 for the hospice of the Great Laura and its kitchen.

64. See *V. Euth.* 9, 18. 2–3 for the monastery of Theoctistus, and *V. Geor.* 12, 108. 12–15 for the monastery of Choziba.

65. In Egyptian coenobia, for example, it was common to locate the refectory next to the church (Walters 1974, 100–2 and Badawy 1978, 38). In the monastery of Alahan in southern Anatolia, a refectory compound (including a kitchen and a bakery) was found near the church's entrance (Bakker, 1985, 140–7). In the Byzantine monastery excavated by Eisenberg (1977) in Mevo Modi'in, halfway between Jerusalem and Tel Aviv, a long refectory was found near the church. In the monastery of Lady Mary in Beit She'an, the refectory is situated opposite the church (Fitzgerald 1939, 1–2).

66. Magen and Hizmi 1985, 72–4.

67. The monastery of Theognius (Khirbet el-Makhrum) was excavated by Corbo (1955, 149–53), as was the monastery of Bir el-Qatt (ibid., 116–17).

68. See *V. Char.* 17, 29. 10–13 for Chariton; *V. Euth.* 39, 59. 7–8 for Euthymius.

69. See *V. Sab.* 13, 96. 15–16 for Sabas; Theod. Petr., *V. Theod.* 14, 37. 7–10 for Theodosius.

70. *Miracula* 1, 362. 11–12. The use of the diaconicon to accommodate guests is also mentioned in connection with the monastery of Euthymius (*V. Euth.* 48, 69. 15–16).

71. *Apoph. Pat.*, Silvanus 5 (*PG* 65, 409C). Another anecdote, related by Moschus, tells of a monk in the laura of Calamon who offered hospitality to a friend of his who came to visit him from Asia Minor (*Pratum* 26, 2872C).

72. On guests taking part in the work, see also *V. Euth.* 50, 72. 18 and *V. Geor.* 14, 110. 3. According to the rules of the Egyptian monks of Mount Nitria, guests could stay a week without working; but if they wished to stay on, they had to do their share of the work (Palladius, *Hist. Laus.* 7, 25. 23–4).

73. Patrich and Di Segni 1987, 275–7.

74. See *V. John Hes.* 6, 205. 28 for the work in the hospice; *V. Sab.* 40, 130–1 for the hospice's location near the core of the Great Laura. Its identification as the remains south of the present monastery was suggested by Patrich 1989, 68.

75. Magen and Hizmi 1985, 78–82.

76. Gough 1967, 37.

77. See *V. Geor.* 25, 124. 125 for Choziba. When Anthony was in charge of hospitality, his office was inside the coenobium (*V. Geor.* 37, 136; 40, 142–3; and 57, 355–7).

78. See *Pratum* 42, 2896C for money; Theod. Petr., *V. Theod.* 15, 39. 11 for food. Wealthy visitors left offerings that helped to maintain the hospice of the monastery of Choziba (*Miracula* 1, 326. 17).

79. See *V. Sab.* 40, 130. 28–32 for the preparation of food for the monks in the Great Laura's hospice; *V. John Hes.* 6, 206. 12 for the preparation of food for the laborers employed by the Small Coenobium.

80. See ch. 3. The infirmary of the laura of Calamon is mentioned by Cyril, who spent several months there (*V. John Hes.* 20, 217).

81. Chitty 1966, 110.

82. See *V. Sab.* 31, 116 for the hospices of the Great Laura and the monastery of Castellion; *V. John Hes.* 20, 217. 6 for the monastery of Euthymius's hospice in Jericho; and Theod. Petr., *V. Theod.* 16, 41. 6–7 for an infirmary of the monastery of Theodosius in Jericho, which is also mentioned by Moschus (*Pratum* 101, 2969B, Latin version). For the monastery hospices in the cities in general, see Corbo 1958, 243–4.

83. See *V. Euth.* 15, 24. 17–18 for the first reservoir and the garden; 44, 66. 9 for the second, larger reservoir. The water system of the monastery of Euthymius was studied by Chitty 1932, 190. For the recent survey of the area surrounding the site, see Hirschfeld 1990b, no. 7.

84. *Miracula* 4, 364. 6; *V. Geor.* 4, 99. 4.

85. *Pratum* 158, 3025C–D. The location of the garden of Marda was identified near ʿEin ʿAneba, north of Masada (Hirschfeld 1989, 262).

86. At the monastery of Alahan, the remains of agricultural terraces were found, together with a well-constructed water system (Gough 1962, 184). In a monastery in upper Egypt, the remains of a garden were found, including a water system, olive presses, and vegetable plots (Arkell 1959, 117). Orchards were found near every one of the small monasteries in southern Sinai (Dahari 1983, 7–10).

87. *V. Cyr.* 15, 232. 4–5. Moschus relates that the abbot of Soubiba of the Syrians on the Jericho plain gave his dog as a guide to a visitor who wanted to go to Soubiba of the Bessians (*Pratum* 157, 3025C).

88. The danger of a strong wind is mentioned by Anthony of Choziba (*Miracula* 3, 363. 16–17). According to Paul of Elusa, the donkey that carried Theognius to his monastery in the desert slipped and fell down the slope (Paul. El., *V. Theog.* 15, 95. 16–17). The same thing happened

to a monk of the monastery of Choziba (*V. Geor.* 26, 125. 8–17) and to a camel in Mar Saba (*V. Sab.* 81, 186. 18–20).

89. Corbo 1958a, 86–7. See *V. Sab.* 67, 168. 8 and 39, 129. 15–16 for the road to the Great Laura; *V. John Hes.* 26, 221. 9–10 for the trees planted along part or all of this road.

90. *Miracula* 4, 366–7. For another version of the same story, see *Pratum* 25, 2869D–2872A.

91. See *V. Geor.* 20, 120. 7 for George walking to his cell; 21, 121. 1 for the monk who met a leopard; and 42, 143. 11 for the monks going on "the path of the Cells" to gather edible plants (capers).

92. Patrich and Di Segni 1987, 272–7.

CHAPTER SEVEN: HERMITS AND THEIR WAY OF LIFE

1. Such is the case with the "Senator's daughter" and the story of Mary the Egyptian told by Sophronius (*PG* 87. 3, 3697–3725). A female hermit is mentioned by Cyril (*V. Cyr.* 17–19, 233–4), a dead hermit in Phasael by Moschus (*Pratum* 92, 2952A), and another, discovered by Sabas on his way back from Galilee, by Cyril (*V. Sab.* 24, 108. 23–5). See also *Pratum* 170, 3077A–B.

2. See *V. Cyr.* 10, 228. 26 for Cyriac's hermitage at Sousakim; *Pratum* 101, 2960C for the return of a hermit to the monastery of Theodosius; and *V. John Hes.* 11–13, 209–11 for the years John spent as a hermit in the desert of Rouba.

3. This is mentioned by the biographer of John "the desert-dweller," who lived in the Great Laura at the beginning of the eighth century (*Jean l'érémo.* 1, 16).

4. Theod. Petr., *V. Theod.* 17, 41–2. A hermit who had lost his mind is mentioned by Palladius in a description of his visit to the monastery of Douka toward the end of the fourth century (Palladius *Hist. Laus.* 53, 145. 9–17).

5. *V. Euth.* 7, 14. 24–7. See also Chitty 1929, 78 and 1966, 82.

6. Euthymius would leave for the interior of the desert as early as 14 January (*V. Euth.* 6, 14. 26–7). However, after Euthymius's death, on 20 January 473, Sabas decided to begin the approximately forty-day fasting period on 21 January, the day after the feast day of his venerated master (*V. Sab.* 22, 106. 15–16). The end of this period, which did not include Saturdays and Sundays, was marked on Palm Sunday, a week before Easter.

7. See *V. Sab.* 22, 106–7 for Sabas's wandering to the desert of Zoar; 24, 108. 11–15 for his journey with Agapetus to one of the sources of the Jordan River. For Stephen Sabaites, see *V. Steph. Sab.* 15. 3, 362 re his walking around the Dead Sea; 17. 3, 365 re his walking to Castellion and other places; and 5. 58 (*Acta Sanctorum*, 527A) re his going to the caves of Douka. Stephen observed three fasts each year: during Lent, from Antony of Egypt's feast day (14 January) to Palm Sunday; from Pentecost to Cyriac's feast day; and from the feast of the triumph of the Cross (14 September) to Sabas's feast day (5 December) (*V. Steph. Sab.* 14. 1, 359).

8. Hunt 1982, 67–8. For the monks' practice of wandering in Palestine and Egypt, see Baynes 1947, 409 and Rousseau 1978, 43.

9. Many early Syrian monks were great wanderers, and their travels often brought them to the Holy Land: Julian Sabas reached Mount Sinai, and Barṣauma of Nisibis led a band of ferocious monks all over Syria, Arabia, and Palestine, destroying pagan temples and Jewish and Samaritan synagogues along the way. Barṣauma visited the Holy Land four times between the end of the fourth century and the beginning of the fifth. His biography has been published by F. Nau in two volumes of the *ROC* (1908 and 1909). For more details, see Vööbus 1960, 196–

207. For Julian Sabas's journey to Mount Sinai, see *Hist. relig.* 2, 1316B. Wandering by Syrian monks was described by Festugière 1959, 299 and Vööbus 1958, 153–6.

10. This opposition found expression in Justinian's laws regarding monastic life, which show a preference for coenobitic life (Gerostergios 1982, 168–74).

11. Chitty 1966, 154. Moschus is our main source on the Judean desert monks' wanderings. He mentions monks going on pilgrimages to Mount Sinai (*Pratum* 1, 2852D; 100, 2948A; and 170, 3036D), Palestine (91, 2948A and 116, 2980C), and Arabia (123, 2985A), as well as monks traveling from Palestine to Constantinople (173, 2031B) and back (174, 3041D).

12. See *V. Sab.* 15, 98. 17–19 for Sabas's cave in the Kidron valley; *V. Euth.* 11, 22. 2–8 for the sojourn of Euthymius and Domitian on Masada.

13. See *V. Sab.* 24, 107. 25 for bread; *Pratum* 179, 3049B for soaked kidney beans.

14. Corbo 1958a, 86–7.

15. This story is told twice: *V. Euth.* 38, 57. 1–11 and *V. Sab.* 11, 94. 29–30.

16. See *V. Euth.* 6, 14. 10–11 for Euthymius's hermitage; *V. Sab.* 42, 132. 24–5 for Sabas's hermitage.

17. Lassus 1947, 281–2 discusses the similar situation in Syria.

18. Blake 1967, 28.

19. In Transjordan a large number of hermitages have been found. See Saller and Bagatti 1949, 230–4; MacDonald 1980; and Frank 1934, 207–8. In Palestine, monks' caves have been found in the Negev desert in the canyon of 'Ein 'Avdat (Tsafrir 1984, 271–2) and in the area close to St. Catherine's Monastery in southern Sinai (Finkelstein 1985).

20. Hirschfeld 1989b, 39–40. The site was discovered by Amos Frumkin.

21. Hirschfeld 1984a.

22. The site was discovered and identified by Marcoff and Chitty (1929, 175–6).

CHAPTER EIGHT: HOLY SITES IN THE JUDEAN DESERT

1. As on her visit to Mount Nebo in Transjordan (Egeria 10–12, 50–4) and to Sedima ("City of Melchizedek"; 13–15, 54–5).

2. Egeria 3–4, 39–43. See Wilkinson 1971, 94–6.

3. The survey was carried out in 1976–7 by Finkelstein (1981).

4. During a survey of the area around the monastery of Chariton, I discovered a number of sites of this type (Hirschfeld 1985 and 1988a).

5. Hirschfeld (1985), 72–4, no. 45.

6. Tzaferis 1983, 49–51.

7. Patrich and Di Segni 1987.

8. *V. Cyr.* 15, 231. 72–8. Just before his death, Cyriac lived in the Hanging Cave of Chariton for another two years (*V. Cyr.* 20, 235. 5–6).

9. Hirschfeld 1985, 53–5, no. 26.

10. It would not be stretching things to connect the burial place of Mary the harp-player with "The Rock of the Crosses," which is located near one of the paths leading from Sousakim to the monastery of Chariton.

11. See Peeters 1930. I wish to thank Leah Di Segni for bringing this text to my attention.

Abbreviations and Bibliography

ABBREVIATIONS

AASOR   *Annual of the American School of Oriental Research*

AB   *Analecta Bollandiana*

BASOR   *Bulletin of the American Schools of Oriental Research*

Bessarione   *Pubblicazione Periodica di Studi Orientali*

Biblica   *Commentarii ad rem biblicam scientifice investigandam*

BZ   *Byzantinische Zeitschrift* (Leipzig)

Cathedra   *Cathedra for the History of Eretz-Israel and Its Yishuv* (Hebrew)

CCSL   *Corpus Christianorum, Series Latina*

Corbo   *Christian Archaeology in the Holy Land. New Discoveries. Archaeological Essays in Honour of V. C. Corbo*, ed. G. C. Bottini et al. Jerusalem, 1990

CSCO   *Corpus Scriptorum Christianorum Orientalium*

CSEL   *Corpus Scriptorum Ecclesiasticorum Latinorum*

DOP   *Dumbarton Oaks Papers*

ENDF   *Échos de Notre Dame de France de Jérusalem*

ESI   *Excavations and Surveys in Israel*

HA   *Hadashot Arkheologiyot* (Hebrew)

IEJ   *Israel Exploration Journal*

ILAN   *Israel Land and Nature*

KvS   *Kyrillos von Skythopolis* (Schwartz 1939)

LA   *Studii Biblici Franciscani Liber Annuus*

La Terre Sainte   *Revue illustrée de l'Orient chrétien*

LCL   *Loeb Classical Library*

Le Muséon   *Revue d'études orientales*

Levant   *Journal of the British School of Archaeology in Jerusalem*

LTS   *La Terra Santa*

PEFQS   *Palestine Exploration Fund, Quarterly Statement*

PEQ   Palestine Exploration Quarterly

PG   Patrologiae cursus completus, Series Graeca, ed. J. P. Migne

PO   Patrologia Orientalis, ed. R. Grafin and F. Nau

Qadmoniot   Quarterly for the Antiquities of Eretz-Israel and Bible Lands (Hebrew)

QDAP   Quarterly of the Department of Antiquities of Palestine

RB   Revue Biblique

ROC   Revue de l'Orient chrétien

RQ   Römische Quartalschrift für die christliche Altertumskunde und für Kirchengeschichte

SC   Sources Chrétiennes

Teva va-Aretz   Bi-Monthly Journal of the Society for the Protection of Nature in Israel (Hebrew)

ZDPV   Zeitschrift des Deutschen Palästina-Vereins

PRIMARY SOURCES

Ant. Plac.—*Antonini Placentini itinerarium*, ed. P. Geyer, *CCSL* 175 (Turnhout 1965) 127–74.

Apoph. Pat.—*Apophthegmata Patrum*, ed. J. P. Migne, *PG* 65, Paris 1864.

Call., *V. Hyp.*—Callinicos, *Vita S. Hypatii*, ed. G. J. M. Bartelink, *SC* 177, Paris 1971.

Cass., *Con.*—Johannes Cassianus, *Conlationes* 24, ed. M. Petschenig, *CSEL* 13, Vienna 1886.

Cass., *De inst.*—Johannes Cassianus, *De institutis coenobiorum*, ed. M. Petschenig, *CSEL* 17, Vienna 1888.

Codex Iust.—*Codex Iustinianus*, ed. P. Krüger, *Corpus Iuris Civilis* 2, Berlin 1877.

De syn.—*De syncletica in deserto Iordanis*, ed. B. Flusin and J. Paramelle, *AB* 100 (1982) 305–17.

Doroth.—Dorothée de Gaza, *Œuvres spirituelles*, ed. L. Regnault et Dom. J. de Préville, *SC* 92, Paris 1963.

Egeria—*Itinerarium Egeriae*, ed. E. Franceschini and R. Weber, *CCSL* 175 (Turnhout 1965) 29–103.

Eusebius, *HE*—Eusebius Caesariensis episcopus, *Historia Ecclesiastica*, ed. E. Schwartz, Leipzig 1903–8.

Hist. Relig.—*Historia Religiosa, Theodoreti episcopi Cyrensis*, ed. J. P. Migne, *PG* 82. 1283–1496.

Jean l'érémo.—*Saint Jean l'érémopolite*, ed. F. Halkin, *AB* 86 (1968) 13–20.

Miracula—*Miracula beatae virginis Mariae in Choziba*, ed. C. House, *AB* 7 (1888) 360–70.

Palladius, *Hist. Laus.*—Palladius, *Historia Lausiaca*, ed. C. Butler, Cambridge Texts and Studies VI. 1–2. Cambridge 1898–1904; repr. Hildesheim 1967.

Paul. El., *V. Theog.*—Paulus Elusinus, *Vita sancti Theognii*, ed. J. van den Gheyn, *AB* 10 (1891) 78–118.

Pler.—*Plerophoriae* by Jean Rufus, ed. F. Nau, *PO* 8, 1, Paris 1911–12.

Pratum—Iohannes Moschus, *Pratum spirituale*, ed. J. P. Migne, *PG* 87.3, 2847–3116

Pratum, ed. Nau and Clugnet—*Pratum spirituale*, ed. F. Nau and L. Clugnet, "Vie et récits d'anachorètes (IVe–VIIe siècles)," *ROC* 7 (1902) 604–17; 8 (1903) 91–100; 10 (1905) 39–53.

Pratum, ed. Nissen—*Pratum spirituale*, ed. T. Nissen, "Unbekannte Erzahlung aus dem Pratum Spirituale," *BZ* 38 (1938) 354–76.

Procopius, *Buildings, Anecdota*—Procopius of Caesarea, *Buildings and Anecdota*, ed. and tr. H. B. Dewing (*LCL*), London 1940.

Theod., *De Situ*—Theodosius, *De Situ Terrae Sanctae*, ed. P. Geyer, *CCSL* 175 (Turnhout 1965) 115–25.

Theod. Petr., *V. Theod.*—Theodorus Petraeus, *Vita sancti Theodosii*, ed. H. Usener, Leipzig 1890.

V. Ab.—"Vita Abramii," in *KvS* 243–9.

V. Char.—*Vita Charitonis*, ed. G. Garitte, "La vie prémetaphrastique de S. Chariton," *Bulletin de l'Institut historique Belge de Rome* 21 (1941) 16–46.

V. Cyr.—"Vita sancti Cyriaci," in *KvS* 222–35.

V. Euth.—"Vita sancti Euthymii," in *KvS* 3–85.

V. Geor.—*Vita sancti Georgii Chozibitae auctore Antonio Chozibita*, ed. C. House, *AB* 7 (1888) 95–144.

V. Ger.—*Vita sancti Gerasimi anonyma*, ed. K. M. Koikylides, Jerusalem 1902.

V. John Hes.—"Vita sancti Johanni Hesychastae," in *KvS* 201–22.

V. Pet. Ib.—*Vita Petri Iberi*, ed. R. Raabe, Leipzig 1895.

V. Sab.—"Vita sancti Sabae," in *KvS* 85–200.

V. Steph. Sab.—*Vita Stephani Sabaitae*, ed. G. Garitte, "Le début de la vie de S. Etienne le Sabaite retrouvé en Arabe au Sinai," *AB* 77 (1959) 332–69; continued in *Acta Sanctorum, Iulii*, 3 (Venice 1748) 524–613.

V. Sym. Sal.—Leontius Neapolitanus, *Vita Symeoni Sali Confessoris*, ed. J. P. Migne, *PG* 96, 1669–1748.

V. Theod.—"Vita sancti Theodosii," in *KvS* 235–41.

V. Theog.—"Vita sancti Theognii," in *KvS* 241–3.

V. Xen.—"Vita Xenophontis," in "De vitae SS. Xenophontis et sociorum," ed. A. Galante, *AB* 12 (1903) 377–94.

SECONDARY SOURCES

Abel (1911)—Abel, F.-M., *Une croisière autour de la mer Morte*, Paris 1911.

Abel (1938)—Abel, F.-M., *Géographie de la Palestine*, II: Géographie politique, Paris 1938.

Aharoni (1954)—Aharoni, Y., "Excavations at Beth Hashitta," *Bull. Israel Exploration Soc.* 18 (1954) 209–15 (Hebrew).

Arkell (1959)—Arkell, A. J., "A Christian Church and Monastery at 'Ain Farah, Darfur," *Kush* (Jour. Sudan Antiq. Service) 7 (1959) 115–19.

Augustinovič (1951)—Augustinovič, P. A., *Gerico e dintorni*, Jerusalem 1951.

Avigad (1977)—Avigad, N., "A Building Inscription of the Emperor Justinian and the *Nea* in Jerusalem," *IEJ* 27 (1977) 145–51.

Avigad (1980)—Avigad, N., *Discovering Jerusalem*, Jerusalem 1980.

Avi-Yonah (1937)—Avi-Yonah, M., "Two Notes on the Jordan Valley," *Jour. Palestine Oriental Soc.* 17 (1937) 252–4.

Avi-Yonah (1954)—Avi-Yonah, M., *The Madaba Mosaic Map with Introduction and Commentary*, Jerusalem 1954.

Avi-Yonah (1958)—Avi-Yonah, M., "The Economics of Byzantine Palestine," *IEJ* 8 (1958) 39–51.

Badawy (1978)—Badawy, A., *Coptic Art and Archaeology: Art of the Christian Egyptians from the Late Antique to the Middle Ages*, Cambridge, Mass. 1978.

Bagatti (1954)—Bagatti, B., "Hircania—Castellion," *LTS* 30 (1954) 311–15.

Bagatti (1955–6)—Bagatti, B., "Scavo di un monastero al Dominus Flevit," *LA* 6 (1955–6) 240–70.

Bagatti (1968)—Bagatti, B., "Un' inedita chiesa al Qasr el-'Abd presso Tequa probabile monastero di Romano," *LA* 18 (1968) 288–300.

Bagatti (1969)—Bagatti, B., "Alla laura di Fara," *LTS* 45 (1969) 18–24.

Bagatti (1971)—Bagatti, B., "La laura di Suka sul Wadi Kareitun," *LTS* 47 (1971) 336–45.

Bagatti (1979)—Bagatti, B., *Antichi villaggi cristiani di Samaria*, Jerusalem 1979.

Bakker (1985)—Bakker, G., "The Buildings at Alahan," in *Alahan—An Early Christian Monastery in Southern Turkey*, ed. M. Gough, Toronto 1985, 75–153.

Ballu (1897)—Ballu, A., *La monastère byzantine de Tebessa*, Paris 1897.

Bar-Adon (1972)—Bar-Adon, P., "The Judean Desert and Plain of Jericho," in *Judea, Samaria and the Golan—Archaeological Survey 1967–1968*, ed. M. Kochavi, Jerusalem 1972, 92–152 (Hebrew).

Baramki (1949–51)—Baramki, D.C., "The Excavations at Khirbet en-Nitla," in "Excavations at New Testament Jericho and Khirbet en-Nitla," ed. J. L. Kelso and D. C. Baramki, *AASOR* 29–30 (1949–51) 50–2.

Baramki and Stephan (1935)—Baramki, D.C., and St. H. Stephan, "A Nestorian Hermitage between Jericho and the Jordan," *QDAP* 4 (1938) 81–6.

Barison (1938)—Barison, P., "Ricerche sui monasteri dell'Egitto bizantino ed arabo secondo i documenti dei papiri greci," *Aegyptus* 18 (1938) 29–148.

Barrois (1930)—Barrois, A., "Une chapelle funéraire au couvent de saint Euthyme," *RB* 39 (1930) 272–5.

Baumgarten (1982)—Baumgarten, I., "Mispe Shivta," *ESI* 1 (1982) 75–6.

Baynes (1947)—Baynes, N. H., "The 'Pratum Spirituale,'" *Orientalia Christiana Periodica* 13 (1947) 404–14.

Beauvery (1957)—Beauvery, R., "La route romaine de Jérusalem à Jéricho," *RB* 64 (1957) 72–101.

Beit Arieh (1981)—Beit Arieh, I., "Tel 'Ira, 1980," *IEJ* 31 (1981) 243–5.

Ben-Arieh and Netzer (1974)—Ben-Arieh, S., and E. Netzer, "Excavations along the Third Wall of Jerusalem, 1972–1974," *IEJ* 24 (1974) 97–107.

Ben-Dov (1973)—Ben-Dov, M., "The Monasteries of the Judean Desert," *Teva va-Aretz* 15 (1973) 143–6.

Ben-Peshat (1990)—Ben Peshat, M., "Baptism and Monasticism in the Holy Land according to Archaeological and Literary Evidence (Fourth to Seventh Centuries)," in *Corbo*.

Blake (1967)—Blake, I., "Dead Sea Sites of 'the Utter Wilderness,'" *Illustrated London News* 4 (1967) 27–9.

Blake (1969)—Blake, I., "El Kuseir: A Hermitage in the Wilderness of Judea," *PEQ* 101 (1969) 87–93.

Blomme and Nodet (1979)—Blomme, Y., and E. Nodet, "Deir Mukelik (1979)," *RB* 86 (1979) 462–4.

Broshi (1986)—Broshi, M., "Demographic Changes in Ancient Eretz-Israel: Methodology and Estimates," in *Man and Land in Eretz-Israel in Antiquity*, ed. A. Kasher et al., Jerusalem 1986, 49–56 (Hebrew).

Bury (1931)—Bury, J. B., *History of the Later Roman Empire*, 2 vols, London 1931.

Butler (1911)—Butler, E. C., s.v. "Monasticism," in *Cambridge Medieval History*, I, Cambridge 1911, 521–42.

Butler (1903)—Butler, H. C., *Publications of the American Archaeological Expedition to Syria in 1899–1900: Architecture and Other Art*, New York 1903.

Butler (1919)—Butler, H. C., *Princeton University Archaeological Expedition to Syria in 1904–1905 and 1909, 2A: Southern Syria*, Leiden 1919.

Butler (1929)—Butler, H. C., *Early Churches in Syria*, Princeton 1929.

Canivet (1977)—Canivet, P., *Le monachisme syrien selon Théodoret de Cyr*, Paris 1977.

Chadwick (1974)—Chadwick, H., "John Moschus and His Friend Sophronius the Sophist," *Jour. Theol. Studies* 25 (1974) 41–74.

Charanis (1971)—Charanis, P., "The Monk as Element of Byzantine Society," *DOP* 25 (1971) 61–84.

Charanis (1974)—Charanis, P., *Church and State in the Later Roman Empire: The Religious Policy of Anastasius the First (491–518)*, Thessaloniki 1974.

Chen (1985)—Chen, D., "Byzantine Architects at Work in Oboda, Nessana and Rehovot," *LA* 35 (1985) 291–6.

Chitty (1928)—Chitty, D. J., "Two Monasteries in the Wilderness of Judea," *PEFQS* 1928, 134–52.

Chitty (1929)—Chitty, D. J., "The Wilderness of Jerusalem," *Christian East* 10 (1929), 74–80, 114–18.

Chitty (1930)—Chitty, D. J., "Excavations at the Monastery of St. Euthymius," *PEFQS* 1930, 43–7, 150–3.

Chitty (1932)—Chitty, D. J., "The Monastery of Euthymius," *PEFQS* 1932, 188–203.

Chitty (1966)—Chitty, D. J., *The Desert a City*, Oxford 1966.

Chitty and Jones (1928)—Chitty, D. J., and A. H. M. Jones, "The Church of St. Euthymius at Khan el-Ahmar, near Jerusalem," *PEFQS* 1928, 175–8.

Colt (1962)—Colt, H. D., et al., *Excavations at Nessana*, vol. 1, London 1962.

Compagnoni (1978)—Compagnoni, P., *Il deserto di Giuda*, Jerusalem 1978.

Conder (1875)—Conder, C. R., "The Survey of the Dead Sea Desert, and a Visit to Masada," *PEFQS* 1875, 125–38.

Conder (1882–3)—Conder, C. R., "Arab Tribe Marks (Ausam)," *PEFQS* 1882–3, 178–80.

Conder and Kitchener (1882)—Conder, C. R., and H. H. Kitchener, *The Survey of Western Palestine*, II: Samaria, London 1882.

Conder and Kitchener (1883)—Conder, C. R., and H. H. Kitchener, *The Survey of Western Palestine*, III: Judea, London 1883.

Corbo (1951)—Corbo, V., "Il romitorio dell' egumeno Gabriele," *LTS* 26 (1951) 202–7.

Corbo (1955)—Corbo, V., *Gli scavi di Kh. Siyar el-Ghanam (Campo dei pastori) e i monasteri dei dintorni*, Jerusalem 1955.

Corbo (1958)—Corbo, V., "L'ambiente materiale della vita dei monaci di Palestina nel periodo bizantino," *Orientalia Christiana Analecta* 153 (1958) 235–57.

Corbo (1958a)—Corbo, V., "Il Cenobio di Zannos e il piccolo cenobio della Grande Laura ritrovati nel Wadi el-Nar," *LTS* 34 (1958) 107–10.

Corbo (1958b)—Corbo, V., "Come abbiamo ritrovata la laura di Geremia," *LTS* 34 (1958) 169–72.

Corbo (1958c)—Corbo, V., "Finalmente identificata la laura 'Eptastomos'?" *LTS* 34 (1958) 85–88.

Corbo (1960)—Corbo, V., "Ritrovati gli edifici della laura di Firmino," *LTS* 36 (1960) 137–41.

Corbo (1962)—Corbo, V., "La Nuova Laura identificata con Kh. Tina," *LTS* 38 (1962) 109–13.

Corbo (1967)—Corbo, V., "L'Herodion di Giabal Fureidis," *LA* 17 (1967) 65–121.

Dafni (1985)—Dafni, A., *Edible Plants in Israel*, Jerusalem 1985 (Hebrew).

Dahari (1983)—Dahari, U., "The Archaeological Excavations at 'Ein Najila in Jebel Bab," *Teva va-Aretz* 25 (1983) 7–11.

Damati (1979)—Damati, E., "Kh. el-Murassas," *HA* 60–1 (1979) 45–6.

Damati (1989)—Damati, E., "Irrigated Gardens in the Monastery of Martyrius," in *The Aqueducts of Ancient Palestine*, ed. D. Amit et al., Jerusalem 1989, 299–304 (Hebrew).

Danin (1983)—Danin, A., *Desert Vegetation of Israel and Sinai*, Jerusalem 1983.

Dar and Safrai (1982)—Dar, S., and Z. Safrai, "Khirbet el-Bireh," *ESI* 1 (1982) 11–13.

de Journel (1946)—de Journel, R., *Jean Moschus: Le pré spirituel*, Paris 1946.

Delau (1899–1900)—Delau, V., "Monastères palestiniens du cinquième siècle," *Bull. de Littérature ecclésiastique* 1 (1899–1900) 233–40, 269–81.

Dembinśka (1985)—Dembinśka, M., "Diet: A Comparison of Food Consumption between Some Eastern and Western Monasteries in the 4th–12th Centuries," *Byzantion* 55 (1985) 431–62.

Desreumaux, Humbert, and Nodet (1978)—Desreumaux, A., J. B. Humbert, and E. Nodet, "La laure de Saint Firmin—1978," *RB* 85 (1978) 417–19.

Diekamp (1899)—Diekamp, F., *Die origenistischen Streitigkeiten im sechsten Jahrhundert*, Münster 1899.

Dinur and Feig (1986)—Dinur, U., and N. Feig, "Qal'at Musa," *ESI* 5 (1986) 86–8.

Di Segni (1986–7)—Di Segni, L., "The Monastery of St. George in Choziba—Selected Sources," in *Eretz-Israel Museum Yearbook*, 4 (Tel Aviv 1986–7) 193–6 (Hebrew).

Di Segni (1990)—Di Segni, L., "The Life of Chariton," in *Ascetic Behavior in Greco-Roman Antiquity: A Sourcebook*, ed. V. Wimbush, Claremont, Calif. 1990, 393–421.

Di Segni (1990a)—Di Segni, L., "The Monastery of Martyrius at Maʿale Adummim (Khirbet el-Murassas): The Inscriptions," in *Corbo*.

Di Segni (1990b)—Di Segni, L., "Nuseib ʾUweishira: The Inscription," in *Corbo*.

Di Segni and Hirschfeld (1987)—Di Segni, L., and Y. Hirschfeld, "Four Greek Inscriptions from the Monastery at Khirbet ed-Deir in the Judean Desert," *Orientalia Christiana Periodica* 53 (1987) 365–86.

Downey (1946-8)—Downey, G., "Byzantine Architects—Their Training and Methods," *Byzantion* 18 (1946–8) 99–118.

Draguet (1946)—Draguet, R., "L'Histoire Lausiaque, une oeuvre écrit dans l'esprit d'Évagre," *Revue de l'histoire ecclésiastique* 1946, 321–64.

du Buit (1962)—du Buit, R. P. M., "Note sur la Palestine byzantine et sur le désert monastique." In *Les moines d'orient*, III. 1, Les moines de Palestine, Cyrille de Scythopolis, Vie de saint Euthyme, ed. A. J. Festugière, Paris 1962, 45–9.

Eisenberg (1977)—Eisenberg, E., "Mevo Modiʿin," *HA* 61–2 (1977) 26–7.

Farmer (1957)—Farmer, W. R., "Soundings at Khirbet Wadi ez-Zaraniq," *BASOR* 147 (1957) 34–6.

Fast (1913)—Fast, T., "Deir el-Mukallik," *ZDPV* 36 (1913) 28–32.

Féderlin (1894)—Féderlin, J. L., "Découverte des laures de saint Euthyme le grand et de saint Théoctiste, dans le désert de Judée, a l'est de Jérusalem," *La Terre Sainte* 11 (1894) 81–5.

Féderlin (1902-4)—Féderlin, J. L., "Recherches sur les laures et monastères de la plaine de Jordain et du désert de Jérusalem," *La Terre Sainte* 19 (1902) 129–32, 152–6, 166–8, 181–4; 20 (1903) 117–20, 132–4, 148–50, 168–71, 180–2, 196–9, 215–18, 232–4, 263–6, 278–9, 299–301, 309–11, 328–31, 342–6, 360–2, 372–5; 21 (1904) 7–10.

Festugière (1959)—Festugière, A. J., *Antioche païenne et chrétienne*, Paris 1959.

Festugière (1962)—Festugière, A. J., *Cyrille de Schythopolis: Vie de saint Euthyme*, Les moines d'Orient, III. 1, Paris 1962.

Festugière (1963)—Festugière, A. J., *Cyrille de Scythopolis: vie des saints Jean l'hésychaste, Kyriakos, Théodose, Theognios, Abraamios; Théodore de Petra: vie de Saint Théodose*, Les moines d'Orient, III. 3, Paris 1963.

Finkelstein (1981)—Finkelstein, I., "Byzantine Prayer Niches in Southern Sinai," *IEJ* 31 (1981) 81–91.

Finkelstein (1985)—Finkelstein, I., "Byzantine Monastic Remains in the Southern Sinai," *DOP* 39 (1985) 39–75.

Finkelstein and Tepper (1982)—Finkelstein, I., and Y. Tepper, "Deir ʿAntush," *Teva va-Aretz* 24 (1982) 28–31.

Fitzgerald (1939)—Fitzgerald, G. M., *A Sixth Century Monastery at Beth Shan (Scythopolis)*, IV, Philadelphia 1939.

Flusin (1983)—Flusin, B., *Miracle et histoire dans l'oeuvre de Cyrille de Schythopolis*, Paris 1983.

Foerster (1978)—Foerster, G., "Yehiam," *HA* 63–4 (1978) 11.

Forsyth (1968)—Forsyth, G. H., "Monastery of St. Catherine of Mount Sinai: The Church and Fortress of Justinian," *DOP* 22 (1968) 3–19.

Forsyth and Weitzmann (1970)—Forsyth, G. H., and K. Weitzmann, *The Monastery of St. Catherine at Mount Sinai: The Church and Fortress of Justinian*, Ann Arbor 1970.

Frances (1963)—Frances, D. J., "Mar Saba," *La Terre Sainte* 43 (1963) 80–5.

Frank (1934)—Frank, F., "Aus der 'Araba, I: Reiseberichte," *ZDPV* 57 (1934) 191–280.

Fritz (1975)—Fritz, V., "Tel Masos: The Iron Age I Settlement (areas, C,H), the Iron Age II Settlement (area G), and the Byzantine Monastery (area D)," *Tel Aviv* 2 (1975) 106–13.

Furrer (1880)—Furrer, K., "Nachtrag zu Baurath Schicks 'Die alten Lauren und Klöster in der Wüste Juda,'" *ZDPV* 3 (1880) 234–6.

Génier (1909)—Génier, R. P., *Vie de saint Euthyme le grand*, Paris 1909.

Germer-Durand (1896)—Germer-Durand, J., "Archéologie Palestinienne," *ENDF* 4 (1896) 71–2.

Germer-Durand (1897–8)—Germer-Durand, J., "'Ain Faouar—la plus belle source de Palestine," *Échos d'Orient* 1 (1897–8) 264–6.

Gerostergios (1982)—Gerostergios, A., *Justinian the Great—the Emperor and Saint*, Belmont, Mass. 1982.

Gibson (1985–6)—Gibson, S., "Ras et-Tawil, A Byzantine Monastery North of Jerusalem," *Bull. Anglo-Israel Archaeol. Soc.* 5 (1985–6) 69–76.

Glueck (1933–4)—Glueck, N., "Explorations in Eastern Palestine, I," *AASOR* 14 (1933–4) 1–114.

Goldfus (1984)—Goldfus, H., "Wadi el-Makkuk," *ESI* 3 (1984) 106.

Goldfus (1990)—Goldfus, H., "Khallet ed-Danabiyeh: A Desert Monastery," in *Corbo*.

Gophna (1962)—Gophna, R., "Ruhamma," *HA* 2 (1962) 23.

Gorce (1972)—Gorce, D., "Die Gastfreundlichkeit der altchristlichen Einsiedler und Mönche," *Jahr. für Antike und Christentum* 15 (1972) 66–91.

Gough (1962)—Gough, M., "The Church of the Evangelists at Alahan," *Anatolian Studies* 12 (1962) 175–84.

Gough (1967)—Gough, M., "Alahan Monastery—Fourth Preliminary Report," *Anatolian Studies* 17 (1967) 37–47.

Griffith (1986)—Griffith, S. H., "Greek into Arabic: Life and Letters in the Monasteries of Palestine in the Ninth Century," *Byzantion* 56 (1986) 117–38.

Guérin (1869)—Guérin, V., *Description géographique, historique et archéologique de la Palestine*, III: Judée, Paris 1869.

Guérin (1874)—Guérin, V., *Description géographique, historique et archéologique de la Palestine*, I: Samarie, Paris 1874.

Guérin (1875)—Guérin, V., *Description géographique, historique et archéologique de la Palestine*, II: Samarie, Paris 1875.

Guillaumont (1979)—Guillaumont, A., *Aux origines du monachisme chrétien*, Bégrolles-en-Mauges 1979.

Hamilton (1932)—Hamilton, R. W., "Mosaic Pavements at 'Ein Fawwar," *QDAP* 1 (1932) 151–2.

Hardy (1931)—Hardy, E. R., *The Large Estates of Byzantine Egypt*, New York 1931.

Heussi (1936)—Heussi, K., *Der Ursprung des Mönchtums*, Tübingen 1936.

Hirschfeld (1979)—Hirschfeld, Y., "A Line of Byzantine Forts along the Eastern Highway of the Hebron Hills," *Qadmoniot* 12 (1979) 78–84.

Hirschfeld (1983)—Hirschfeld, Y., "Judean Desert, Survey (Map 106)," *ESI* 2 (1983) 58–9.

Hirschfeld (1984)—Hirschfeld, Y., "Monastery of St. Euthymius, Survey and Excavation," *ESI* 3 (1984) 80–2.

Hirschfeld (1984a)—Hirschfeld, Y., "Sousakim—A Monument to St. Kiriakos in the Judean Desert," in *Sefer Zev Vilnay*, ed. E. Schiller, Jerusalem 1984, 281–5 (Hebrew).

Hirschfeld (1985)—Hirschfeld, Y., *Archaeological Survey of Israel—Map of Herodium (108/2)*, Jerusalem 1985.

Hirschfeld (1985a)—Hirschfeld, Y., "Khirbet el-Quneitira—A Byzantine Monastery in the Wilderness of Ziph," in *Eretz Israel* 18 ("Avigad Volume"), Jerusalem 1985, 243–55 (Hebrew).

Hirschfeld (1987)—Hirschfeld, Y., *Dwelling Houses in Roman and Byzantine Palestine*, Jerusalem 1987.

Hirschfeld (1987a)—Hirschfeld, Y., "The 'Hanging Cave' of St. Chariton," *ILAN* 12 (1987) 149–58.

Hirschfeld (1987b)—Hirschfeld, Y., "The Judean Desert Monasteries in the Byzantine Period—Their Development and Internal Organization in the Light of Archaeological Research," Ph.D. Diss., Jerusalem 1987.

Hirschfeld (1988)—Hirschfeld, Y., "La grotte de saint Chariton," *RB* 95 (1988) 270–2.

Hirschfeld (1988a)—Hirschfeld, Y., "Memorial and Venerative Sites of Saints in the Vicinity of the Chariton Monastery," in *Jews, Samaritans and Christians in Byzantine Palestine*, ed. D. Jacoby and Y. Tsafrir, Jerusalem 1988, 112–30 (Hebrew).

Hirschfeld (1988–9)—Hirschfeld, Y., "Jerusalem Desert and Samaria, Survey of Monasteries—1987," *ESI* 7–8 (1988–9) 3–4, 95–104, 149–50.

Hirschfeld (1989)—Hirschfeld, Y., "Masada in the Byzantine Period—the Monastery of Marda," *Eretz Israel* 20 ("Yadin Volume"), Jerusalem 1989, 262–74 (Hebrew).

Hirschfeld (1989a)—Hirschfeld, Y., "Monasteries of the Judean Desert in the Byzantine Period," *Qadmoniot* 87–8 (1989): 58–87.

Hirschfeld (1989b)—Hirschfeld, Y., "Monastery Survey in Judea and Samaria (II)," *HA* 94 (1989) 39–43.

Hirschfeld (1989c)—Hirschfeld, Y., "Wandering Desert Monk," *Eretz Magazine* 4 (1989) 18–33.

Hirschfeld (1989d)—Hirschfeld, Y., "The Water Supply System of the Monastery of Chariton," in *The Aqueducts of Ancient Palestine*, ed. D. Amit et al., Jerusalem 1989, 305–12 (Hebrew).

Hirschfeld (1990)—Hirschfeld, Y., "Edible Wild Plants: The Secret Diet of Monks in the Judean Desert," *ILAN* 16 (1990) 25–8.

Hirschfeld (1990a)—Hirschfeld, Y., "Life of Chariton in the Light of Archaeological

Research," in *Ascetic Behavior in Greco-Roman Antiquity: A Sourcebook*, ed. V. Wimbush, Claremont, Calif., 1990, 425–47.

Hirschfeld (1990b)—Hirschfeld, Y., "List of the Byzantine Monasteries in the Judean Desert," in *Corbo*.

Hirschfeld and Birger (1986)—Hirschfeld, Y., and R. Birger, "Khirbet ed-Deir (désert de Juda)–1981–1984," *RB* 93 (1986) 276–84.

Hirschfeld and Kloner (1988–9)—Hirschfeld, Y., and A. Kloner, "Khirbet el-Qasr: A Byzantine Fort in the Judean Desert," *Bull. Anglo-Israel Archaeol. Soc.* 8 (1988–9) 5–20.

Hirschfeld and Schmutz (1987)—Hirschfeld, Y., and T. Schmutz, "Zur historisch-geographischen Entwicklung der monchischen Bewegung in der Wüste Judäa," *Antike Welt* 18 (1987) 38–48.

Hunt (1982)—Hunt, E. D., *Holy Land Pilgrimage in the Later Roman Empire, AD 312–460*, Oxford 1982.

Iliffe (1935)—Iliffe, J. H., "Cemeteries and a Monastery at the Y.M.C.A., Jerusalem," *QDAP* 4 (1935) 70–80.

Isaac (1984)—Isaac, B., "'Listim' in Judea and Arabia," *Harvard Studies in Classical Philology* 88 (1984) 171–203.

Johnson and West (1967)—Johnson, A. C., and L. C. West, *Byzantine Egypt: Economic Studies*, Amsterdam 1967.

Jones (1964)—Jones, A. H. M., *The Later Roman Empire*, 2 vols, Oxford 1964.

Jullien (1896)—Jullien, P. M., "Une vallée des anciens solitaires de Palestine," *ENDF* 4 (1896) 291–300.

Kallai (1972)—Kallai, Z., "The Land of Benjamin and Mt. Ephraim," in *Judaea, Samaria and the Golan—Archaeological Survey 1967–1968*, ed. M. Kochavi, Jerusalem 1972, 153–93 (Hebrew).

Karmon (1971)—Karmon, Y., *Israel—A Regional Geography*, London 1971.

Kasser (1967)—Kasser, R., *Kellia 1965. Recherches suisses d'archéologie copte*, 2 vols, Geneva 1967.

Kopp and Steve (1946)—Kopp, C., and A. M. Steve, "Le désert de saint Jean près d'Hebron," *RB* 53 (1946) 547–75.

Krauthheimer (1965)—Krauthheimer, R., *Early Christian and Byzantine Architecture*, New York 1931.

Kühnel (1984)—Kühnel, G., "Wiederentdeckte monastische Malereien der Kreuz-fahrerzeit in der Judäischen Wüste," *RQ* 79 (1984) 163–88.

Kurtz (1894)—Kurtz, E., "A. Dmitrijevskij, 'Die klosterregeln des hl. Sabbas,'" *BZ* 3 (1894) 167–70.

Lagrange (1894)—Lagrange, M.-J., "Excursion à Sebbé (Masada)," *RB* 3 (1894) 263–76.

Lagrange (1895)—Lagrange, M.-J., "Chronique de Jérusalem," *RB* 4 (1895) 88–96.

Lampe (1961)—Lampe, G. W. H., *A Patristic Greek Lexicon*, Oxford 1961.

Lassus (1947)—Lassus, J., *Sanctuaries chrétiens de Syrie*, Paris 1947.

Leclercq (1929)—Leclercq, H., s.v. "Laures Palestiniennes," in *Dictionnaire d'archéologie chrétienne et de liturgie*, ed. F. Cabrol and H. Leclercq, 8.2, Paris 1929, 1961–88.

Lenoir (1852–6)—Lenoir, M. A., *Architecture monastique*, 3 vols, Paris 1852–6.

Lombardi (1958–9)—Lombardi, G., "Alcune questioni di topografia," *LA* 9 (1958–9) 272–82.

MacDonald (1980)—MacDonald, R., "The Hermitage of John the Abbot of Hamman 'Arfa,' Southern Jordan," *LA* 30 (1980) 351–64.

MacMullen (1963)—MacMullen, R., *Soldier and Civilian in the Later Roman Empire*, Cambridge, Mass. 1963.

Mader (1929)—Mader, A. E., "Conical Sundial and Ikon Inscription from the Kastellion Monastery on Khirbet el-Merd in the Wilderness of Juda," *Jour. Palestinian Oriental Soc.* 9 (1929) 122–35.

Magen (1984)—Magen, Y., "The Water Systems in the Byzantine Monastery of Martyrius at Maʿale Adummim," *Mivnim* 23 (1984) 38–45 (Hebrew).

Magen (1990)—Magen, Y. "A Roman Fortress and a Byzantine Monastery at Kh. el Kilya," in *Corbo*.

Magen and Hizmi (1985)—Magen, Y., and H. Hizmi, "The Monastery of St. Martyrius at Maʿale Adummim," *Qadmoniot* 18 (1985) 62–92.

Magen and Talgam (1990)—Magen, Y., and R. Talgam, "The Monastery of Martyrius at Maʿale Adummim (Kh. el-Murassas) and Its Mosaics," in *Corbo*.

Malone (1950)—Malone, E. E., *The Monk and the Martyr*. Washington, D.C. 1950.

Mango (1974)—Mango, C., *Byzantine Architecture*, Milan 1974.

Mann (1969)—Mann, S., "The Magna Laura or the Monastery of Mara Saba," *Christian News from Israel* 20 (1969) 64–8.

Marcoff and Chitty (1929)—Marcoff, M., and D. J. Chitty, "Notes on Monastic Research in the Judean Wilderness, 1928–9," *PEFQS* 1929, 167–78.

Marrou (1964)—Marrou, H., "Origins of Monasticism," in *The Christian Centuries*, ed. J. Daniélou and H. Marrou, London 1964, 1. 269–80.

Marti (1880)—Marti, K., "Mittheilungen von Baurath C. Schick über die alten Lauren und Klöster in der Wüste Juda," *ZDPV* 3 (1880) 1–43.

Mateos (1963)—Mateos, J., "L'Office monastique à la fin du IVe siècle: Antioche, Palestine, Cappadoce," *Oriens Christianus* 47 (1963) 53–88.

Mayerson (1986)—Mayerson, P., "The Saracens and the Limes," *BASOR* 262 (1986) 35–47.

Mazor (1984)—Mazor, G., "Ramot Survey," *ESI* 3 (1984) 56.

Meimaris (1977)—Meimaris, Y. E. "Khan el-Ahmar," *HA* 59–60 (1977) 34–5.

Meimaris (1978)—Meimaris, Y. E., "The Hermitage of St. John the Chosibite, Deir Wady el Qilt," *LA* 28 (1978) 171–92.

Meimaris (1986)—Meimaris, Y. E., *Sacred Names, Saints, Martyrs and Church Officials in the Greek Inscriptions and Papyri Pertaining to the Christian Church of Palestine*, Athens 1986.

Meinardus (1964–9)—Meinardus, O., "Notes on the Laurae and Monasteries of the

Wilderness of Judaea," *LA* 15 (1964–5) 220–50; 16 (1965–6) 328–56; 19 (1969) 305–27.

Meinardus (1966)—Meinardus, O., "Anachorètes modernes en Palestine," *RB* 73 (1966) 119–27.

Milik (1960)—Milik, J.T., "Notes d'épigraphie et topographie Palestiniennes," *RB* 67 (1960) 354–67, 550–91.

Milik (1961)—Milik, J.T., "The Monastery of Kastellion," *Biblica* 48 (1961) 21–7.

Negev (1983)—Negev, A., *Tempel, Kirchen und Zisternen. Ausgrabungen in der Wüste Negev, Die Kultur der Nabataer*, Stuttgart 1983.

Netzer (1975)—Netzer, E., "Cyprus," *Qadmoniot* 8 (1975) 54–61.

Netzer (1990)—Netzer, E., "The Byzantine Churches of Herodion," in *Corbo*.

Netzer and Birger (1990)—Netzer, E., and R. Birger, "A Byzantine Monastery at Nuseib 'Uweishira, West of Jericho," in *Corbo*.

Nir (1965)—Nir, D., "Geomorphological Maps of the Judean Desert," *Scripta Hierosolymitana* 15 (1965) 5–29.

Nir (1975)—Nir, D., *Géomorphologie d'Israel*, Mémoires et Documents, n.s. 16, Paris 1975.

Noret (1971)—Noret, J., "Une Homélie inédite sur les rameaux par Theognios, prêtre de Jérusalem (vers 460?)," *AB* 89 (1971) 113–42.

Norris (1950–1)—Norris, H.T., "Mediaeval Monasteries of Eastern Palestine," *PEQ* 82–3 (1950–1) 31–9.

Oren (1971)—Oren, E., "Hagiva Ha-Zarfatit (The French Hill)," *HA* 38 (1971) 16–17.

Orestano (1956)—Orestano, R., "Beni dei monaci e monasteri nella legislazione giustinianea," in *Studi in onore di Pietro De Francisci*, 3, Milan 1956, 563–93.

Orni and Efrat (1966)—Orni, E., and E. Efrat, *Geography of Israel*, Jerusalem 1966.

Ovadiah (1970)—Ovadiah, A., *Corpus of the Byzantine Churches in the Holy Land*, Bonn 1970.

Ovadiah and de Silva (1981–2)—Ovadiah, A., and C.G. de Silva, "Supplement to the Corpus of the Byzantine Churches in the Holy Land," *Levant* 13 (1981) 200–61; 14 (1982) 122–70.

Patlagean (1977)—Patlagean, E., *Pauvreté économique et pauvreté sociale à Byzance, 4ᵉ–7ᵉ siècles*, Paris 1977.

Patrich (1983)—Patrich, J., "Mar Saba Map," *ESI* 2 (1983) 65–6.

Patrich (1984)—Patrich, J., "Judean Desert, Secret Passages and Caves," *ESI* 3 (1984) 61–2.

Patrich (1985)—Patrich, J., "Deir Mukallik," *ESI* 4 (1985) 21.

Patrich (1985a)—Patrich, J., "Dissidents in the Desert—the Cave Encampment of Simeon Son of Gioras," *Eretz Magazine* 1 (1985) 51–61.

Patrich (1986)—Patrich, J., "Hyrcania—A Hasmonean Treasure House in the Judean Desert," *Eretz Magazine* 2 (1986) 46–55.

Patrich (1988)—Patrich, J., "Hermitages of the 'Great Laura' of St. Sabas," in *Jews, Samaritans and Christians in Byzantine Palestine*, ed. D. Jacoby and Y. Tsafrir, Jerusalem 1988, 131–68 (Hebrew).

Patrich (1989)—Patrich, J., "The Monastic Institutions of Saint Sabas—An Archaeological-Historical Research," Ph.D. Diss., Jerusalem 1989 (Hebrew).

Patrich (1989a)—Patrich, J., "Refuges juifs dans les gorges du Wadi Mukhmas," *RB* 96 (1989) 235–8.

Patrich (1990)—Patrich, J., "The Cells (*to kellia*) of Choziba, Wadi el-Qilt," in *Corbo*.

Patrich and Di Segni (1987)—Patrich, J., and L. Di Segni, "New Greek Inscriptions from the Monastery of Theoctistus in the Judean Desert," *Eretz Israel* 19 ("Avi Yonah Volume"), Jerusalem 1987, 272–81 (Hebrew).

Patrich and Rubin (1984)—Patrich, J., and R. Rubin, "Les grottes de el-'Aleiliyat et la laure de Saint Firmin," *RB* 91 (1984): 379–87.

Peeters (1930)—Peeters, P., "La passion de S. Michel le Sabaïte," *AB* 48 (1930) 66–77.

Peña, Castellana, and Fernandez (1983)—Peña, I., P. Castellana, and R. Fernandez, *Les Cénobites syriens*, Jerusalem 1983.

Perrone (1980)—Perrone, L., *La chiesa di Palestina e le controversie cristologiche*, Brescia 1980.

Phokylides (1927)—Phokylides, J., *Hē iera laura Saba*, Alexandria 1927.

Piccirillo (1985)—Piccirillo, M., "Rural Settlements in Byzantine Jordan," in *Studies in the History and Archaeology of Jordan*, ed. A. Hadidi, Amman 1985, 2. 257–61.

Preusser (1911)—Preusser, C., *Nordmesopotamische Baudenkmaler altchristlicher und islamischer Zeits*, Leipzig 1911.

Prignaud (1963)—Prignaud, J., "Une installation monastique Byzantine au Khan Saliba," *RB* 70 (1963) 243–54.

Pujol (1958)—Pujol, C., "Il monachesimo bizantino nella legislazione del MP. Postquam Apostolicis Litteris," *Orientalia Christiana Analecta* 153 (1958) 57–97.

Quasten (1963)—Quasten, J., *Patrology,* III: The Golden Age of Greek Patristic Literature, Washington, D.C. 1963.

Quibell (1912)—Quibell, J. E., *Excavations at Saqqara (1908–9, 1909–10), the Monastery of Apa Jeremias*, Cairo 1912.

Restle (1979)—Restle, M., *Studien zur frühbyzantinischen Architektur Kappadokiens*, 2 vols, Vienna 1979.

Rousseau (1978)—Rousseau, P., *Ascetics, Authority and the Church*, Oxford 1978.

Rousseau (1985)—Rousseau, P., *Pachomius*, Berkeley, Los Angeles, and London 1985.

Rubin (1982)—Rubin, R. B., "The 'Laura' Monasteries in the Judean Desert during the Byzantine Period," *Cathedra* 23 (1982) 25–46.

Saller (1941)—Saller, S. J., *The Memorial of Moses on Mount Nebo*, Jerusalem 1941.

Saller and Bagatti (1949)—Saller, S. J., and B. Bagatti, *The Town of Nebo (Khirbet el-Mekhayyat)*, Jerusalem 1949; repr. 1982.

Sauneron and Jacquet (1972)—Sauneron, S., and J. Jacquet, *Les érmitages chrétiens du désert d'Esna*, Cairo 1972.

Savramis (1962)—Savramis, D., *Zur Soziologie des byzantinischen Mönchtums*, Leiden 1962.

Schick (1987)—Schick, R., "The Fate of the Christians in Palestine during the Byzantine-Umayyad Transition, A.D. 660–750," Ph.D. Diss., Chicago 1987.

Schiwietz (1913)—Schiwietz, S., *Das morgenlandische Monchtum,* II: Das Monchtum auf Sinai und in Palästina im vierten Jahrhundert, Mainz 1913.

Schneider (1931)—Schneider, A. M., "Das Kloster der Theotokos zu Choziba im Wadi el Kelt," *RQ* 39 (1931) 297–333.

Schneider (1931a)—Schneider, A. M., "Die byzantinische Kapelle auf Masada (es-Sebbe)," *Oriens Christianus* 28 (1931) 251–3.

Schneider (1934)—Schneider, A. M., "Zu einigen Kirchenruinen Palästinas," *Oriens Christianus* 31 (1934) 219–25.

Schneider (1938)—Schneider, A. M., "Das Kalamon-Kloster in der Jerichoebene," *Oriens Christianus* 35 (1938) 39–43.

Schürer (1979)—Schürer, E., *The History of the Jewish People in the Age of Jesus Christ (175B.C.–A.D.135)*, rev. ed. G. Vermes and F. Millar, II, Edinburgh 1979.

Schwartz (1939)—Schwartz, E., *Kyrillos von Skythopolis*, Leipzig 1939.

Tarchnischvili (1955)—Tarchnischvili, M., "Le iscrizioni musive," In V. Corbo, *Gli scavi di Kh. Siyar el-Ghanam (Campo dei Pastori) e i monasteri dei dintorni*, Jerusalem 1955, 135–9.

Tchalenko (1953)—Tchalenko, G., *Villages antiques de la Syrie du nord*, 3 vols, Paris 1953.

Testa (1982)—Testa, E., *Herodion*, IV: I graffiti e gli ostraka, Jerusalem 1982.

Testini (1964)—Testini, P., "The Church and Monastery of the 'Kathisma,'" in *Excavations at Ramat Rahel Seasons, 1961 and 1962*, ed. Y. Aharoni, et al., Rome 1964, 101–6.

Tinelli (1973)—Tinelli, C., "Il battistero del S. Sepolcro in Gerusalemme," *LA* 23 (1973) 95–104.

Tobler (1854)—Tobler, T., *Topographie von Jerusalem und seinen Umgebungen*, II, Berlin 1854.

Tristram (1866)—Tristram, H. B., *The Land of Israel, A Journal of Travels in Palestine*, London 1866.

Tsafrir (1971)—Tsafrir, Y., "Monasticism at Mount Sinai," *Ariel* 28 (1971) 65–78.

Tsafrir (1982)—Tsafrir, Y., "The Desert Fortresses of Judaea in the Second Temple Period," in *The Jerusalem Cathedra*, Jerusalem 1982, 2. 120–45.

Tsafrir (1984)—Tsafrir, Y., *Eretz Israel from the Destruction of the Second Temple to the Muslim Conquest*, II: Archaeology and Art, Jerusalem 1984 (Hebrew).

Tsafrir (1985)—Tsafrir, Y., "On the Pre-Planning of Ancient Churches and Synagogues. A Test-Case: The Northern Church at Rehobot in the Negev," *Eretz Israel* 18 ("Avigad Volume"), Jerusalem 1985, 392–8 (Hebrew).

Tzaferis (1983)—Tzaferis, V., *The Excavations of Kursi-Gergesa*, 'Atiqot 16, Jerusalem 1983.

Ussishkin (1986)—Ussishkin, D., *The Village of Silwan—The Necropolis from the Period of the Judean Kingdom*, Jerusalem 1986.

Vailhé (1897)—Vailhé, S., "La laure de Saint Sabas," *ENDF* 5 (1897) 112–23, 135–44.

Vailhé (1897–8)—Vailhé, S., "Les premiers monastères de la Palestine," *Bessarione* 3 (1897–8) 29–58, 209–25, 334–56.

Vailhé (1897–8a)—Vailhé, S., "Saint Theognius, évêque de Béthélie," *Échos d'Orient* 1 (1897–8) 380–2.

Vailhé (1898)—Vailhé, S., "Monastère de Saint Théoctiste (411) et l'évêque de Parémboles (425)," *ROC* 3 (1898) 58–76.

Vailhé (1898–9)—Vailhé, S., "Les écrivains de Mar-Saba," *Échos d'Orient* 2 (1898–9) 1–11, 33–47, 332–41.

Vailhé (1898–9a)—Vailhé, S., "Les laures de Saint Gerasime et de Calamon," *Échos d'Orient* 2 (1898–9) 106–19.

Vailhé (1898–9b)—Vailhé, S., "Les monastères de la Palestine," *Bessarione* 4 (1898–9) 193–210.

Vailhé (1899–1900)—Vailhé, S., "Répertoire alphabétique des monastères de Palestine," *ROC* 4 (1899) 512–42; 5 (1900) 19–48, 272–92.

Vailhé (1901–2)—Vailhé, S., "Jean Mosch," *Échos d'Orient* 5 (1901–2) 107–16.

Vailhé (1907–9)—Vailhé, S., "Saint Euthyme le grand, moine de Palestine (376–473)," *ROC* 12 (1907) 298–312, 337–55; 13 (1908) 181–91, 225–46, 389–405; 14 (1909) 189–202, 256–63.

Vailhé and Pétridès (1904)—Vailhé, S., and S. Pétridès, "Saint Jean le paléolaurite, précédé d'une notice sur la vieille laure," *ROC* 9 (1904) 333–58, 491–511.

van den Heyden (1986)—van den Heyden, A., "Monasteries of the Judean Desert," *Ariel* 65 (1986) 77–90.

van Kasteren (1890)—van Kasteren, J. P., "Aus der Ungegend von Jerusalem," *ZDPV* 13 (1890) 76–118.

Veilleux (1980–2)—Veilleux, A., *Pachomian Koinonia*, 3 vols, Kalamazoo, Mich. 1980–2.

von Riess (1892)—von Riess, M., "Das Euthymiuskloster, die Peterskirche der Eudokia und die Laura Heptastomos in der Wüste Juda," *ZDPV* 15 (1892) 212–33.

Vööbus (1958)—Vööbus, A., *History of Asceticism in the Syrian Orient*, I: The Origin of Asceticism and Early Monasticism in Persia, *CSCO* 184 (Supplement 14), Louvain 1958.

Vööbus (1960)—Vööbus, A., *History of Asceticism in the Syrian Orient*, II: Early Monasticism in Mesopotamia and Syria, *CSCO* 197 (Supplement 17), Louvain 1960.

Vööbus (1960a)—Vööbus, A., *Syriac and Arabic Documents Regarding Legislation Relative to Syrian Asceticism*, Stockholm 1960.

Walters (1974)—Walters, C. C., *Monastic Archaeology in Egypt*, Warminster 1974.

Ward (1975)—Ward, B., *The Sayings of the Desert Fathers*, London and Oxford 1975.

Ward-Perkins (1981)—Ward-Perkins, J. B., *Roman Imperial Architecture*, Harmondsworth, Middlesex, 1981.

Weigand (1914–19)—Weigand, E., "Das Theodosioskloster," *BZ* 23 (1914–19) 167–216.

Weitzmann (1935)—Weitzmann, K., *Die byzantinische Buchmalerei des 9 und 10 Jahrhunderts*, Berlin 1935.

White (1932)—White, G. E., *The Monasteries of the Wadi 'n Natrûn*, vol. 2: The History of the Monasteries of Nitria and Scetis, New York 1932.

Wilkinson (1971)—Wilkinson, J., *Egeria's Travels*, London 1971.

Wilkinson (1975)—Wilkinson, J., "The Way from Jerusalem to Jericho," *Biblical Archaeologist* 38 (1975) 10–24.

Wilkinson (1977)—Wilkinson, J., *Jerusalem Pilgrims before the Crusades*, Jerusalem 1977.

Wright (1961)—Wright, G. R. H., "The Archaeological Remains at el-Mird in the Wilderness of Judaea," *Biblica* 42 (1961) 1–21.

Yadin (1965)—Yadin, Y., *The Excavations at Masada 1963–4, Preliminary Report*, Jerusalem 1965.

Yadin (1966)—Yadin, Y., *Masada, Herod's Fortress and the Zealots' Last Stand*, New York 1966.

Zeisel (1975)—Zeisel, W. N., *An Economic Survey of the Early Byzantine Church*, Princeton 1975.

Zias (1986)—Zias, J., "Was Byzantine Herodium a Leprosarium?" *Biblical Archaeologist* 49 (1986) 182–6.

Index